Growing Pains

USES OF SCHOOL CONFLICT

John P. De Cecco and Arlene K. Richards

ABERDEEN PRESS, NEW YORK

Contents

Preface

THIS BOOK HAS MANY AUTHORS. They are the students and school adults who described their dilemmas and conflicts for us. Their words are the bulk of each chapter. Their viewpoints define the scope of the book.

Our adults, in this drama of institutional conflict, are parents, school officials, and teachers. Our young people are the almost 8,500 high school, junior high and elementary school students who described for us their school problems. Our dramatic setting is the high school—the territory in which society has contained young people and that is now the stage for violence or apathy.

This book is *not* a disciplinary prescription for adults who believe that they must meet student dissent with mounting repression. It is *not* a revolutionary manual for students or adults who believe that they must break adult rule with force and violence. It is *not* a systems analysis for school officials, political leaders, and social scientists who want to restructure the school from the top. It is *not* a breviary of meditation and retreat for those who believe the problems are insoluble or will magically solve themselves.

The book *does* provide a practical framework for the work of adults and young people who would improve the schools.

1

People who have been reading criticism of our school system and have become dissatisfied with the schools may use this book in constructing their own new models on the basis of what is available in their own schools and communities. The book is an alternative to copying models that have succeeded elsewhere but may not be suitable to local needs. People who are looking for the humanistic reform of the school may use this book in dealing with problems of real teachers and real students. Their idealistic efforts need not end with frustration or compassion.

This book is about how to *use* ideas about school rather than how to correct them. It neither shows how to identify a "correct" point of view nor how to persuade others to accept one's own point of view. The book deals with ways to use different viewpoints to generate new options for resolving conflict. It shows how these resolutions can be choices neither students nor adults imagined they had when the conflict started. It demonstrates how the same aggression aroused by the conflict can be the wellspring for creative resolutions of it. It concludes with a description of how these resolutions can be the means for reforming the high school as an institution.

We view with compassion the inevitable conflicts which arise when human beings try to change old institutions. Those whose ambitions and lives are tied to the old ways collide with those whose hopes and satisfactions are embodied in change. All parties to the conflicts, however, have human needs and democratic rights which the changes must respect and fairly treat. If we want schools that place individual before institutional needs then we must also honor that priority in the process as well as in the product of change.

We believe, therefore, that democratic changes in the school must be made piecemeal from the long term, joint efforts of parents, teachers, school officials, and students who feel the pressure and pain of their own daily frustration and conflict and who know best the particular changes they need to make.

A glance at the table of contents shows how school conflict has been classified and analyzed. Chapter 1 is introductory. It describes the dilemmas of high school as seen by students, teachers, school officials, and parents now entangled in them.

It provides a political, social, and moral perspective for reading and evaluating the findings, interpretations, and conclusions that follow.

Chapter 2, on classroom and curriculum conflict, describes the dilemmas of teachers who try to make all the decisions and do all the teaching without any help. It distinguishes between survival teaching which emphasizes *amount* and gourmet teaching which emphasizes *choice*. In gourmet teaching the teacher can enlist the help of students in developing new ways of teaching and learning.

Students describe school conflicts in Chapters 3 and 4 and apply to them the democratic rights or constitutional principles they consider most relevant: the civic choices of participation in decision-making and dissent and the civic rights of equality and due process.

There are two chapters that deal with anger, verbal threats, and with the violence and vandalism that surround school conflict. Both chapters are based on new affect codes derived from psychoanalytic dynamic theory of aggression. Chapter 5 shows the need for all parties to conflicts to give direct verbal expression of anger as a way to open negotiations. Chapter 6 shows the alternatives to verbal expression of anger: physical violence, vandalism, threats of violence, and institutional coercion.

The conflicts described in Chapter 7 show how students and school adults depict the various parties to conflicts and the differences and similarities between their points of view. The conflict analysis in this chapter is based on Piagetian theory of cognitive development and decentering.

Chapter 9 describes how to resolve school conflicts. It tells how to bargain by using the various means for analyzing conflict described in the previous chapters. It presents a model of negotiation that has practical application to the handling of school conflict.

Chapters 8 and 10 extend the data analysis and represent our willingness to learn from the students and teachers things we did not go out looking for. Chapter 8, based on Piagetian theory, describes and analyzes the differences in writers' time perspectives, using the new concepts of sequencing, duration, and dating of events in time. Chapter 10 has three purposes. First, it integrates the various levels at which high school conflict can be analyzed—institutional, interpersonal, and intrapsychic. Second, it presents some facets of a psychoanalytic theory of adolescence. Third, it states our position on high school change. We argue for a constant renewal process that must always involve conflict.

There are two appendices. Appendix A, *Paying Attention: Conducting and Analyzing Interviews on Conflict,* provides a conflict interview form and a checklist that can be used in transforming partisan statements into forms more suitable for the production of a mutually acceptable statement. An example of the use of both forms is included. The discrepancies between statements revealed by the checklists can become the starting points for negotiation between the parties.

Appendix B is a summary of the original research. It presents both the original and subsequent methods for analyzing the data. The description of methodology should enable others who wish to do so to replicate our study. The description of results, including the tables, provides statistical details for those interested in them.

We have described how to use this book. We now talk about who can use it. Teachers who are finding it increasingly difficult to handle the anger expressed in words or deeds in school conflict may find Chapter 5 on anger especially practical. Together with Chapter 6, it outlines the alternatives, showing how anger is *always* expressed, either directly or indirectly, in words or in actions, in school conflict. These chapters illustrate the usefulness of verbal expression of anger by both students and teachers.

School administrators may give particular attention to Chapter 9 on negotiation. This chapter argues for substituting partial and imperfect solutions to concrete problems for global solutions to abstract problems. Using the negotiation model can help them channel student dissent into school reform. Even imperfect solutions will require the sacrifice of some administrative power for the sake of running a better school.

Students may use Chapter 7 on the good guys and the bad guys in soliciting the points of view of others involved in their conflicts, particularly the views of school adults. Chapters 3 and 4 may show them how conflict can be used to clarify democratic rights and improve the political socialization of both adults and students.

Parents may find Chapters 3 and 4 on participation in decision-making most useful in supporting their efforts to get a better education for their children. The whole book intends to show them that their views of the school are shared by other parents, teachers, students and school officials. They can defend themselves from the charge of being uninformed outsiders when they attempt to enter into school decision-making by demonstrating the similarity between their views and those of the people presently in the school. Chapter 5 on anger, will support their decision to be involved even at the cost of seeming intrusive.

School counselors who want to do more than diagnosis and referral may find alternatives in this book. The alternatives aim at reconciliation of student and school through open discussion of differences and common interests rather than the expectations that the student must always adjust to the needs of the school in order to be considered "healthy."

Professors, including those in education, psychology, sociology, and political science, and in the various disciplines taught in high schools, who are involved in teacher preparation, will find the book useful in several ways. It provides their students with a realistic preview of high schools and high school students. It will help avert the complaints of neophyte teachers that their programs did not prepare them for dealing with classroom discipline and the institutional and political realities of the school. The book will be helpful in teacher preparation programs that require students to spend large amounts of time in the schools. It will help the student teachers to make sense of what they observe and the consequences of what they do in the classroom.

Research professors who face the growing resistance of students, schools and parents to being research subjects may find our research model a way to get immediate results for both subjects and investigators. School people can obtain resolution of conflicts and investigators can obtain research data. Investigators who have become dissatisfied with the superficial results that can be obtained from questionnaires and checklists may find the close analysis of open-ended questions used here a more satisfactory way of getting subjects to respond in depth and without the distortions inevitably introduced by prestructured formats.

Chapter 10, on levels of conflict, may be particularly useful to students and investigators interested in the relationship of intrapsychic, interpersonal, and institutional conflict. The chapter emphasizes the parallel nature of the concepts of individuation, coordination, and integration and the concepts of separation, differentiation, and separatism.

School consultants, when asked for their expertise in psychiatry and the social and behavioral sciences, may find the book a means of transferring their special knowledge and skill to students and the school. They can gather data from large numbers of students before making recommendations for change.

We want to express our appreciation to the many people who helped us with this book. Our appreciation goes to Alan F. Westin, Professor of Political Science and Law, Columbia University, who directed the Center for Research and Education in American Liberties in which our original research was done and kept us constantly aware of the political implications and potential social value of the work. The late Louis M. Levine, Professor of Psychology, San Francisco State University, was co-director of the Center and deserves our thanks for bringing one of the authors to the Center. We thank all of the students who described their school conflicts and dilemmas for us. We thank all the graduate students from San Francisco State University, Columbia University, City College of the City University of New York, the New School for Social Research and New York University who gathered and coded our data.

We greatly appreciate the help of our many consultants. First, our thanks to those who helped us in the course of the original research. Professors Arno Bellak and Dale Mann of Teachers College, Columbia University, James Fargannis of Brooklyn College, Kent Jennings and Mark Chesler of the University of Michigan, Alan Guskin of Clark University, Hanan C. Selvyn of State University of New York at Stony Brook all contributed valuable comments. The statistical advice of Murray Tondow of the Palo Alto School System was helpful. Belvin Williams, the Director of Teachers College Computor Center, now at the Educational Testing Service, Princeton, was unfailingly generous with his time and clear in his advice.

One person contributed uniquely to both the original research and this book. We thank Arnold Richards, M.D., for his advice, his endless patience, and his generosity in arranging for us to have the time to write the book. His constant trust and belief in the value of our efforts enabled us to complete the work in the face of all sorts of difficulties.

Many other people gave us the benefit of their critiques of particular chapters, parts of chapters, or contributed in other ways to the understanding and support of our work. Among these we especially wish to thank Jacob Arlow, M.D., Harvey Bezahler, M.D., Mrs. Deborah Bezahler, Charles Brenner, M.D., Judith Brooks, Ph.D., Lawrence De Cecco, James Duggins, Ph.D., Mr. Frank Foreman, M.A., Harold Ladas, Ph.D., the late Professor Edward Ladd, Ph.D., Herbert Lehmann, M.D., Mrs. Walter Menninger, Arthur Peterson, M.A., Rebecca Richards, and Alan Wrightsman, Director, American Civil Liberties Union.

Finally, our thanks go to Mrs. Betty Gardiner who generously responded to our requests for finished typed copy and who, as a parent of high school students, felt personally involved in the project.

Mondello, Sicily, 1972
New York and San Francisco, 1973

1 High School INSTITUTIONAL CONFLICT

THIS CHAPTER DESCRIBES high schools as we now see them. It describes some of the roles and choices presently available to school adults, parents, and students. It provides an overview of the institutional conflicts they face and some of the options they have in dealing with these conflicts. It also introduces the research upon which the book is based and it briefly describes our social, political, and moral perspective for the school.

High School as Warehouse

The American high school has been the warehouse for the temporary storage of young people until the factories, stores, offices, armed forces, and households needed their labor. It allowed the large number of compliant students to remain through graduation, when they were duly certified and stamped for the job market. It even rewarded and provided more education for the small number of students who combined academic talent with conformity, grooming them for positions of status, money, and power. By allowing students to drop out of the school, while providing no alternative, the school

9

maintained the illusion that the students had a choice. The illusion of choice was supported by the large market for unskilled labor. Even when jobs were available, the students at best traded the constraints of the school for those of the job. One student said about his job:

It may be no better than school but, at least, I'll be paid for being miserable.

As today's students point out, there is not even a miserable job. For them the new alternatives seem to be joining the drug culture and living on welfare. The warehouse is not a place for learning and enjoyment and the warehouse-school does not provide the pleasure students could derive from pursuing their own goals.

With the safety valve of ample employment, the governance of the warehouse-school remained authoritarian. It fed the malcontents to the occupational furnaces a little sooner than the compliant and apathetic. The rapid development of automation, however, has now closed that valve. There is little need for unskilled labor anywhere—in the factory, store, home, or office. The warehouse-school sometimes has more goods than room or time to store. One student told us:

The principal's bulletin says that we will have to go to the lunchroom if we come to school early. This lunchroom seats only 112 people and there are 3,000 students in our school.

Another student:

They schedule 50 of us into class with 30 seats. Man, they just don't want us there. You go a couple of days but then you cut out.

Students today know that jobs are difficult to obtain. They can hang around the school building and grounds, occasionally attending class, but mostly just talking and fooling around. They can leave the building and hang around street corners, pool halls, hot dog stands, and drive-ins—at least until the merchants and police chase them away. Within the school building they can vent their rage against teachers and principals, protesting the decisions and conditions which bother them. They can attack other students as individuals or as members of rival gangs, teams, or races.

Students can also use drugs to avoid awareness of their internal and external conflicts. It is more comfortable to feel the sensation of the drugs than the pain of conflicts. Conflict is a universal source of pain for all of us but particularly for adolescents who have stronger needs and less developed ways of coping with them. Drugs are also a way for students to avoid the feelings aroused by the conflicts they have with the school.

Without these escapes they would have to face their despair —the despair of not developing their talents, not learning anything personally satisfying and useful to themselves and others, and not doing anything that would improve the school. For these students the alternative is to know what they want, become aware of their alternatives and follow their own choices.

Are the choices of the school officials better? Most of them feel trapped by school boards, conservative faculties, vocal parents, community pressure groups, and unruly students. Their attempts to change the school run into opposition from all sides. In addition, school regulations make them responsible for control of space and movement within the building. They are expected to keep the students corralled in classrooms, counseling cubicles, cafeterias, libraries, study halls, gymnasiums, and auditoriums and inventory them every forty or fifty minutes for possible transit losses. And they hear about the losses— from the teachers and parents and from the merchants and the neighbors near the school whose property and businesses are menaced by the missing students.

The teachers occupy a pivotal role. In handling students they seem to have three options from which to choose. One option is to try to teach the required curriculum in the way they always did. When they do not believe in that curriculum teaching it erodes their morality (Adler and Harrington, 1970). The exercise of this option appears arbitrary to those students who feel they are denied any choices.

There are two different reasons why teachers choose this option. First, they believe that the curriculum they have been teaching is the only or best one. Or they believe that innovations are likely to be short lived because of the vagaries of budgets.

Other teachers follow a second option. These teachers let students do whatever they like. Some teachers choose this course because they feel powerless. They feel they have no allies among school officials, parents and students. Some see school officials as mere figureheads and politicians, transmitting orders they receive from above and appeasing irate parents and community pressure groups. Other teachers choose this course because they believe in students taking full responsibility for their own learning.

Still others choose a third option. They try to negotiate with students in order to meet their needs. Their difficulty is often that students are apathetic and will not describe their needs. Conscientious teachers who try to negotiate with them find it difficult to get them to respond. Neither teachers nor students have much understanding and experience of negotiating with each other. To the extent that negotiation preserves both teacher and student responsibility, it is a compromise between the first two options.

In dealing with parents what options do teachers seem to have? One option is to avoid dealing with parents. Those who choose this are content to keep things as they are. Or they want to change the school as only they think best. They view parents as being uninformed outsiders.

A second option is to seek parental involvement. Some teachers who want it, cannot get it. These teachers want to change the school and realize that parents can help them. They sometimes feel that parents use the school to keep their children off the streets. Some get parental help but must negotiate carefully to insure that parents are involved in ways that further student learning.

Parents are dismayed by the spectacle of a venerable institution falling apart. They cling to an idealized fantasy of what the school was for them: obedient, respectful students, solicitous, dutiful teachers, powerful, persuasive principals and lessons well-planned, well-executed, obligatory and worthwhile.

They think they learned something—the substance of their knowledge and skill and "industry" and "self-application." Yet, they recall with considerable relish the "creative" pranks they played on teachers and fellow students and the satisfying ways in which they violated hated rules.

Now parents see some grim realities they believed were absent in their schools. They see that some of their children hate school and learn nothing. The school appears disrupted, dirty, and dangerous. The vandalism and pranks in the halls and restrooms constantly threaten their children. Some resent school authorities' limiting their involvement to busy work, excluding them from real decision-making and responsibility. Parents fear involvement. Some fear appearing too pushy. Some poor parents fear the exposure of their educational deficiencies and alleged social inadequacies.

What are the parental choices in dealing with this situation? Some parents try to prop up the tottering authority of the school and support the school's containment and punishment of their children (low grades, failure, detention, suspension, and physical punishment). Other parents support the rebellion of their children and encourage them to use whatever means necessary for making teachers miserable and forcing their transfer and early retirement. Some remove their children from public schools and install them in private schools and end up only paying more for the same bad treatment and neglect. A few parents (a very few, we found) mediate disputes between their children and the school, attempting to get the fairest treatment possible in very grim situations.

Another group of adults involved in the school are educational psychologists. How can they help to resolve school problems? For over fifty years studies of the behavior of rats in mazes have dominated educational psychology. Once the experimenter places the rat in the maze, it must do whatever the experimenter wants. Experimenters can make rats do self-destructive things by forcing choices between survival (hunger) and punishment—traverse an electrified grill to obtain food morsels, attack other rats, and gnaw off their own tails. The school today has become that maze and the students are the trapped rats. The school officials and teachers have become the macabre experimenters. In this ironical way the school and traditional educational psychology have at last achieved the long-sought mutual relevance.

We want our educational psychology as used in this book to help adults and young people find a way out of the educational maze. Students have to be lived with, not ruled. Young people achieve individuality by separating themselves from old biological and institutional dependencies and integrating themselves with new group endeavors that ultimately become the new social institutions. Students, as young people, must clash with adult society on the road to becoming members of it. Their impatience with social and political imperfection, as annoying as adults find it, becomes the energy they use to renew institutions.

The clashes between young people and the school can result in apathy, bitterness or reform. They result in apathy and/or bitterness when the school denies students opportunities to express their frustration, impatience, and criticism and fails to confront them. They can result in genuine reform when the school recognizes and respects both the conflict and compatibility in the goals of adults and young people.

Interviews and Findings*

Under leadership of the authors, as research directors of the civic education project at Columbia University, a large staff of undergraduate and graduate students interviewed about 7,000 students in urban and suburban junior and senior high schools, both public and private. The students varied in socioeconomic status, race, nationality, religion, and entrance requirements. The original data were collected in the New York and Philadelphia metropolitan areas in 1969. Since that time (1970-1973) we have collected data in high schools in the San Francisco Bay area, interviewing about 1,500 more students.

---

* A detailed summary of our methodology and findings appears as Appendix B.

The data collected during 1970-1973 also have included interviews with teachers, school officials, and parents.

Our collection of data probably represents one of the most abundant sources now available of information about the breakdown of adult-student interpersonal relations and of present-day high school governance. Because the respondents tell us in *their own* words how they perceive and feel about the chaos and the choices, it is a first-hand description of what is happening.

In the following chapters, quotations from students and school adults are not identified by name, age, race, religion, or socioeconomic status. We decided in the beginning of the research to protect the confidentiality of those interviewed. Name of school and grade were used only in the statistical analysis of data. The quotations have not been corrected for spelling or grammar, but where clarity demanded it, one or two words were inserted in brackets. Proper names, omitted to protect anonymity, have been replaced by a dash.

The Columbia interviewers asked students to describe "democratic dilemmas" with which they were personally acquainted. We defined dilemmas as incidents in their own experience in which individuals or groups tried to do old things in new ways or to do new things and had difficulty in deciding "the democratic thing to do" when there were at least two choices. After writing the incidents, students were asked to rank from 1 to 4, four titles for their incidents, assigning a rank of 1 to the best title, 2 to the second best, and so on. The four titles were decision-making, equality, dissent, and due process. The interview form provided simple definitions of each title, as follows:

Dissent: Criticizing, protesting, or refusing to take part in a group.

Equality: Getting the same chances in life no matter what your race, religion, sex, or how well off your parents are.

Decision-making: Having a voice in what rules should be made and how they should be enforced.

Due process: Giving a person who has been accused of something a fair chance to defend himself.

Various codes were developed for analyzing and summarizing these data. The original codes are described in the research summary appearing in Appendix B. These codes have been modified as the use of new theory suggested new codes and new analyses.

A Social, Political, and Moral Perspective

The traditional Civics and Problems of Democracy courses focused attention on problems *outside* the school. Our findings pointed to the serious problems of democracy *within* the school's daily operational realities. Yet, we know that when we tell students one thing and they experience another thing, that they learn what they experience and not what they are told. Of all the injustices students felt their incidents exemplified, the most frequent was their exclusion from the decision-making processes in their own schools—their subjection to rules they could not help to formulate, change, or enforce. There was the widespread belief that even their student governments and organizations left them powerless. Yet they were not demanding power over teachers and principals. When students had opportunities to participate in decision-making, they often showed an awareness of and respect for the problems and rights of school adults. A senior student showed such awareness and respect in this passage:

Every school has poor teachers, and ours is no exception. I had, in 9th and 11th grades, a very old, very poor (bad) teacher. She had no contact with the students (generation gap?), no concept of what we were, as people and students, with ideas. In other words, the classes were frighteningly dull, and everyone agreed (other teachers included) that she should not be teaching. She had, however, been teaching for over 45 years. Many students called for her dismissal, saying that it wasn't fair (democratic) to subject so many students to a complete waste of time. The answer was that she had been teaching for so long, and had tenure.

The teacher was kept. Question: Is it "democratic" to make many suffer at the hands of a poor teacher, in order to protect her from joblessness and/or retirement and/or unhappiness? Question: Is it "democratic" as long as we, as a society, have no provisions for the old in terms of jobs and social set-ups, to fire a teacher who has no life but her teaching? I have no ideas and I can side with neither view. The answer, obviously, is to find an alternative to the system of tenure which somehow protects the interests of teachers and students.

Should schools continue to employ tenured teachers who either cannot or will not change but who have given many years of faithful service to past generations of students? School boards, teacher unions, and state legislatures have not dealt with this problem. By discussing this problem with students, the teachers helped the students examine this dilemma from the tenured teacher's as well as their own point of view.

Problems of the larger society are reflected in the problems of the smaller school society. Consider this incident:

I think this school is undemocratic. The principal is very afraid of the kids who act tough. One day a group of Negro kids were up on the top of the stairs and were throwing bottles at any kids they didn't like. It was dangerous because if the glass hit anyone he might have been seriously injured. No one was around to stop them and they must have broken nine bottles. But if any white kid is caught even lighting a match near the stairs, he is suspended. It happened to a friend. The principal is afraid of a few Negroes and they know it and they take advantage. There was a fight the other day between two Negro girls and they weren't suspended just warned. I bet if they were white they would have been. I feel they should get someone who isn't afraid, yet will understand today's kids and make them understand the rules of the school. I'm not against Negroes. Some of my best friends are black. I just think the kids who are causing the trouble should be expelled—black or white.

This student resents the failure to enforce school rules consistently. Far from being rebelliously angry at all school rules, this student demands only their fair enforcement. His request is for more, not less, "law and order" in the school. The problem of equality before the law is brought into the school by adults and students from the larger society.

Our subsequent research (1970-1973) has concentrated on student and teacher perceptions of alternative ways of resolving school conflict. These follow-up studies were suggested by two findings in the original study: (1) relatively few students described courses of action alternative to the ones taken in the incidents they described, and (2) in those relatively few cases in which negotiation (with both sides gaining and losing) was tried, students perceived outcomes as good and the immediate tension level as lowered. These later studies showed that when we gave students and teachers specific suggestions on how to handle conflicts, that they chose the negotiation modes over decision by authority. The later findings are a source of realistic optimism: even though the collapse of school authority left us with a bleak picture in 1970, it appears in 1973 that students and school adults can learn to share power in ways that respect mutual interests. But they need to deepen and expand their experience with negotiation in settling conflicts in which they are directly involved. Each shared, negotiated conflict resolution makes the collapse of the old hierarchical school authority and the spread of decision-making a less fearful and painful experience for everyone.

Our book is about the need and the ways to resolve problems *within* the school. But we know that the pressure for these changes is the result of forces outside as well as inside the school. In many of the passages that follow, students say they are *not* willing to postpone changing the school until we finish changing society. Many of them even believe that the school should be the first institution to change and that it should provide a change model for business, industry, government, the armed forces, and the church.

Historical changes occurring in the last two decades have altered the economic, political, and psychological conditions of the lives of everyone—particularly the lives of young people in their teens and twenties. These changes, which many adults view as a break with the past and many young people view as a generation gap, present the broadest array of personal and institutional goals and ways of achieving them that we have ever had.

In the economic sphere, the historical change is the increasing capacity of a growing technology to provide now and in the future the basic conditions of human survival—food, shelter, clothing, and care for the sick. More and more people now believe that the poverty of our cities and underdeveloped nations is more a political and moral problem than a material and economic necessity. Everywhere the poor believe that their suffering is not the result of natural and supernatural acts but of archaic institutional arrangements that prevent more aggressive attempts to solve problems of human survival.

In the political sphere, with the rapid spread of education, people everywhere are gaining confidence in their ability to govern themselves—they want to participate in making decisions that directly affect their lives as well as the institutions which govern them. Monolithic pyramids of power, which concentrate decision and authority at the top and work and responsibility at the bottom, appear more arbitrary than necessary.

Herbert Marcuse (1962), in his synthesis of psychoanalytic and political theory, provided a bridge between the larger social and political context and the psychological state of the contemporary individual. He believes that we are moving from a society of scarcity, in which much repression was justified to assure human survival, to a society of abundance, in which that amount of restraint becomes surplus repression. Scarcity in present society is due to poor planning and allocation rather than lack of capacity for production.

Marcuse's belief has both institutional and personal implications. His picture of future society as Nirvana is not one that we share. Nor do we agree that violence is an inevitable requirement for social change. Yet, we accept his idea that now is the time for change because of the social transformation from scarcity to abundance. In the psychological sphere the beauty of nature and the pleasures of the body are choices that more and more individuals are unwilling to be denied. Students, as part of that larger society, now expect more choice and a wider range of choice.

It should not be surprising that the high school should feel most acutely the pressure of these enormous historical changes. The lives of today's high school students are uniquely a product of those changes. High school students, far more consciously than most adults, embody the beliefs of the civil rights, peace and ecology movements. More and more high school students almost unconsciously combine their reservoir of talent and energy with a ready critique of institutions whose failures all of us have experienced and, to some extent, acknowledged. Adolescents traditionally are quick to observe adult imperfections and to criticize. Today, their biological maturation combines with real institutional dysfunction to produce extraordinary and powerful pressures for change.

2 Survival Teaching and Learning CLASSROOM CONFLICT

STUDENT PRESSURE FOR changing the school is seen in their classroom conflicts with teachers. This chapter shows those aspects of classroom decision-making that provoke conflict.

What these classroom conflicts had in common was the students' perceptions that their needs and interests were ignored. Student discontent with classroom teaching has been extensively documented in the school reform literature of the sixties and early seventies (e.g., Herndon, 1968, 1971; Silberman, 1970). Most of the school critics have advocated school reforms that would provide students opportunities to select goals and make choices (Glasser, 1969; Fantini and Weinstein, 1968). The conflicts in this chapter, described by teachers and students, will give specific instances of how the absence of choice led to conflict. Some incidents will show how the presence of choice sometimes led to pleasure in learning.

Some adults believe that learning cannot be pleasurable. This belief may be a result of experiences in which learning was not fun for them. Some teachers believe that teaching is only a matter of doing something *to* students (e.g., lecturing, drilling, assigning seatwork and homework) rather than doing something *with* students. But the process of teaching and learning can

21

be both pleasurable and educative for both teacher and student. Making learning and teaching a joint process requires that students have a range of options from which to choose.

Jean Piaget (1969, pp. 150-51) who, for thirty years, has studied the intellectual development of children and adolescents, contrasts the ways in which the "traditional" and "new" schools handle student interests and choices:

The traditional school imposes his work on the student: it "makes him work." And it is doubtless true that the child is free to put a greater or lesser degree of interest and personal effort into that work, so that insofar as the teacher is a good one the collaboration that takes place between his students and himself will leave an appreciable margin for genuine [mental] activity. But in the logic of the system the student's intellectual and moral activity remains heteronomous [i.e., under outside control] because it is inseparable from a continual constraint exercised by the teacher, even though that constraint may remain unperceived by the student or be accepted by him by his own free will. The new school, on the contrary, appeals to real activity, to spontaneous work based upon personal need and interest. This does not mean, as Claparede so succinctly put it, that active education requires that children should do anything they want; "it requires above all that they should will what they do; that they should act, not that they should be acted upon" (*L'education fonctinnelle*, p. 252). Need, the interest that is the resultant of need, "that is the factor that will make a reaction into an authentic act" (p. 195). The law of interest is thus "the sole pivot around which the whole system should turn" (p. 197).

In order to delineate the sources of pain and pleasure in learning we use two metaphors: survival teaching and learning and gourmet teaching and learning. Both are based on a simile: teaching and learning are like cooking and eating. Cooking provides the materials, conditions, and methods of feeding and eating. Teaching provides these same elements for learning. Eating for the child is the process of incorporating what the cooking and feeding provides. Learning is the process of incorporating what the teaching provides.

Choice is what distinguishes survival and gourmet cooking and eating. In survival cooking and eating the purpose is to prepare and eat enough food to stay alive and to avoid as much hunger as possible. In gourmet cooking and eating the purpose is to enjoy experimenting with a variety of distinctive foods. Whereas survival cooking and eating emphasize *quantity,* gourmet cooking and eating emphasize *quality.*

Choice is what also distinguishes survival and gourmet teaching and learning. In survival teaching and learning the teacher must provide and the students must study as much as possible of whatever is available and required. To guard against possible scarcity of knowledge in the student, the school defines the requirements largely in terms of amounts of course content and skills that the student must consume before he moves on to the next school year and finally graduates. In survival teaching the teacher is always the cook, following the required recipes, and the student always the consumer, eating whatever is provided by the teacher.

In gourmet teaching and learning the roles of cook and consumer are shared by both teacher and student. The purpose of gourmet learning is to develop goals, needs and talents that will guide future learning efforts. But the goals are chosen by student and teacher. Any particular subject matter or skill can be a gourmet choice or survival obligation. Computer programming, if the teacher enjoys teaching it and the student enjoys learning it, becomes gourmet teaching and learning. It is still gourmet learning when students decide to use a whole learning package (e.g., textbook, programmed lessons, kits) or only parts of it—the exercise of choice is still possible.

Marcuse's (1962) conceptions of pretechnological and contemporary societies are the basis for the teaching and learning metaphor. The earlier societies were based on realistic fears of scarcity. Their social institutions, including the schools, were hierarchical and coercive, because social survival was at stake. Contemporary societies, through the development of technology, achieve affluence and abundance. A major source of social conflict, according to Marcuse, is the retention of social and political forms of scarcity societies in ways that prevent the enjoyment of abundance in affluent societies. As societies move from scarcity to abundance, survival eating must give way to gourmet eating if we are not to choke on a glut of useless and non-pleasurable material.

Piaget's theories of cognitive development neatly dovetail with Marcuse's political and social theories. New teaching methods, Piaget (1969, p. 150) states in the following passage, respond to the child's impulses and own activity:

To educate means to adapt the individual to the surrounding social environment. The new methods, however, seek to encourage this adaptation by making use of the impulses inherent in childhood itself, allied with the spontaneous activity that is inseparable from mental development. And they do so, moreover, with the idea that society itself will also thereby be enriched.

According to Piaget the two basic processes in adaptation (or learning) are assimilation and accommodation. Assimilation is the filtering or modification of whatever is taken in (Piaget and Inhelder, 1969). Accommodation is the modification of the organism in response to that which is taken in. The child accommodates to the assimilation of the milk he drinks by growing taller. There is not an unlimited capacity in the child to use his environment. If drinking one cup of milk allows him to grow to his genetic capacity, a quart of milk will not make him grow taller. He could even get sick from the oversupply of milk.

In order to learn the child must maintain a balance between assimilation and accommodation. Piaget (1969, pp. 153-54) describes the nature of this balance:

Moreover, this adaptation is a state of balance, an equilibrium whose achievement occupies the whole of childhood and adolescence and defines the structuration proper to those periods of existence— between two inseparable mechanisms: assimilation and accommodation. We say, for example, that an organism is well-adapted when it can simultaneously preserve its structure by assimilating into it nourishment drawn from the external environment and also accommodate that structure to the various particularities of that environment: biological adaptation is thus a state of balance between an assimilation of the environment to the organism and an accommodation of the organism to the environment. Similarly, it is possible to say that thought is well adapted to a particular reality when it has been successful in assimilating that reality to its own framework while also accommodating that framework to the new circumstances presented by reality. Intellectual adaptation is thus a process of achieving a state of balance between the assimilation of experience into the deductive structures and the accommodation of those structures to the data of experience. Generally speaking, adaptation presupposes an interaction between subject and object, such that the first can incorporate the second into itself while also taking account of its particularities; and the more differentiated and the more complementary that assimilation and that accommodation are, the more thorough the adaptation.

Most learning theorists, in contrast with Piaget, see the students as "stimulus-bound": they learn in response to various stimuli and continue to learn as long as stimulation is available. The external environment controls the students' learning. Learning theorists shy away from theories that assume the presence of "mental frameworks" that enable students to select from the environmental stimulation available at any one time and to accommodate the environment in ways compatible both to these frameworks and the environment.

B. F. Skinner (1971) believes that students are stimulus-bound: the control of their behavior (and presumably their learning) is in the hands of the "behavior modifiers." These individuals manage the environment by dispensing rewards in ways that make the students learn patricular responses. Skinnerian theory views students as being in a state of knowledge scarcity (i.e., response deficits) that must be gradually removed by building a vast storehouse of knowledge (i.e., response repertories).

Knowledge scarcity (or ignorance) was once grim reality: a rudimentary science, the absence of schools and books, and limitations in travel and communication. Learning in large amounts when knowledge was available was the only way of storing enough knowledge to protect oneself against periods when knowledge was less readily accessible. "Study all you can whenever you can" appeared to be the model of survival learning. There are currently popular "learning packages" and "computerized lessons" that allow us to increase the bulk of our knowledge with great savings of time and effort so as to avoid growing up empty-headed. Speed reading allows us to read large amounts in short time periods.

Information can be stored in easily accessible packages, computers, books, tapes, film and libraries so that students no longer need to store it in their heads (Coleman, 1971). It is now more important that the student know where to find information rather than trying to store all the information in his head and cluttering his mind with excess baggage. And this information burden impedes the student's ability to think critically, creatively, and effectively (Getzels and Jackson, 1962). According to Coleman, the society and schools are information-rich but activity-poor. Students need more options for doing things in order to use knowledge they have and discover what new knowledge they need to acquire and invent.

This chapter identifies four aspects of school and classroom decision-making which lead to conflict by excluding choice: (1) the amount of time and effort spent on various parts of the curriculum; (2) the particular courses, materials, and activities; (3) the order in which various requirements are met; and (4) the standards by which work is judged. Each aspect is an attribute of survival teaching and learning.

Conflicts Over Amount

Survival teaching measures the amount of learning in terms of time spent in physical and mental labor. School attendance, therefore, as the measure of time spent within the school building becomes a major educational priority. The following conflict, described by a student, shows the importance the school attaches to the control of time and movement:

It happened during October. The project was Communalism. Annie (a very close friend) and I decided that in order to write about Communes and the way the people in communes lived, we would have to observe and go to some. We had already been to one when we decided to go to Oakland to visit the M—— Commune.

Before I go on I must tell you that the rule of the school is:
1: No independent field trips before 12:00 and 2: all three teachers,
along with the vice-principal and attendance office must be
satisfied. Alright, so we're going to Oakland, right? Wrong! In
order to get there on time for the appt. we had to leave at 9:00.
Well according to the rules we can't leave. Well, we don't give up
so easily. And because of our persistence we had to go through
a bunch of crap down in the office. After 30 minutes of running
off mouths and signing "permits to leave" we got on a streetcar
and head for the Buses to Oakland. Well, we got there O.K.
(an hour late) but O.K. And the people were fantastic (6 houses
on —— St.) and we were invited to stay for lunch. (This surprised
us, because the house rules said no guests aloud.)

In the writer's view, the school's priority is amount of time.
Students are to remain in school during the morning hours
despite the nature and time demands of field trips. School
adults must also be certain that the students will actually
take the trips they have planned. Even this concern about
amount of time is ironic to the writer because of the amount
of time (thirty minutes) spent in securing and signing permits.
The writer's view of the cordiality and flexibility of the commune members contrasts sharply with his view of the rigidity
of school rules and procedures.

The limitations of survival teaching are especially clear
when students are required to practice for arbitrary and uniform amounts of time. A physical education teacher describes
this conflict:

Student X was selected as a member of the basketball team.
The coach made a rule that students attend practice otherwise
student would not play in matches. Student X missed a number of
practices and explained to the coach that absence was due to fact
of mother not allowing her to stay for practices after school.
Student X was, in spite of missed practices, still the strongest player
to fill a vacant spot on the team. Other students grumbled that
coach would be breaking her own rule by allowing student X to
play in match. Coach sent letter home to student's mother to explain
situation and ask if student could remain after school for practices.
Coach also talked with other members of the team and explained
student X's absences. Coach played student X in match on the

understanding that she would be able to attend future practices after school and all practices during the lunch breaks.

This teacher never asked whether "student X" *wanted* or *needed* more practice. Since the rule required uniform amounts of practice for each team member, both coach and students expected student X to comply. Student X had two reasons for not practicing as much as the other players: she needed less practice for top performance and her mother apparently wanted her to return home after school. In the end, the coach had to break her own rule about required practice. Instead of negotiating with students a new rule that would permit more flexibility and choice, student X was required to practice even during her lunch periods. In survival teaching quantity (e.g., of practice) takes precedent over individual need and quality.

The previous incident dealt with the amount of time spent in physical work. The following one, described by a student, was over the amount of time spent in mental work:

It all began when I was a teacher's aide for a speech class in summer school. I was really excited as I never had a chance to work in a summer program before. I really enjoyed every minute of it. In the end I gained patience and initiative. This to me was a great beginning. I was then asked to help the teacher during the fall. We made plans and discussed the time and place that she would need me. We did not know if I would get paid or if I would do it for working experience or just credits. This is when the trouble started.

My counselor got all upset as she thought I was not going to discuss the matter with her but with the head counselor. I had told her that I would like to go on a half-day basis and she blew up. She told me that an education was more important than working. I told her that I only needed ten more units to graduate and she was still in disagreement with me. She had felt that it would probably be all right if I went over to the other school two periods a day. In the end she told me to let her know my decisions after I talked with the other counselor as she wanted things her way or else! I told her I would let her in on the discussion as I would have to make changes in my class schedule anyway. What made me so mad was the fact that you never get to make your own decisions. Counselors are continually hasseling you. They never give you a chance to make up your own mind. They think that nothing is better for you than learning. My feelings are that they just can't teach you to be a good teacher. You get experience for me as well as for others. I enjoy helping little children and am interested in this kind of work. If I were to explain this to my counselor she would agree but she would still have to doubt it. I should know as I have had many experiences as well as problems with her before. As far as anything goes counselors to me are always right; they never make a mistake. Well, they're not making this mistake for me and my chances of getting work experience. Now my feelings still hold and I know I have a big decision to make. Who knows? I might be making a big mistake, but this is a big chance for me and I don't want to lose it for anything.

The counselor could have been justifiably angry if she believed the student was passing over her by first discussing with the head counselor his arrangement for assisting the speech teacher. But the issue over which the writer describes the counselor's "blowing up" concerned his request to attend school on a half-day basis. The counselor equated amount of time spent in class to learning. Helping the speech teacher was working but not learning. In survival learning, school work must be done in school where the amount of work can be measured and re-warded and inadequate amounts can be punished.

In the previous conflicts, school adults were concerned about amounts of time spent in classroom work. In the following conflict, described by a teacher, the teacher's concern is that each student should do the same amount of work:

The problem that I had isn't really a dilemma but I will discuss it anyway. I had a pupil in Grade 5 last year in my Math class— a very bright student. I had greater expectations of him. On his first reporting period I marked him "down" in computation. I was the first teacher in his school career who didn't dote on him and make him teacher-pet. He got the idea that I was much harder to please—I probably was. Anyway he started acting up, crying, tantrums, etc. Talks-reasoning didn't really help. And so the year ended. We built up between us a "block" because I couldn't seem to get through to him and he wouldn't respond well to me. The year ended and it would have ended this way but I started

teaching Grade 6 this year. One of my classes was the enriched
Reading-Language group and, of course, this same child was in
the class. The situation went from bad to worse. He refused to
work for me at times. Then for a few weeks he'd work. Time
went on. My class was upset because of him. I was cross and not
natural. I had interviews with him, his mother, the principal, etc.
Nothing helped. I thought that since he was an intelligent child
that I could reason with him. I felt that I had not been mistreating
him—in fact probably the opposite. I bent over backward to
make him feel good. He was a very strong willed, head-strong boy.
My dilemma was what to do with him. Nobody gave me advice.

The principal couldn't help me nor could the mother. If I moved
the child to a lower class I felt he (being clever) wouldn't do
anything at all in class where he'd be bored. Also, if I put him
on his own in the library, I felt he would think he could get
away with his bad behavior. I will add that I am on an
individualized reading program where he could pretty well work
on his own. One other point was that for a child so bright
he needed constant reinforcements.

It is not clear why the teacher marked him down in the first
report period. It could have been for several reasons: (1) his
refusal to do as much work as the other students; (2) her
setting higher standards for the bright student; and (3) her
using a purely punitive measure to prove her refusal to favor
him. This teacher did not question the assumption that the
teacher should determine the amount of effort and time the
bright student should put in. The student apparently failed
to meet her standard of effort if he can learn the same material
with less time and labor. Then the student's going to the
library on his own becomes an opportunity to pursue choices
of his own.

Survival teaching too often forces teachers and students to
adhere strictly to school schedules even in situations that clearly
warrant exceptions. Consider this conflict described by a high
school student:

I, myself, often have little or no time to study outside of class.
At the beginning of the semester, one of my teachers told us
that if we had to study for a big exam, we didn't have to come

to class. One day I didn't go to class because I had to study for
a math test. I went into the Library and began to study. The next
day, when I went to class my teacher told me never to cut class
again because he was teaching something that no one had ever
taught before. I soon discovered that he was teaching us something
I had learned in the eighth grade. I was a little annoyed with
this so I went and told the teacher. He said he didn't mind if
I cut, but at the end of the week I had to take a test, to see if I
knew it. When the test came I passed with flying colors.
The teacher said I could cut whenever I wanted to.

The apparent vacillation of the teacher (granting, revoking,
and again granting cutting privileges) suggests the dilemma
the teacher faces: his concern for protecting the student's time
competed with the school schedule. Again, as we saw in the
previous conflict, the problem was resolved *for* the teacher
by the student at a sacrifice made almost entirely by the
student. In the school's emphasis on students' learning particular bodies of information in required amounts, the same
information is often needlessly retaught. The school's emphasis
on required amounts to be learned often removes from the
student the responsibility for deciding where he can best invest
his learning time.

In the following conflict, described by a teacher, we see
how a conscientious teacher is frustrated by the survival emphasis on amount:

I was teaching grade 12 vocational mathematics course to a group
of ten students. The course is required as a prerequisite to entrance
to the Post Secondary Technical Institute. The students in the
course were of poor mathematical ability and background but
many had no intention of pursuing a course in the area of
mathematics. The particular math course was being offered for the
last time that semester and was being replaced by a considerably
more difficult course which few if any students could handle.
Should I lower the standards of the course to enable all of the
students to pass and thus continue on to Tech, or should I maintain
my previous standards thereby, in effect, closing the door for future
education for those who failed to measure up? There could be
no second chance for those who failed as that course
would be offered no more.

I discussed the problem with the students in an effort to encourage more work so that they would reach the standard. I held extra classes for those who had problems with the course. I spoke with the math department head and several instructors from the Technical Institute to determine why the present course was being replaced by a more advanced one. After considering these factors, I tried to give students every opportunity to succeed and finally evaluated as I had done in my previous classes failing those who did not reach the standard. One student failed to pass.

Here the measure is not the amount of work or time, as in the previous incidents, but the amount of acquired knowledge. The solution adopted by the teacher, although sensitive to the painful situation in which the students are trapped, shows how little teachers can do within the survival curriculum and even how modest remedial action wastes more of teacher and student time. At least this teacher did not entirely give up. He grappled with the problem to the best of his ability and managed to pass all but one student.

Conflicts Over Requirements

Survival teaching implies that society, as represented by adults, knows best what learning is needed. Survival teaching emphasizes the learning of "basic" knowledge and skill even though curriculum committees have endless debates on what is "basic" for a single grade, course, or program. In the gourmet society, rich in knowledge and skill, the school continues to stuff as much information as possible into the mental storehouse of the child to protect him against a scarcity of information that no longer exists. Using the rhetoric of survival, teachers and schools coerce students to do things for which they have little ability or inclination and even punish them when they resist or use subversive measures.

In gourmet learning the students' need to think critically and creatively is more important than learning particular information which may, moreover, be wrong and irrelevant tomorrow. More and more teachers are seeing the value of gourmet teaching and learning even in memory courses such as foreign languages. Gourmet teachers allow students to develop their particular gifts. With the freedom to try many options and to find out what does appeal to them, they grow clearer about their capabilities and the skills they need to practice. Even the exclusive pursuit of a single option that is later discarded helps the student clarify his interests and goals. The survival emphasis on getting enough of many different things interferes with individual choice.

"Individualized" programmed learning was supposed to restore choice to teachers and students. Yet, too often all that is chosen is how fast you go through the exercises. All students in programmed classrooms are expected to complete about the same exercises in about the same order and perform well on identical tests. The students have no choice about the use or non-use of the program and about the requirement to meet a minimum standard test performance. Little effort was made by the program writer or the teacher to develop skills in a context of personal and group student interests, talents, and goals in a format which may stretch beyond the classroom to realistic uses of the skills the students are learning.

Because they are required to learn so many different things, students are confused and overburdened. They often say "I don't have time to do this because I have to do so many other things." We included incidents in which students complained about not getting what they wanted because they were required to take a little of everything the school had selected for them.

Survival teaching prescribes the ingredients and dosage for the student. It presumes to know what future hoard of ingredients he needs and the crucial ingredients for his growth.

The fact that students wanted a variety of ingredients for physical education was made clear in this resolution passed by a student executive council:

Whereas: This school's policy on P.E.-evaders has been one of severe punishments such as suspensions, threats of continuation school and probation officers, and

Whereas: We feel that a student's entire education and future should not be jeopardized by punishments of this magnitude and

Whereas: If the physical education department had a program that attracted students rather than repelled them, there would be no attendance problem,

Therefore: We recommend the following changes be instituted in the P.E. program at T—— High School:

1. Less resemblance to the military. More specifically, students should be treated as individuals and not as recruits in a boot camp; uniforms should no longer be required; and overall, there should be less regimentation.
2. Less stress on competition.
3. More emphasis on the "education" in physical education.
4. More flexibility in programming.
5. An independent-study P.E. program should be instituted.
6. Freshmen and sophomores should be allowed to take alternatives such as Bicycling, Modern Dance, etc.

Until these recommendations are implemented, we find it necessary to form a committee called E.S.C.A.P.E. (Experienced Students Counselling Against Physical Education.) The purpose of this committee shall be to advise students methods of avoiding or escaping P.E. Membership shall be open to any person interested in aiding and abetting P.E. resisters.

The next incident depicts a central tenet of survival teaching: the educator knows the essential ingredients of the skills to be learned. This is his justification for force-feeding the students. In this conflict, the student wants to select the ingredients:

My previous english teacher gave us nothing but grammer papers and tests and things like that. I wanted to learn how to write well and express my own feelings on paper, but he didn't let us do that. All he wanted was neat handwriting and good grammer. I charged out of his class and I got a teacher who taught me what I really wanted to learn. I'd like more teachers that taught good writing with expression of your thought, and not just grammer and spelling.

Well, we can agree that this student could use a little help in spelling, grammar, and syntax. But the teacher may have believed that these were the indispensable ingredients for all writing.

Another way of requiring ingredients is to deny students access to alternatives—in effect, locking up the pantry. One junior high school student made this complaint:

My biggest hassle is when we want supplies the "old lady" in charge wouldn't work with students because she thought students weren't capable of handling themselves with responsibilities of this nature. And that is the prime thing of the alternative school is that students do most of the work and the students handle supplies, mailing, money and these sort of things. She said that "the teachers should handle these things and the children should sit in a class and do your work without any gripe." And the teachers came to my rescue and sat down to talk to the "old lady" and the administrator in charge of the alternative school.

We have seen various ways in which the school prescribes ingredients: by requiring certain courses for graduation, by specifying the components of the skills learned, and by controlling the materials of learning. Prescribing ingredients in these ways caused conflicts by excluding choice. Later (in Chapter 9) we will explore how negotiation can resolve conflict by opening up choices for all parties.

Conflicts Over the Order in Which Requirements Are Met

Not only does the school supply recipes that list all the ingredients but also it prescribes the order for adding them. The school requires students to follow a prescribed order for several reasons of survival. It requires students "to take turns" at the cup of knowledge because it assumes that there is not enough knowledge to go around. To deal with so many knowledge requirements and for so many students, it must rely on all students "doing what they're supposed to do." Finally, the school can use the following of this prescribed order as a way of evaluating without looking at the products.

Studies in learning revealed that we forget at least 65 percent and sometimes even 90 percent of what we have learned
(Underwood, 1959). Therefore, the emphasis on particular
courses as prerequisites for other courses has found little support
in learning theory. Since students remember so little from one
course it is useless to require it for the next course. What
we remember appears to be linked to the satisfaction of genuine
curiosity that existed at the time of learning (Berlyne, 1960).

Learning is based on learning. But there has to be *real*
learning to begin with—something that the incidents show
prerequisite courses hardly guarantee. Jerome Bruner (1966)
has described how each learner, in one sense, must be his own
programmer. He must organize information into mental patterns that are meaningful to *him*. To deprive the student of this
opportunity robs him of intellectual competence. The "modi-
fying" of behavior that Skinner advocates and that is characteristic of survival teaching is learning at a low, concrete level.
Bruner believes that man's full intellectual ability is developed
by learning complex thinking skills.

The fear of leaving something out by skipping around lies
at the base of this conflict over student initiative:

I accidentally discovered that a student in my grade eleven class
did not pass his grade ten course and was taking the two
concurrently. He outlined for me a proposed project for a unit
on "tradition and change" using Indians as his topic. He told me
that he was also doing a topic on Indians for his grade ten work
but from the aspect of "poverty". I told him that he would have
to differentiate his approach and he answered me that he would
do that. Incidentally, he was working with another student on the
grade eleven topic. He had grandiose plans for multi-media
presentation, dubbing in a sound track commentary
with film clips, etc.

When presentation of report was due he was absent several days,
kept overdue several films from the National Film Board
(about which I was phoned) and finally handed in a half-dozen
pages of written material and a film he chose. The film was
shown without commentary and was not by any means the best

of the ones he selected. The other boy—a victim of circumstances—
did little or nothing. When I checked with the grade ten teacher
—the work handed in to him was word for word the same
as the one I was given.

I gave the second student 20% of the mark assigned and the
principal author of the project zero, explaining briefly that he
would get his grade ten mark from his grade ten teacher, and
furthermore that I considered his behavior unacceptable and
irresponsible. The truth of it was that I did *not* get through. He
saw nothing reprehensible in his action, though he accepted
my decision without much fuss.

In this survival conception of teaching, grade-ten work is
entirely distinct from and clearly prerequisite for grade-eleven
work. It appears that the teacher mentioned this in the first
sentence because she considered it very important.

Following the prescribed order is imposed on teachers as
well as students:

I had assigned a research paper for a class of Social 20 students.
It was to be handed in on the last day of the semester. I had
one girl who was a grade 12 student so I had one day to mark
her paper and send in her year's mark to the Dept. of Ed. She had
copied this report from one of the grade 11 boys but this
I did not find out until two days later when I corrected his paper.
Who was I to fail? She deserved to be given a lower mark as a
failure but I had sent in her marks. I did seek out both students
and made it known to them what I had found. The boy's paper
I did mark lower deliberately but I did not fail him.

For the student the need to meet the deadline may have led
her to believe that she had to cheat. For the teacher the required rigid time schedule for grading prevented negotiation.
Student and teacher could have at least agreed that an extension
of time was preferable to cheating.

In survival teaching the *sequence*, when compared with the
quality of the product, becomes disproportionately important.
This insistence on a pre-established sequence prevents negotiation by imposing a non-negotiable demand on teachers and
students.

Conflicts Over Judging the Product

Using test scores as the exclusive measure of learning is like judging a meal by how much the diners ate, how long they stayed at the table and whether they ate all the courses. It ignores the diner's feelings of delight, satisfaction or disinterest. Test scores may be accurate, but they certainly are not all inclusive.

The testing and grading system fails for three reasons: (1) It measures only the *quantity* of learning and this is like judging a meal only by how much we have eaten. (2) It ignores the quality of experience and this is like ignoring the taste of the food in judging a meal. (3) It too often entirely misses the target and renders a judgment on something other than the meal.

Who shall judge—since teachers and students so differently evaluate their school experience? Guskin (1971) found that the teachers, who on other counts voiced a liberal, progressive educational rhetoric, favored more rigid measures of discipline while the students believed that rules were applied unfairly and wanted less discipline. Whereas 52 percent of the teachers believed that they treated students as responsible, 50 percent of the students believed that teachers did *not* treat students as responsible. And while 55 percent of the teachers believed they helped students do their best, only 30 percent of the students agreed with them.

Parents and students challenge the school's reliance on test scores and grades:

I am a junior high principal. One of my teachers received a long phone call and a follow up letter from a parent criticizing her scoring of one item on a test and asking what answers were expected on a number of other questions. The parent is presently a grad student and has shown the school what we call an overconcern for her 7th grade daughters work. Her demands are—"so that I can help my daughter." The teacher's feeling was "I will help the girl who really needs a little help in my own way. Mother is just trying to show off her new learning." The teacher has been upset by this challenge—not sleeping well, etc. I asked the teacher not to answer the letter. I intend to fend off the mother by trying to convince her that the daughter must learn at her own (now quite good) level. Trying to impose adult standards of work on this youngster will create tensions beyond her ability to handle them. The dilemma will not really be solved—I will relieve the teacher but add another dissatisfied parent to the school community.

The principal objects to the parent's having a part in judging the child's success and satisfaction. He believes that school adults, not parents or students, should set standards for judging products.

In the previous incident the parent objected to low standards set by the school for her child. In this incident, the teacher objects to the school rather than teachers judging products:

I think that it is the teacher's prerogative to report to parents on the student's progress the way he sees fit. The reporting in our school was to be based on a set of scholastic Christmas, Easter and final exams, for which date and (to a large extent) content was predetermined by the administration or department head. This was unfair to the students whose teachers did not follow this rigorous administrative pattern. Here personal differences in teachers and students were sacrificed to a "desirable" uniformity of product. I went ahead and evaluated on total involvement on the philosophy that the main measure of a student's work is his work. I told the administration that I refused to evaluate any students on one or two exams and, to my surprise, this was accepted and more teachers are doing the same thing.

Standards are set by school authorities who are not involved in either preparing or using the curriculum. When teachers try to free their students and themselves from these external standards they run into considerable opposition even from parents:

I gave a grade 12 class the right to evaluate (group and individual) their own learning experience. The vast majority (100% of vocalizing) agreed to try the experiment. The father of a student complained bitterly that no one should evaluate his daughter but me. I felt the student wanted to try the experiment but father was against it. I didn't know whether to evaluate the

pupil or get her to involve herself in the experiment. I ended up
by evaluating her yet felt badly that, of all my students, she most
of all could have benefited from participating. I really think I
cop'd out. I phoned parent but met a brick wall. He didn't want
to hear any explanation of the "experiment." He wasn't willing
to even allow his daughter to try. Because it was an "experiment"
I didn't feel too secure. I feel I would handle it differently now
that I am more sure of the value of self-determination of marks.
I discussed it (after I had made the decision) with my Principal.
I felt more secure again that he would have backed me up
because he'd had *other* difficulties with the same man.

This particular parent appears to be particularly difficult to
communicate with, especially about self-evaluation. Self-evaluation is a necessary step toward gourmet learning. It develops
the critical skills students need to determine how they like
what they learn. Even self-evaluation by someone else's standards does not reveal to students their own personal gain and
satisfaction. The use of standard testing and grading procedures also precludes choice by requiring every student to
perform in the same way. By limiting student options divergent
resolutions of conflicts become impossible.

Summary

Using an analogy derived from Piaget and Marcuse, the
chapter shows the central role of student choice in teaching
and learning. The similarity between Piaget's theory of cognitive development and Marcuse's theory of political and social
development has been shown. Their concepts have been used
in order to understand classroom conflict. Four aspects of school
decision-making that lead to conflict, by excluding choice, were
identified: (1) amount of time and effort spent on various
parts of the curriculum; (2) particular courses, materials, and
activities; (3) the order in which the various requirements are
met; and (4) the standards by which work is judged. The
presence of student choice will not always prevent conflict.
But the absence of student choice seriously obstructs the negotiation of conflict.

This conception of curricular choice is closely linked to the democratic rights discussed in the next two chapters. Choice requires student participation in decision-making. They must have a choice in selecting educational experiences inside or outside the school. Dissent, if not silenced and if heard, can be the students' first articulation of their own particular tastes and interests. By appreciating the value of different talents in individuals, providing for choice respects student equality. Finally, due process protects choice by providing democratic procedures for resolving conflict.

3 Civic Choice DECISION-MAKING AND DISSENT

THE AMERICAN HIGH SCHOOL is expected to provide the political education of young people living in a democratic society. Our major research objective was to discover how well the high school was fulfilling that objective. We also wanted to discover how well students' perceptions of their high schools squared with their conception of democratic institutions.

Our own conception of democracy is a society which gives priority to individual over institutional needs. It provides individuals a wide array of opportunities for creating and selecting their own choices. It avoids convergence of thought, feeling, and behavior and even fosters divergence and pluralism. From its early, post-Revolutionary days, American society has tried to maintain unity within this pervasive pluralism by developing a basic value consensus. These values are widely shared democratic principles which guide the thoughts and actions of individuals who have considerable personal liberty in the pursuit of personal satisfaction.

Westin (1968) divides his conception of democracy into four democratic rights or constitutional ideals which many political scientists believe are its major components: participation in decision-making, equality, dissent, and due process. These rights are also the names of our political socialization codes.

Two of these rights, equality and due process, involve *civic status*. They are rights automatically given to every citizen without laying an individual claim to them and without exercising them. The other two, participation in decision-making and dissent, involve *civic choice*. These rights allow the citizen the option of participation or non-participation in civic affairs.

This chapter relates and analyzes school incidents in which students believed civic choice was at stake; the next chapter deals with civic status. Both chapters place the incidents in the context of other research.

Since the ultimate goal of civic education is to enable students, as adults, to understand and act on their own experience, we needed to know how well they were able to do this in school. As stated in Chapter 1, *after* they wrote their incidents they were asked to rank from 1 to 4 these four rights as titles highlighting the central issues of the conflicts described. This procedure encouraged them to write about incidents that were meaningful to them rather than about incidents preselected to fit these concepts. To check the fit between the students' perceptions of these concepts and those of political scientists, we compared the students' rankings with those of trained coders. For all four democratic rights, students and coders agreed on rankings as to the relevant titles. The one exception to this pattern of agreement will be described later.

In the remainder of this chapter we will look at two of the four democratic rights as categories of political socialization. These are the civic choices of decision-making and dissent. First, for each category, we will provide a short rationale for including the right as a category in the analysis of the experience of high school students. Second, we will look at the way students describe and understand their own experiences.

Participation in Decision-Making

What distinguishes democracy from other forms of government is the right to general participation in decision-making. All periods of American history have had their own participatory forms. They range from the original town meetings to the present-day television debates. We have even divided large political units into small ones so that face-to-face debate can continue to influence local and national policy.

Participation in the making of decisions is one of the ways individuals and groups keep institutions responsive to their changing needs and interests. When institutions deny any individual or group member access to decision-making, they tend to serve the interests only of governing elites. Participation in decision-making would have helped the dissatisfied students to voice their complaints and expectations, hear those of others, and negotiate changes which reconciled old and new demands. Our democracy provides the opportunity but not the obligation to participate in decision-making whenever any individual feels vital interests are at stake.

This participatory view of democratic society and citizenship has radical implications for the school and civic education. It is reasonable to expect that the high school, as an institution in a democratic society, should respect the rights and values of that society. As the chief agency of civic education, the high school should embody in its own governance the constitutional ideals of participation in decision-making, dissent, equality, and due process. Civic education in a democracy should not separate students from participation in school governance or from involvement in community affairs.

A democratic conception of the school and civic education is fundamentally opposed to the authoritarian conception in two crucial respects. First, it views the school as a pluralistic institution. Decisions should not be made only by the administration to be carried out only by teachers and students. Each of these groups has a stake in school decisions. Each has a right to a meaningful voice in making those decisions. Second, it views the school as an integral part of the community which it serves. It is more than a building which isolates students. It is the staging area for the students' entry into the community. The school, in a democratic society, has a major responsibility for helping students find effective ways of participating in the civic affairs of their communities and society (Everett, *et al.*, 1938).

As early as 1943, Jones found that over two-thirds of the high school seniors he interviewed said that they had no interest in talking with fellow students about government and politics. We can assume that these students understood that politics and government were socially approved, adult, and masculine topics. Therefore, their self-reported lack of interest probably reflected their real avoidance of these topics. Student interest in politics, therefore, is not to be taken for granted. Disinterest is not new, not a characteristic of the current generation and not to be dealt with by deploring it. Schools must evoke student interest in political issues and forms by encouraging their participation in the political processes embodied in their own lives.

Over two-thirds of the students in our study selected decision-making as the best of four possible titles for their incidents. Students selected decision-making as the crux of the issue more often than equality, due process and dissent in every school, at every level, for every social class. The incidents they described in fact do show that high school students rarely participate in making the school policy and rules they are bound by. In less than one-fifth of the incidents did the students perceive that they had any voice in the resolution of problems. There was no difference among elementary, junior high, and senior high school students in how often they mentioned lack of participation in decision-making as the central issue of their incidents.

More than half of the students interviewed wrote about issues classified by our content codes as issues of school governance and individual (civil) rights. This finding confirmed the evidence of the political socialization codes that participation in making and enforcing school regulations is of vital interest to high school students.

As early as 1925, Meltzer found that 51 percent of high school students believed that "government by the people" was a major aspect of democracy. Although these students were thinking about the national level, his finding is similar to ours. Wolfson and Nash (1968) discovered considerable discrepancy between teachers and students in their perception of who was making the decisions. Even when teachers thought that the students made a large share of the decisions, the students thought the teacher was still in control. They explain this finding as follows:

Teachers seldom check their perception against their pupils' perceptions. This lack of communication may contribute to the extensive differences in perceptions of decision-making in the classroom. On the one hand, children may not be aware of the opportunities to decide for themselves; on the other hand, the teacher may communicate indirectly the idea that decisions have to satisfy him even though he thinks that he allows children to decide (p. 93).

The lack of student participation in decision-making is exemplified in this incident:

There is a problem in my electronics class in which the teacher uses a point system for grading. The idea is that each student is required to have at least 200 points by the end of the school year. Each student receives a point each day he is present in class. In this manner the student would receive a total of 184 points just for being present in class every school day. The work done in class constitutes no points. The remaining 16 points needed to pass the course can only be obtained by building electronics projects, of which the material needed is not supplied by the school. A person may top the course and have all his work done with an A, he may fail purely on account of absenteeism. Projects cost money for the material the school does not supply. Each project gives a maximum of 5 points. . . . The students of his class have gotten together to fight this system of grading. The teacher refuses to change or even talk to the principal.

The teacher excluded the students from participation in making decisions about the projects and the grading system. Poor students are discriminated against for lack of money to pay for project materials. Had they been allowed to participate, they could have suggested a less discriminatory grading system. Student participation could have made this grading system more fair.

Parents and teachers together can exclude students from participation in decision-making:

A portion of the students would like to have a voice in the Parent-Teachers Association. They would like to have a voice in what laws should be made and how they should be enforced. This opportunity came a few weeks ago. A student panel was selected from the body to speak on the current issues concerning the students and the school. A few of the issues raised included cutting classes, after school activities, various courses and smoking. The parents argued with the students. The students feel they should have more voice in making and enforcing laws. The sessions ended by one student saying that the students were not going to discuss anything else with the parents until the parents were ready to listen. I think the parents could have listened more to what the students have to say than arguing with them.

In the two preceding incidents, adults excluded all students from a voice in the decision. The next incident shows how adults can co-opt a few students to exclude most students:

The G.O.* President is traditionally elected from the upcoming senior class. There have been four nominees, and the student who gets the most votes is President, next highest is vice-president, and on down to secretary and treasurer. However, this year in the constitutional convention, the method of electing a G. O. president is being changed: each candidate runs with 3 other people for the 3 other offices. The only undemocratic thing about this is that the rest of the student body has little voice in making rules for the new constitution. Part of the problem is that candidates must have a C+ (or something) average. I don't think this should be a qualification, especially if someone's average is being pulled down by physical education. There is a group of seniors and faculty members who pick the nominees (usually students who bring them flowers and apples, or their best friends).

It appears that good grades were the means the adults used to "co-opt" the students.

Students without adult intervention sometimes formed and preserved their own elites by excluding other students from participation in school decisions:

* General Organization. In New York City this term refers to the student government in high schools.

This incident is between the Senior Councils and the students. This was the argument. The council member suggested that the senior trip be taken on the bus. The students wanted to go on a boat ride. This wasn't fair toward the students bcause this was their senior trip, and they should have something to say about it and where they should go. The Senior Council members decided where they should go, that was final. The Seniors have to go along with them if they like it or not. This wasn't fair to the students.

Students may learn to exclude others from participation by following adult models. The students in the last two incidents appear to have done just that!

There were very few incidents in which individuals or groups were willing to give up power and status to others in order to share the decision-making. The following incident shows how a decision was reached in a participative manner:

It is the custom in high school for the senior term president and vice-president to lead the term in the traditional Senior Sing. The Sing Committee chairman had spoken with the officers before about the possibility that he could lead the sing instead of the officers. When the officers said they would resign, it was decided that they would never bring the subject up again. However, at a rehearsal a few months later, a motion was made that the Sing Chairman lead the sing instead of the two officers. The treasurer of the term immediately took charge of the meeting. She said there would be no discussion on the matter, yet immediately went into a personal attack on the two officers saying that they didn't do any work at all so why should they have the honor of leading the sing. A vote was taken and the motion was passed. . . .

The incident raised many problems and questions. First of all, a promise was broken when the matter was taken up. The two co-chairmen and the treasurer acted in collusion in an attempt to gain control for themselves. The question of who should lead the sing could have been brought to the term and discussed openly. . . . The manner in which the question was handled was definitely undemocratic yet it shocked me at that time that none of the students in the group moved to stop what was happening.

A term meeting was called for the following day. The President and Vice-President put themselves up for a vote of confidence.

The term voted confidence in the officers by an overwhelming margin. The term then voted on who should lead the sing. The officers then were still voted to lead the sing. . . .

The problems could have been handled in a manner other than the democratic way. The officers could have used the vast power that they possessed to decree that they would lead the sing with no questions asked.

The fact that these two girls saw and acted upon the possibility of participation by all the girls is evidence of a democratic thinking not readily found in high school students. This type of decision-making is what many students wanted to be involved in.

Participation in decision-making is the essential democratic right because it distinguishes democracy from other governmental forms. It is particularly basic in a pluralistic society in which there is great variety of individual needs and goals to which institutions should respond. The family is decisive in early political socialization in determining political attitudes. Liberal families tend to produce liberal children and conservative parents conservative children (Keniston, 1968). But young people only become ready for the more abstract ideas of fair play, social justice and rule governed participation with responsibility to uphold ideals in adolescence during which they have already become more responsive to school than to family mores (Kohlberg, 1966). Therefore, the high school plays a crucial role in both the teaching and practice of democratic rights.

The incidents here show who the students perceive as rulers. They are sometimes teachers excluding students from making classroom decisions. They are parents and teachers formulating schoolwide policy without listening to students. They are school adults and co-opted students denying other students a voice in school governance. They are students excluding other students by insisting on the privileges of status. One incident showed the positive value of decision-making. When the student officers of an organization shared decision-making power with the student members issues were clarified and the officers obtained a vote of confidence.

The Right to Dissent

Dissent is criticizing, protesting, or refusing to take part in a group. Reasonable dissent stops short of physical violence and verbal threat. There are strong political and psychological arguments for the value of dissent. Consider first the political argument. Dissent is the spark of social change. It is vital to the functioning and self-regulation of large and small groups. It can change specialized functions of small institutions and the multipurpose functions of large institutions. Institutions change only when the governing group becomes aware of their failure to function. To keep even small institutions viable someone must point to their flaws so that the governing group can make improvements. In the larger society, also, some individuals must be the social critics who point to the flaws of large institutions that have not performed the functions for which they were established.

In the political arena, social criticism is called dissent. Dissent serves society by revitalizing outmoded institutions. By stimulating institutional re-evaluation, dissent even provides support for those institutions that appear outmoded but actually serve society in unappreciated ways (Rice, 1969).

Arno Bellack (1956) describes the constant requirement for institutional change:

The content of our culture, then, is a complex intricate web composed of many modes of thought and behavior, intimately and organically related, dynamic and constantly undergoing reconstruction. Each generation builds on the heritage it inherits, *sloughs off certain elements of it* and adds to it on the basis of its own unique experience as new discoveries are made, new theories are formulated and adaptations to changing conditions become necessary [emphasis added].

The "sloughing off" of the obsolete and archaic institutional forms is the crucial function of political dissent.

A viable society requires that schools produce at least a few dissenters who will point to institutional flaws and thereby release their fellow citizens' energy for change. Those student dissenters who learn how to evoke constructive school change can become gadfly-leaders who keep the community and nation growing and alive. School dissent, therefore, is useful both inside and outside the school.

Yet the role of dissenters is often difficult. Their society often subjects them to ridicule and rejection. They must always face and endure the threat of ostracism. They are often persons who believe in human freedom and self-fulfillment (Keniston, 1968). Their own institutional alienation is expressed today in their rejection of the occupational and political world of corporate values and in withdrawal from constructive change efforts. Isolated in their communes, apartments, or rural retreats, they try to build a world of repose, decency, and mutual love and concern. Their fierce concentration of energy and fantasy on their small communities often reaches explosive intensity. It often becomes necessary for them to leave one commune to build another or to try again the larger society.

Prolonged alienation and apathy are the unfortunate result of repeated failure to find workable alternatives to perceived institutional imperfections. Many dissenters are young people who are just entering institutional life and are neither blind to its imperfection nor despairing about its change. When the institutions do not provide opportunities for dissent, the resulting alienation may threaten to destroy or reduce them to absurdities.

The high school must meet the same political challenges as other social institutions. Students voice dissent within the school just as young citizens voice their dissent outside the school. The school, therefore, faces a very real choice. It can use student dissent for its own reform in response to new social realities and, in this way, gain vigor and renew itself. Or it can thwart student dissent to preserve a superficial calm that hides subterranean turmoil and despair. In the perceptions of many students, high schools usually make the second choice.

There are strong psychological arguments for the value of dissent in the development of character. It is the verbal and behavioral forerunner of personal independence. To the extent that dissent is reasonable criticism of group behavior and goals, it is evidence of what Freudians call ego autonomy or strong character. Modern theorists of moral development postulate "independent," "personal," or "self-directed" morality as the highest stage of moral growth (Kay, 1969). The internalized personal standard is the ultimate goal of moral development. Theorists agree that the school is responsible for promoting this moral growth. Dissent allows students opportunities to make public their private moral standards when these standards are in conflict with the public standard of school and peer group. Dissent, in this way, leads to the opportunity for the students to compare standards and to know and experience the full range of moral choice. Dissent, as the result of the conflict of individual, group, and school standards, can change institutional morality and foster the moral development of students. John Stuart Mill recognized the dual value of dissent for individual and society:

It is not by wearing down into uniformity all that is individual in themselves, but by cultivating it, and calling it forth, within the limits imposed by the rights and interests of others, that human beings become a noble and beautiful object of contemplation; and as the works partake the character of those who do them, by the same process human life also becomes rich, diversified, and animating, furnishing more abundant aliment to high thoughts and elevating feelings, and strengthening the tie which binds every individual to the race, by making the race infinitely better worth belonging to. In proportion to the development of his individuality, each person becomes more valuable to himself, and is therefore capable of being more valuable to others.

Kay (1969, p. 34), asserts that the school actually retards the appearance of independent moral judgment in students by demanding their submissiveness to an authoritarian structure:

The empirical evidence suggests that there is a period of moral decline, or at least a period of arrested moral growth in early adolescence, but it must be made perfectly clear that the evidence can be interpreted in another way. These moral agents are school children. They belong to an essentially authoritarian, heteronomous organization. In view of this it is equally true to argue that the development of moral autonomy in this context will *inevitably appear to be* a decline in morality.

With the authoritarian structure of the school, Webb (quoted in Kay, 1969) believes it is "not too much of an exaggeration to say that sanity is only possible [for students] by being, when not working, irrepressible, spontaneous, and rule-breaking." The views of both writers argue for schools that open avenues of free expression and channel it in ways that foster the students' emotional independence and moral autonomy. In the Freudian view, we can expect that allowing the verbal form of dissent will provide students the choice of constructive reform behavior.

The school can be measured against the criterion of how well it produces independence of moral judgment in students. One way to produce moral independence is to encourage students to act on their own judgments. Another is to encourage them to verbalize those judgments. Toleration of dissent is not enough. The school should actively evoke and reward it rather than fear and suppress it.

Much fear of dissent comes from the implicit understanding that independent and original thought is dangerous. The dissenter does not go along with what everyone accepts as the social reality. His ideas sound new and strange and even a little terrifying. The new ideas challenge old group credos that form the bases of old relationships. Dissent, therefore, threatens the lines of communication from one person to another within the group. Thus, it seems to be a threat to the security and cohesiveness of the group as a whole as well as to each member of it.

Describing the "intellectual" student whom he specifically defines as the divergent thinker, Liam Hudson (1966, p. 172) suggests why the dissenter makes school adults uncomfortable:

In searching for crises, therefore, the intellectual plays a solitary game in which, in a sense, the integrity of his personality is at stake. He abandons himself, and finds, once the crisis is past, that he has survived intact. This is not thrill-seeking for its own sake, but thrill-seeking of a kind which enables a man to stir the embers of a primitive desire: the longing to be engulfed totally by someone else. His difficulties (and our apprehension) arise both from the fear of abandoning his autonomy, and from the more specific horror that his impulse was originally incestuous. It was directed toward his mother. Some readers will doubtless find this train of thought preposterous. To my mind, nevertheless, it encompasses neatly our intuition that intellectual discovery is dangerous; the fascination that it exerts over a small minority; the inhibitions which they may experience; and the much greater inhibitions which the prospect of discovery evokes in the rest of us.

The idea that divergent impulses come from some part of the personality that most of us find uncomfortable and avoid dealing with partly explains why the dissenter arouses so much hostility.

Studies of the political lives of American teachers have shown that they were models of conformity (Zigler, 1966). Although compliance helps teachers fit into the school system, it leaves students without models of dissent and independent moral judgment. The moral conformity of teachers even counteracts the biologically-based tendency of adolescents to turn a fresh gaze on old institutional arrangements, question them, and even rebel against them. Schools which provide neither the adult model nor the adult encouragement of dissent fail to inspire moral independence in students.

Hess and Torney (1967) believe that we do not yet know how the school as an institution and the teacher as an adult model shape the political attitudes of American students. But they write about this likelihood:

The tendency to evade some realities of political life seems to be paralleled by the school's emphasis upon compliance with respect to both itself and the community—although teaching children to obey is certainly an important function of the school. For some children, the combination of complacency and compliance may contribute to political inactivity and the failure to progress from early levels of involvement (attachment to nation) to a more vigilant, assertive involvement in political activities.

How can the school embark on the seemingly risky practice of encouraging dissent? In the beginning, students only need the time to talk and to discover where their disagreements lie. This student asked for such time:

Ethics class is all right when you can talk about what you want. But Mr. —— makes us pick subjects where there are two sides. Sometimes you can just talk about your ideas and learn about other people's without two sides. He wouldn't let us talk about abortion because of that.

The author, who observed this incident, saw that the teacher had a choice between allowing a general class discussion or of imposing a debate on the abortion laws. He had placed debate topics on the board and the class proceeded to ignore these, embarking instead on a discussion. It appeared that his decision was to have a debate while the students' decision was to have open discussion. Rather than their differing views on values and the specifics of the abortion laws, the true expression of dissent was their objection to being forced to debate. The teacher could have insisted on sticking to a debate that he was confident had two sides. He could claim that debate would give students practice in dealing with controversy. He could have set up two teams. For the students, however, such exercises could never have attained the reality of having experienced dissent. For the practice of dissent, deciding how to talk about the issues was more important than their substance.

We found relatively few incidents in which dissent was handled in ways fair to both dissenters and their opponents. This scarcity of positive incidents strongly indicates that, of the four rights, dissent was the least successfully handled, presumably because it is the most threatening. For about one-half the incidents, dissent was ranked first or second as the best title for the incident. This was true for urban as well as suburban senior high schools. More senior than junior high school students used the higher ranks for dissent (see Appendix B, Tables 2 and 3).

Relatively few alienated students could be interviewed. Board of education statistics show that Manhattan high schools graduate less than a tenth of the students who enter the tenth grade. Only about a tenth of those who do graduate achieve an academic diploma, the only credential accepted by most colleges and trade schools as proof of satisfactory educational achievement. The 99 percent who do not obtain the academic diploma have given us the most convincing proof of their alienation. They are registering their dissatisfaction in the most unmistakable terms.

Not to participate is a substitute for vocal dissent. Sometimes students felt general hostility toward the school:

> In this school many students are starting to feel that what's going on in the school is unfair, such as detention, suspension, the smoking rules, dress code, and many other school policies, personally I don't give a damn. I hate school very much and I am waiting patiently until the day I get out. . . . Starting something such as sending a paper to all students saying strike for what they want is bullshit, because even if everyone felt that way nothing would ever become of anything. . . .

This form of dissent, resulting in the student's withdrawal from the school, cannot renew the school.

But those who stay in school and register their dissent are not apathetic. They show by their staying that they hope to change the school. The mildest form of dissent is voicing dissatisfaction with an existing practice. Consider the complaint of this student:

> A few months ago I was suspended from classes because of my dress. Shit. I really can't see how dress has any connection with education. Blue jeans, bare-footed, and tee shirts will not reck my study habits. It's such a hassel to come well-groomed to school. Also my hair was quite long and I was forced to get a trim. Wow, like who the hell do they think they are. Your dress and your length of your hair have no connection with the individual's education.

When such verbal dissent meets with resistance from school authorities (and the angry, uncompromising tone almost insures strong negative reactions from teachers), the dissent may escalate to the level of student rebellion. The next student faces the same legal limits to his actions, yet he went to the level of behavioral dissent—he actually did something:

This year students took matters into their own hands and started a movement to totally ignore the "existing" dress code. Girls wore pants to school, boys wore their hair at lengths which they liked and some (those who could) wore beards and moustaches. The general trend was towards much more casual dress creating a more relaxed atmosphere. When the "authorities" realized what was happening they started taking measures to curb the movement by prohibiting certain "un-school like" dress modes. This created a feeling of dissent among the students and a more intense fight against the dress code. With some research it was discovered that legally school authorities can not punish students for the clothes they wear. In fact they cannot restrict dress unless it becomes physically detrimental to the student's education. When this was discovered authorities were forced to give up their dress code which was illegal in its existing form.

After official repression of student dissent over the dress code, the next step for the students was to use legal (verbal) means to obtain the change. The legal system provided a channel for dissent that was both effective in changing an outmoded policy and educative in reinforcing rational dissent among the students. Even though issues must change, the school must always make provision for dissent. The right to dissent, indeed, the *obligation* to dissent when one is convinced that the institution needs change, will remain.

The suppression of dissent can deepen alienation as shown in this principal's account of a student's exclusion from class:

A French teacher excluded a student from her class because he refused to become involved in the learning process. His presence in the classroom interfered with the normal positive atmosphere for learning, until he could voluntarily involve himself in learning. I considered the possibility of placement in another option but none were open that were of any interest to the student. I then held several counseling interviews with the student in an effort to get him to see the wisdom of his returning to class as his own idea and learning what he could. During the interviews I uncovered a much deeper problem of rejection by his peer group and called in his parents from whom I deducted there was a high level of non-acceptance in the home because of his uncooperative behavior. I recommended (1) transfer to another school to solve the peer group rejection situation, (2) the parents to take a positive approach to make the boy (adopted) feel more accepted in the family and (3) that the parents seek professional counseling for the boy whose whole attitude toward life and society in general was negative. The student was transferred. I accepted the exclusion as reasonable on the teacher's part and resolved not to allow the student to return. . . .

Rather than deal with the dissent in the classroom and the school, the teacher and principal excluded the student. By defining the problem as mental illness, the principal was able to see his action as beneficial for the student. If the principal was implying that the mere silent presence of the student in the class disrupted the learning of other students, then we can say that the principal was suppressing dissent. His alternative was to allow the student to discuss what he wanted for himself.

Dissent was also suppressed by students, as we see in the following two incidents. Just as the teacher and principal dealt with a student's dissent by sending him out of the classroom and, finally, out of the school, students can sometimes deal with the intolerable anxiety aroused by the dissent of other students by telling them to accept the majority view or to go away. The writer of this incident advocated just that:

On Tuesday, April 1, this high school was exposed to the stupid and asinine message that was handed out. A group of radicals who are afraid to expose themselves and speak out. The problems were the students or aliens were complaining about privelages that any person in another country would be glad to have. These pupils are free to leave this country at any time or they can shutup.

This student accuses the radicals of being afraid to speak out and then suggests that they leave if they don't like it. But the price for maintaining the open exchange of ideas is to face the pain of dissent.

Students more than school adults found dissent hard to tolerate. In the following incident the student refuses to tolerate the teacher's expression of a dissenting view:

When I sit in Social Studies and we are studying a country that
has communist government our teacher gives us a bunch of
communist propaganda. And when we try to speak up for our
country, she shuts us off. I believe people should be able to speak
their mind but when someone starts chopping down our country
they should go to hell. I hate it when our communist teacher
tells only one side of it. And when the class comes to the aid of
there country their is a real problem. And she won't let it be
handled in a democratic way. We could of had a good discussion
if everybody spoke but no she had to speak.

Students are more easily threatened with loss of belief than
the teachers because they are still in the formative stages of
developing character structure. Teachers can provide models
of tolerating dissent. With threats to job and reputation and
security hanging overhead, teachers can become fearful and
defend themselves from attack by stifling the verbal opposition
of their critics. The real test of the strength of our conviction
about dissent is our ability to engage in our own advocacy of
new and critical ideas while we tolerate the criticism of our
opponents.

Allowing students to wrestle with dissent can increase
student awareness of its costs and gains. The following incident
illustrates how students may attack this dilemma:

Our school's student organization (G.O.) had many elections
on all scales, large and small. One of the smaller elections took place
in our homeroom for a person who is supposed to represent our
class. Many times the elections will be very close like 10-11 and
the minority will be left out when it's only one less than majority.
If the election was 5-16 then it would be better. Perhaps
one way to try and solve this problem would be that in order
to be a majority your election has to have at least 5 more votes.
The number set for how much votes should decide elections
would depend on the number of people in the election. Example:
If candate A runs against candate B and they will be 40 people
voting in order for either A or B to win they must win by
ten votes in order to make a clear majority. I am saying that a
minority cannot express itself. Minniroties have acted in the past.
Our revolution (American) was started by a minniroty. This
problem could also be solved by having the runner up represent

the minnirty at a counsel and this offer opposing positions. If there was no minnaroty there would be no opposition and you would have one view on everything which would not work. When my homeroom election came up it was very close 15-17. Our alternate (runner up) is supposed to represent us when the winner is absent. Our winner was never absent so the runner up never represented the minority.

By having the opportunity to consider the dilemma of majority rule, the writer was stimulated to consider alternatives, devise strategies, and thereby to learn.

For the next student dissent was worth facing the anger of irate adults. He had dissented by gathering petition signatures for a war moratorium:

I was really expecting everybody to sign up but a lot of people didn't. They asked us how old we were. They said it was just what they expected, a bunch of fifteen-year-old kids trying to tell them what to do. They wouldn't listen to anything we had to say. But a lot more signed. There are a lot of people against the war. I guess it really did some good that we went.

We can contrast the satisfaction derived from dissent on a national political issue with the resentment engendered in those school situations above in which there was no opportunity to participate in the political process.

Summary

The second civic choice is dissent. In the political realm it sparks institutional change and increases the values placed on some institutional practices. In the psychological realm it develops independent political and moral judgment. It is important for the school not only to allow but also to encourage dissent. Dissent becomes the bridge between the political and psychological—between individual character development and the development of institutions.

The incidents showed three forms of dissent in the schools: verbal dissent (criticizing the dress code), behavioral dissent (disregarding the dress code), and non-participation. They showed that school officials, teachers, and students suppress dissent. Those suppressed were also teachers and students. The last two incidents showed the positive value of dissent—how it clarified a school issue and carried over to a national issue.

Participation in decision-making has two major consequences: (1) it can keep the school responsive to changing student and teacher needs and (2) it prepares students for democratic roles in other institutions. Our data showed that the school is the ideal place for teaching democratic decision-making because this is where the students said they wanted and needed it. They seldom wrote about national political conflict.

Non-participation and withdrawal pose the dilemma of balancing one civic choice against the other. They are a form of dissent (one civic choice) but they remove the individual from participation in decision-making and reduce his chances for satisfying his own needs and interests. One resolution of this dilemma is to participate in the group if only to voice publicly one's dissent.

As will be seen in Chapter 10, the psychological development of school age children requires continuously expanding interaction with peers, peer groups and adults other than one's own parents. And, in order to form group relationships which bind, the anger exposed by dissent has to be established. The kind of dissent adults sometimes dismiss as arguing just for the argument's sake is a necessary part of adolescent development. Dissent in a supportive environment allows the open verbal expression of anger, discussed in Chapter 5. Dissenting is the first step in any negotiation, as will become clear in Chapter 9. Participation ties the remaining chapters of this book together. The only way to teach and learn—the best way to run a school or a country—is to be in there participating.

4 Civic Status EQUALITY AND DUE PROCESS

UNLIKE THE RIGHTS OF participation in decision-making and dissent, the rights of civic status belong to the individual regardless of the form of government or the person's choice. One has no right to either the choice to exploit or the choice to be exploited because choosing either limits the freedom of others. To behave like the inferior stereotype is to pretend that we have the choice of inequality. To choose the role of the exploited is to force others into the role of the exploiters. Due process is not a matter of choice either. If one person gives up the right of due process or if we as a society deny due process to a single member, it erodes that right for all. Since equality and due process are rights of status rather than individual choices, they cannot be surrendered by individuals.

The Right of Equality

The right of equality asserts that particular types of heritage, abilities, desires, talents, and personal values are neither superior nor inferior to other types. It provides for the equal acceptance of each member of society. As a tradition of rugged individualism, equality has often clashed with historical pressure to amalgamate the diverse subgroups of American society. The civil rights movement asserted the right of people who are black, brown, white, yellow and red to human relations of equality and reciprocity. The civil rights advocates ask school adults and students to discard not only the color stereotypes but also the stereotypes of nationality, sex, status, class, money, dress, and physical appearance.

Various writers have suggested that the school can and should promote socioeconomic equality by encouraging lower-class students to seek upper- and middle-class status. Friedenberg (1963), for example, advocated sending ghetto blacks to prestigious prep schools. Dewey (1916) pointed to the high school's responsibility for encouraging upward mobility as the path to social integration.

Increased status is only part of the equality issue in the high school. The pressure for racial and ethnic equality is exerted in two directions. First, there is the push toward integration in the hope that some of the status of the white children can be shared with their non-white schoolmates. Second, there is the push toward separation—the idealism of ethnic pride as a means of establishing a distinctive group identity within which the high school student can establish a personal identity. Ironically, "equal but separate" becomes the motto of young separatists.

The simultaneous pressure for integration and separation creates painful ambivalences in the people of the ghetto and slows their drive to improve their social and economic status. The demands for integration and separation both began with black people. We can still see "the faces of black domestic servants window shopping later at night in fashionable white suburban shopping centers" (Lelyveld, 1970). Other non-white groups, American Indians, Chicanos, Puerto Ricans, Orientals, have now followed blacks in demanding a share in the larger society.

Middle-class status is attractive to many non-white people and motivates their integration. The high schools have taught them to feel worthless and envious of the middle class. Yet society spent less on schools for them, built new schools in suburbs from which they were excluded, gave them the worst books, least experienced teachers and fewest opportunities for academic achievement. Thus society has frustrated the very desires it raised in non-whites.

Speaking of those in American schools who deride black youngsters' interest in fancy clothes, Bayard Rustin (1970) asked:

Might they then show some compassionate understanding of black youngsters who dream of better things even when crippled by poor education? Broken families, and the disabilities caused by slum life? If it is true that a Negro boy is nobody unless he owns alligator shoes and an alpaca sweater, who created these symbols? Who whetted his appetite? Who profited from the sale of these commodities and who advertised them? And who is victimized?

The high schools that expelled these young people expressed the middle-class attitude toward them. For the few blacks who didn't accept expulsion, the right costume expressed their willingness to "go on." While the South African servants want the clothes on sale in the white men's shops, the American high school dude can and does buy and wear them. Having realized that the clothes don't facilitate social acceptance, the dudes created a fashion for Afro-style clothes. These clothes were symbols for the black culture and wearing them expressed their pride.

Their separatist movement in the high school has led to the institution of ethnic studies courses. These courses have not only bolstered group esteem and changed the ideas of students about their own goals, but also have begun to change notions of what is desirable in our whole culture.

The tensions produced by simultaneous pressures toward integration and separation also apply to women and the young. Driven by the need for integration, women asked for equal job opportunities and believed that having the same work would give them equal status with men. Women, like blacks, tried to integrate first by dressing more like men (which is a cause of the seemingly irrational reactions first encountered by women wearing pants!) and later by working more like men. A high school woman complained that she was "forced to conform to

the Board of Education's image of her sex. At seven co-ed
vocational schools, boys can learn clerical work, food preparation, and beauty care along with the girls. But the courses that
would normally be found in a boy's school are not open to
girls" (De Rivera, 1970, p. 370).

But neither dressing nor working like men could satisfy that
need for a separate identity which women have for the same
reason blacks do—the need to become seriously themselves
instead of comical imitations of others. To achieve this identity,
women separatists have had to view all men as oppressors.
Their separatist Redstockings Manifesto proclaims (pp. 533-34):

Because we have lived so intimately with our oppressors, in isolation
from each other, we have been kept from seeing our personal
sufferings as a political condition. This creates the illusion that
a woman's relationship with her man is a matter of interplay
between two unique personalities, and can be worked out
individually. In reality, every such relationship is a *class* relationship,
and the conflicts between individual men and women are *political*
conflicts that can only be solved collectively.

Women may have different as well as some of the same needs.
The institution of women's studies courses could parallel ethnic
studies courses as a serious high school reform aimed at helping
women identify their group goals by examining their past
history and present problems.

The young are simultaneously engaged in the fight for
integration with and separation from adults. They were once
perceived as miniature adults living by adult standards and
conforming to adult choices. They were expected to dress and
act like adults and even referred to as young women and young
men. Like women and ethnic groups, youth culture has mani-
fested itself in dress first. The young are constantly instituting
new styles that differentiate them from previous youth. The
idea of the young as a separate group is relatively modern
and has taken the form of institutions that segregate the young
(Aries, 1965). There have been writers like Paul Goodman
(1960) and Ivan Illich (1971) who have advocated doing away

with schools as one form of institutional segregation and integrating young people into the adult society.

There have been several advocates of a separate youth culture. The youthful separatists have asserted their identity by their distinctive modes of dress, music, food, work, and travel. Erikson (1968) and Coleman (1971) emphasized the need for adolescents to form a peer consensus that is different from the adult culture in order to form a group identity as an alternative to the family identity. Blos (1962) describes how the adolescent vacillates between identification with adults significant in his life (integration) and identification with peers (separation from family). We suggest that young people have a right to organize some school time to pursue interests unique to their age group even when these interests will be abandoned as they grow older.

High school textbooks contribute to the problem of failing to help the attainment of equality through the process of integration and separation. An examination of forty-five social studies textbooks, published since 1965, showed inadequate treatment of living conditions and heritage of the blacks and gave no mention of problems of women and young people (Kane, 1970). They even failed to treat the problems of the poor and of other ethnic minorities. These are the books most likely to be purchased by school districts and used by the schools in the seventies. Even though we have limited our treatment to the current issues of equality for minority groups, including black people, women, and the young, we know there are many other forms of inequality that we have not even mentioned. As students become aware of inequalities that they were not aware of before, these are likely to become issues in the school setting. The raising of new issues can replace the always out-dated published materials and become the renewed content of civic education. And if we never published the materials at all, we would save a lot of taxpayers' money.

The school's attempts to incorporate the forces of both integration and separation of all ethnic groups, of women, and of the young can induce students to think seriously about what it means to be equal—about who wants equality, for what reasons, and the price in individuality one is willing to pay for group membership. Serious attempts of the school to practice as well as to preach equality can make radical changes in curriculum and school governance.

Does school change really make a difference in student attitudes toward and practice of equality? Recent studies (Katz, 1972) show that institutional change produces changes in students:

1. Black students were accorded higher status by their white classmates when they were assigned high status roles by the teacher.
2. Girls in all-female groups were listened to more often by women when the leadership role was assigned to female students.
3. A teacher succeeded in changing the power relations in his classroom by voluntarily removing himself from the role of authority.

All of these positive outcomes were responses to the classroom problems arising when students faced the forces of integration and separation. Attaining equality may be very difficult, but these small beginnings do give hope that change is possible.

Our findings showed that 45 percent of the students ranked equality as the first or second best label for their incident. Equality ranked higher in the senior than in the junior high schools. Equality also ranked higher in the urban than in suburban schools. There were no consistent differences between integrated and segregated schools (De Cecco, Richards, *et al.*, 1970).

Student demand for equality in the high schools began with the demand for black equality just as the national demand for ethnic and sexual equality began with the black citizens. There were differences in our findings between the segregated and integrated high schools, differences between schools in poverty areas of the inner city and schools in the affluent suburbs. Yet all of the schools faced the problem of social equality.

The first demand for black equality was for school integration. By 1969, however, students were asking for courses in black history. As the following incident illustrates, the demands for black history courses were an assertion of the need for a racial identity of equal value to but separate from other races:

I am a black student. This is the first year they have given us black history and now they say they aren't going to give it to us again. I couldn't take it this half of year because I already have a full schedule. So my guidance tells me to take it next year. They only taught it for half a year anyway. You tell me one black student who wants to learn about white history all their lives! They call it world history, American history and 20th century history but they might as well say white history because all they teach us about blacks is they were slaves.

Black students often asked for racial separation. Black and white students, however, often wanted the benefits of racial integration. The next incident shows that students can perceive how much they lose when the racial barriers divide them:

One of the utmost problems in today's American society is the conflict between the races of black and white. Blacks feel they have been penalized all these years for something that is beyond their control. Of course they have been penalized—but to a certain extent. Recently John's sister was dating a Negro, her parents found out and sent her to Missouri. As a result a gang of Negroes grouped together around John. They told him unless he fought his parents store would be damaged. So he did, with his sister's boyfriend. John won the fight. The blacks couldn't let it go at that. The next day in the school, 7 to 10 blacks beat John up. Fair? Unfair? To begin with, it was unfair of John's parents, they couldn't accept this new thing. But there was no reason for John to be involved and then attacked. The whole situation was unrelated and almost ridiculous. It should have stopped with the white girl and the colored boy being separated. The hurt was John's parents were prejudiced, but it was over with them. The fighting should never have occured. This story shows problems of equality first off.

The last two incidents involved confrontation between blacks and whites. Other ethnic groups now make demands similar to those made in 1969 by the black students.

In the following incident the writer demands preservation of ethnic identity as a prerequisite to integration:

The students do not like the idea that another student has to be put in a class where the student does not understand the subject. The teacher said that this is the best way to teach that student how to understand or speak English. The other students do not like the teacher's idea because how can a student be taught how to speak English if the words being used are too hard for the student to *understand*.

At some schools attended by black students, there were significantly more issues of racial equality than in the general sample of schools. A most striking finding, however, was that incidents of racial equality usually involved adult administration of rules in unequal ways. One student, for example, stated:

When the colored kids sit on the radiators (which is forbidden) none of the teachers tells them to get off because, as one teacher said, "I'm afraid one might stab or knock me out." One white girl sat on the radiators and received detention. Another was suspended for the same act. I feel that if any student, whether black or white, breaks a rule, equal punishment should be administered for both. Being afraid has led to a touchy situation. Another time, one Negro student wrote on a girl's room: "For Blacks Only." Then both girls and boy Negro students piled into the adjacent boys' room. Though the teachers knew, not one tried to stop it.

This incident was described by a white student in a "working class" school. She could easily be identified as part of the "silent majority." Yet she was dissatisfied. What was she angry at? Not the black students' behavior, but the injustice of the adults in not punishing it. She reacted to the arbitrary, abject failure of the adults to deal with the situation caused by their own rules. If the adults made the rules and enforced them for one group of students, she felt that they should be enforced for all students. This is a simple enough expectation for someone who has been taught that the Constitution provides equal protection under law. Schools have the responsibility both to teach the realistic limitations of the judicial system and to provide a model of justice closer to what they preach.

The pattern of white school officials and teachers who "cool it" when black students break rules that they enforce for white students, inevitably leads to increased resentment and raises tension levels. But, since there is covert permission to vent rage on other students and strong overt prohibition against using violence toward authorities, the violence that ensues pits student against student, white against black, and group against group, as the following incident, reported by several students at the school illustrates:

A fuss, commotion or a problem started in our school shortly after the assassination of Dr. Martin Luther King. Prior to this, the black and white kids here were on good terms and were really "brothers." After this, disagreements and tensions mounted, so much so that people were afraid to go into the lavatory alone for fear of trouble. Many felt uneasy and could not communicate with their black friends after this because we felt that there was no longer an equity between us. This was seen later in 1968, *when a white* girl was cut with a razor at a school dance because she finally got disgusted and spoke out about the situation and what she felt should be done.

Maybe you would by now call me a bigot, but I am sick and tired of all the mess and I simply want things back the way they were. The colored people never worried about equality before and did nothing. Equality is something that is not achieved overnight, but gradually.

The crisis over the celebration of King's birthday was reported by many students, both black and white. One black student described how he viewed the handling of the incident:

It happened in my school the day of Martin Luther King's birthday. We the black students wanted that day off. We thought why shouldn't we? The Jewish have their holidays, the Italians, and so on. So we said we should have our own too. We're not worse than anybody else. Our first problem was that we have a club, the Black Student Coalition, and our president didn't agree with

that. Even though she didn't we went ahead and we talked with
our principal and he said that he'll see about it. But we
didn't see nothing done.

So the day before King's birthday we made a kind of riot, not
exactly, because everything was quiet but all we did was refuse
to go to classes until something was done. Our principal came and
told us that we had to talk with the supervisor so there we went,
until we had the day. And we made a program, which everybody
went to, even the white kids, and after the program all the black
kids left for their homes and the white kids stayed in school.
Now, we had part of what we wanted but not all, because we
wanted it to be a holiday just like Kennedy's day and so on. We
wanted everybody to participate in it. In my opinion the black
students went along with that, they said they fought for that,
so they were the ones who were supposed to get the prize.
But I don't think so. Because on that day you could see and feel
clearly the problem of prejudism. And I don't think there was
another way of solving that problem, but in the way we did.

White students saw the principal's reaction to the black students'
refusal to take part in the normal school activities as an abdication of responsibility. To abdicate responsibility is not the
same as to honor equality. The following example is typical of
student reactions to abdication of responsibility:

It happened in school. The negroes started it. They didn't bother
going to classes and they did what they pleased. No white girls
could go in the girls' room. The teachers to me seemed afraid
of them and did absolutely nothing. This problem could have been
handled with plain discipline, but nothing was done. And to
this very day nothing has been done.

The black student poignantly describes how he and his friends
were driven to "riot" by the inaction of the principal, were
rewarded for their misbehavior by finally getting someone to
negotiate with them and wound up causing bad feeling and
prejudice. The capitulation of the principal was seen by the
white students as inequitable enforcement of school rules.
Racial feelings erupted at a school dance a few days later, and
the white girl was knifed at a dance.

It is easy to interpret the knifing incident as pure racial hatred. But that ignores the part that the school principal played in creating a situation of fear and distrust by unfair administration of the rules. Too often school administrators avoid any kind or degree of confrontation and thereby sweep a small problem under the rug only to have it work its way into a big problem. It is also easy to blame the increase in bad feeling between white and black students on social and political forces beyond the control of school officials. But blaming such incidents on the students' own prejudices or the pressures of the larger society, while failing to make sure that the school is run in such a way as to keep students in contact with each other as people and not just as subjects in the same dictatorship, is a clear abdication of responsibility.

Students do bring prejudices they have learned at home to school. As they grow older their political beliefs more and more resemble their parents' beliefs. School officials, teachers, parents and student leaders who exploit the undemocratic beliefs of students call grave trouble down upon themselves and their schools.

One of the bitter myths about high school unrest is that racial strife among students themselves is the source of much of the trouble. Our study showed that relatively few of the students believed that their incidents dealt mainly with the issue of equality.

Minority and even majority subgroups often suffer a difficult polarity. At one pole there is the pull toward integration with the institutional mainstream. At the opposite pole there is a pull toward separation. This polarity creates conflict even when the issue is the equality of women and men:

I don't think it was right to pass the law about girls wearing slacks to school, because some can't wear slacks to school, because of their figure, or home life. Some parents won't let their kids wear pants to movies or bowling and of course school. The girl who started the petition did not make it clear to everyone that there was a petition going around. I do love to wear pants anyplace but it was unfair to other kids. Some kids that are very fat and sloppy are wearing slacks to school and it looks horrible. It makes

everyone ashamed of the girls and the boys make fun
of the girls in slacks now.

The issue of sexual equality underlies this girl's complaints
about the school dress code. She talks of women's dress in
terms of pleasing others. Her objection to fat girls wearing
pants is that the sight of them in pants will offend other people.
The notion that fat boys in pants could be equally offensive
never occurs to her. Like the society around her, she doesn't
seem to regard the idea of pants only for thin women as male
domination. She does not question the right of fat boys to
wear pants, accepting that male prerogative. The value conflict
is entirely internalized for this girl. She is just beginning to
want equality as a woman. High schools, like the rest of
society, can oppress women far more easily than men simply
by spoofing the issues. By laughing at the girls in pants, high
school boys merely protect their superior status in ways the
media have found effective.

A third category of incidents in which there were complaints
about inequality dealt with the issue of age status. Discrimination by age leads to inequality of opportunity for younger
children. The following incident illustrates age discrimination:

I found upon going to a meeting for the first time that many of the
students who attended were being completely ignored when
they wanted to present their point of view. After listening for
a while, I found that there were four or five older individuals,
of the thirty members attending, always being called on for remarks
while other students had been trying to speak for a long time.
Usually when one of the students was talking he would have
five or ten minutes to speak leaving no time for anyone else.
Many of the students there were in the grades ten to twelve. This
incident took place in a school classroom and was instigated by a
faculty member. The problem was not handled well and no
matter what was said the same four or five students still were doing
most of the talking. This problem could have been handled much
better by the faculty member prohibiting the same four or five
students to speak and let the people who were not as well known
as the others speak. If he did this the meeting might have
been more democratic.

Here, older students were given speaking priority while younger students were ignored.

Because demands for equality began with the complaints of black students, the first attempts to remove school inequalities addressed their complaints. We found that establishing black studies courses at several schools with black students did reduce conflict over the curriculum. None of the students interviewed in the black studies classes complained of dissatisfaction with these classes. When they got what they wanted they were satisfied—a conclusion supported by teachers and students who could observe the change.

In the following incident the teacher recognized the connection between the assembly called to hear the grievances of black students and the effect that positive action had on the school curriculum:

Democracy and the struggle for democratic rights has been in the news in this high school—taking the form of minority and majority rights conflicts. Prior to Martin Luther King's birthday, the black students in the school attempted to bring about a change in the Social Studies curriculum and to have King's birthday declared a school holiday. In trying to secure these demands, their protests took the form of a virtual strike—cutting classes, walking through the halls, holding meetings in various parts of the building. As the Social Studies Dept. had been making an effort the year long to include the role of the black man in courses offered— including a functioning black student curriculum committee—the protest by the black students did not seem to bring about any substantial change, but rather an increased awareness on the part of the teachers and students alike of some problems faced by this minority. The demand for a school holiday was met—not by declaring a day off, but instead by the holding of a special assembly, arranged by the black students.

Since that time, with a variety of pressure tactics seemingly being used by the black students (walking through the halls in groups of 2-5, pressuring white students for money, restricting the use of lavatories by intimidating white users, issuing threats, etc.) a white backlash has been developing among the majority. Students speak of being afraid, feeling tense and uneasy,—to my knowledge, this reactionary movement has not been organized.

As a Social Studies instructor, hopefully somewhat aware of the needs of students to become involved in a democratic way in decisions that affect them, I have tried (both in regents and non-regents classes) to have students plan the material. In the non-regents classes, this effort has been continued throughout the year—and seems to have been met with some success. The students in two classes—when asked what they wanted to study—have suggested mostly current topics (riots, the draft, the Kennedy's, the civil rights movement, black history, the war in Vietnam, the Pueblo incident, Middle East crisis, etc.) and their requests have been met. For the most part student interest has been maintained—traditional forms of testing or grade giving (grade determining) procedures have not been successful, i.e. only on the war unit did the students seem to take exceptional interest and perform well in testing. As long as material becomes required, enthusiasm seems to decline when the time comes for me to have to grade performance.

Since the curriculum, by virtue of the importance placed on regents, becomes more structured in regents classes, various discussion days are held when topics of interest to the students are brought up. As these days involve no note taking or graded efforts, they have been met with enthusiasm. Students volunteer to secure information on the topic ahead of time and though the contribution depends on the individual, their effort generally is noteworthy.

The age status of teachers no longer was used to justify the prescribed curriculum in this school. By respecting the black students' demand for changes in the social studies curriculum, the school demonstrated how equality becomes the basis for reform.

Incidents for which equality was chosen as the best label dealt with issues of separation, such as wanting to take black studies and have a holiday dedicated to the memory of a black leader. They also contained issues of integration such as a white student wanting to date a black student and non-English speaking students wanting to learn English. There were several incidents where the handling of school conflict by school officials converted an issue of fair administration of rules (due process) to issues of racial inequality.

The Right of Due Process

The right of due process is the bedrock of democratic law and order. To ignore or abrogate this right is to cause widespread social disorder. Due process can be defined as basic fairness in procedure whenever sanctions against individuals or groups are applied by governmental or institutional authorities. It is particularly important that the right of due process be protected for those students who dissent to school practices.

Instituting due process in the schools means adding institutional structures to an already complex organization. It complicates running the school, for example, to have a student court. Having a court composed of student, teacher, administrator, board of education and parents is even more complicated. The whole judiciary practice seems cumbersome, and it is, and the judicial system has numerous flaws of which students have to be aware and critical. But consider the alternatives: either capricious, arbitrary discipline with teachers defending themselves from the onslaughts of the "barbaric" students or some students tyrannizing over other students, teachers and school officials. Neither of these choices is appealing. Robert Havighurst (1969, p. 103) belives that:

The high school and junior high school years are probably the most important ones for learning social responsibility through conscious effort.

He favored programs that would give students the opportunity for service to society and the presence of adult models of self-esteem and social responsibility. A student court might supply the former, but only an all-school court could supply the latter. Both kinds of social responsibility would evolve in a school regulated by due process. A series of lower courts could be set up in each homeroom or social studies class. Superior school courts could deal with situations outside the classroom and with appeals from the lower classroom courts.

Such judicial systems have also been established spontane-
ously by the teenage "clubs" and "gangs" now forming on the
streets of large cities. One gang member told one of the
authors:

We don't take no s—— from any of the guys. A brother is on dope,
he makes all the brothers mad. We get him, we rap. He raps.
We take turns sitting with him till he forgets it. If not, he gets out.
You can't trust a guy on junk to follow any rules man. He gotta
make it with the brothers, not with dope.

If the street clubs could learn to temper justice with mercy
and make the punishment fit the crime, then they could reha-
bilitate their criminal members. By employing a system of
justice in the school, students could learn to police themselves
and to become responsible. School adults, acting as advisors,
could make the difference between success and failure for the
street gangs.

Due process is the most deeply entrenched of all the civil
rights. It has received the most vigorous support, partly because it is the right that links the conflicts of the present
most securely to the past precedents for resolving them. The
Fourteenth Amendment guarantees the right of due process to
students facing school charges (Reitman, Follman, and Ladd,
1972). This report (pp. 7-8) identifies four aspects of due
process:

1. notification of charges,
2. the right to counsel,
3. opportunity to rebut charges in a fair hearing,
4. a separation among accuser, judge and executioner.

After defining the school as a governmental body in the sense
of the Fourteenth Amendment, the report specifically states
that:

While schools cannot be expected to provide formal procedural
due process whenever a classroom regulation is flouted, in
administering justice teachers should be guided by the requirements
of due process. The classroom offers the ideal environment to

inculcate in children the concept of democratic behavior within a framework of rules. Children have their first close continuing contact with formal authority in the schools; here they acquired attitudes toward liberty and equality that are of lasting influence. As an advocate of the constitution and an exponent of its principles, the teacher has a unique opportunity to exemplify the spirit and practice of fair play and procedures. Such exemplification is ill served by the sweeping dispensation of summary justice by force which deprives students of liberty and due process of law and undermines respect for the democratic process.

There is a psychological as well as political rationale for due process in the school. The opportunity to engage in the procedures of due process can motivate students to understand, use, and preserve them.

Schools have tried less radical alternatives. In the late sixties, students were given case materials from which to deduce general legal principles from the study of particular events (Oliver and Shaver, 1966). The case materials derived from the authors' concerns rather than the students' experience and conflicts. Case studies have been particularly fruitful in teaching due process. The model courtroom and mock jury trial have a long and honorable history in American education. They have relieved the tedium of lectures for generations of students.

Like other textbook authors, Oliver and Shaver provide the students materials on approved methods of analysis and on pre-selected sets of social values. Their materials are better than conventional texts because they combine concrete examples with general rules and historical generalizations. In format, however, their materials are conventional—detailed unit sequences. The units are completely pre-planned. The number of class periods (e.g., six weeks for project and one week for non-project materials) to be spent on each topic (e.g., "Settling of the West") is determined long before school starts. Packaged units easily become stale for students occupied with their own immediate interests.

Our findings showed that due process was least frequently ranked as first or second best title for their incidents by all students. The proportion of incidents for which due process was selected as first or second best title was lower for students than for trained coders ranking the same incidents. Since there was considerably more student-coder agreement for the other three rights, this finding suggests that students are most confused about the meaning of due process. Coders gave high ranks for about 47 percent of the incidents, while students gave high ranks to due process for only about 40 percent, a significant difference. Suburban students ranked due process high as a title for more incidents than urban students.

Even in a school district in Kansas which publishes a booklet for students on their rights, few students bother to read about them. The concepts of due process are difficult in their abstract form. Only by teaching those concepts in terms of actual classroom and schoolwide conflicts can the school discharge its responsibility to students.

The incidents which students labeled as problems in due process were examples of all four aspects of due process, either singly or in combination.

The following incident shows how the school ignored the student's right to notification of charges:

When I was in eighth grade, I had a incident with a teacher. My teacher's name was Mr. N. . . . and the teacher next door to us name was Mr. K. This particular day our class was extra noisy, so Mr. K. came into the class and asked what was going on. Mr. N. told him that he asked a girl to get out and she wouldn't move. So Mr. K. asked him which girl he did want out. Mr. N. pointed to the girl next to me but Mr. K. came to me and told me to leave. I told him I wasn't the one who was supposed to be leaving so he pulled me up out of the chair and pushed me out of the room. When we got outside I hit him and cursed him out so he took me to the assistant principal's office and I had to sit there all day.

The principal told me I had to stay after school for what I had done. But I went back home and brought my mother back with me. Of course the teacher denied everything and my mother was even against me. So I was suspended. Nothing was done about the teacher.

The problem should have been handled in a different way. I think that even though the principal believed the teacher my mother should have believed me. Something should have been done about the teacher for pulling and pushing on me.

The student complains bitterly about an incident that took place in school over a year ago. What bothers her most is not the suspension, but the lack of proper identification and notification. In asserting control over a class that had gone beyond the regular classroom teacher's power to control, the neighboring teacher did not care *which* student was thrown out. Someone had to be thrown out to intimidate the rest of the class. The teacher very likely avoided chaos involving many students at the price of injustice to one student. The incident is typical of situations in which students claimed that one person was punished for the rule infraction of another. The writer confesses to the use of violence. But cursing and hitting the teacher is described as the writer's reaction to the teacher's pushing and pulling. It reflects the most primitive notion of justice, the *lex talionis* rule of "an eye for an eye."

The second aspect of due process is the right to counsel so that the accused may answer and rebut the charges against him. Students rarely mentioned the lack of counsel, be it a sympathetic third party (peer or adult) or a lawyer. Few students seemed to know that they even had the right to counsel. Outside of school students belonged to groups which made them aware of this right. The following incident illustrates this awareness of a student in his role of employee:

I work in a supermarket not far from my school. Since this store is part of a chain the company can afford to hire people for security purposes, but I feel in some cases they act like a gestapo. There was one incident which happened several weeks ago which I was not directly involved in, but heard a lot about. A girl who works as a cashier at the store gave a large discount to one of her friends on meat. A security man caught her and she was taken off her register. This was her first offense, but they didn't think about that, but called the police so they could book her on petty larceny. The girl happens to be sixteen years old. The security squad, five men, took her in the back and questioned her for several hours. To get her to talk they promised that if she confessed it wouldn't hurt her future career and it would be better for her. They not only made her confess and sign a paper after being under such strain, but to tell names of other people who had done something similar. They called this girl many names and made her feel like a really bad kid when she hadn't done anything wrong before. She could have been able to have a union representative during the questioning, but they didn't even tell her her rights. Later that night, after putting the girl in jail they called the other girls into be questioned. These girls also didn't know they could have a union representative there. The security accused the other girls of being tramps, bums and many other things and got them very upset so they would confess to something and then gave it to them to sign. Two girls didn't get in trouble, but one confessed and got suspended, perhaps fired from work.

The third aspect of due process is the right to a fair hearing. Students often complained that they did not have the chance to tell their adult accusers their side of the conflict. The next incident illustrates the anger students felt about not having a fair hearing:

There is no set discipline system—each teacher imposes her own ideas of discipline in her own highly individualized method. I am able to relate more than one incident in which one teacher has imposed what students feel is a "too strict" system of discipline, which is unfair to the students. For example, in our school it is customary to attend homeroom at 3 p.m. so that the teacher may relate any information necessary for the class to receive. Many days there is no need for homeroom, and the teacher tells the president (of the homeroom) to inform the girls or the teacher tells any girls who come to homeroom that they can leave. Last week, the teacher of whom I am speaking had nothing to do in homeroom. However, she did not contact her president and took attendance. One girl, who had stayed after her math class to arrange for tutoring, was two minutes late. Even though the girl explained why she was late she was made to stay an hour after school. The students feel this is unfair because the teacher did not take into account the reasons for the girl's lateness. The girl is treasurer of the class and always goes to homeroom to collect dues. If I were the teacher, I would establish some method of contacting the students if they do not need to come back. There were other girls who could vouch that the girl was asking for help.

The next incident shows how parents can intercede with the school on their children's behalf to protect their right to due process:

I remember when I was in seventh grade, I was working on an award for a certain civic group. It was a very high honor and took 18 months to complete. I had finished the preliminary and first step requirements, and was therefore assigned a day to be tested by an examiner. (The steps were written in a sort of scrapbook) After completing the examination, the examiner wrote down in my book some information including whether I had passed or not. He said something to me, but I didn't hear him, and because I was nervous, didn't ask him to repeat it, but just answered "Yes, sir." When I left the office, there were some other kids waiting to be tested, and they flocked around me, asking if I had passed. I said I didn't know, so I went to look in the book to see if I had or not. Just as I was pulling out the piece of paper, the examiner opened the door and began saying, "You cheat, sneak, etc, etc, You're unworthy, blah, blah. I told you not to tell anyone what the result was until you got home and told your parents!"

He had me so stupefied, shocked and frightened that I began to cry, saying, "I didn't hear what you said. I didn't realize . . . I wouldn't have taken out the paper if I had heard you I sorry but I was afraid to ask you to repeat yourself."

Well, my parents went down that evening and explained to him the situation and he said, "It was a misunderstanding." I was determined to finish it and that May I received the award.

This person I consider an ignorant fool. People who loose their temper and don't bother to listen to both sides of a story gain no respect in my eyes. The whole situation would not have occurred if he had been open-minded.

The student is correct in blaming his unfortunate experience on the behavior of the examiner. But the larger issue is the right to a fair hearing. In this instance the violation of that right is especially ironic because the examiner was giving a test on civic behavior to honor students. Unfortunately the student sees the event as a personal matter, rather than as failure of due process.

The fourth aspect of due process is the need to separate accuser, judge and executioner. Lewis Carroll gave the best picture of this aspect in his account of a trial of the dormouse by the cat. "I'll be the judge and I'll be the jury says the cunning old fury." And one need not ask about the results of *that* trial. Nor does one wonder who the executioner will be. No one would intimate that his need to be judge and jury could be motivated by any considerations more noble than a wish for a tender little mouse for dinner. Most school adults really do begin their careers with the wish to be more helpful than punitive. Yet failure to separate prosecutor, judge, and executioner leads them to inflicting harsh punishments on students. The next incident illustrates how an educator's wish to be helpful can be perverted into a harsh punishment by the failure to separate judicial roles:

My incident is mainly about school. All the girls were in homeroom and our official teacher politely said there would be a raid on our locker rooms and if any locker was found open all their books and personal belongings would be taken. During our class period most of the girls keep them open because there is not enough time. Some girls don't even have locks and I myself don't have a locker, so right now I am sharing one with my girl friend. Well, the day of the raid came while all the girls were at English class. Since I was like the first one out, I went down to the locker room and actually saw our official teacher throwing books against the wall, pushing them with her feet into the room and really damaging them greatly. Most girls whose lockers weren't locked were emptied out completely and now these girls have no books to study with or use. Now to me, I don't care who it is, they have no right to just take away everything and just throw it into a room.

We explained our story to most of the girls and some are on our side. The issue was brought to discuss it yet nothing really happened. What are they going to do, I don't know. Most of the students are afraid to go to our official teacher and ask for their things.

Our official teacher took some girls' coats so one of the other sisters gave her raincoat to this girl. The faculty better come to a solution quick.

The teacher was a dedicated teaching Sister in an excellent parochial school for girls. Ironically, the teacher's concern with the lockers was aroused by some thefts. Her rage over the students' failure to heed her warnings for locks was triggered by her concern for their property! The books and coats were too valuable to leave unlocked. As the writer implied in her last sentence, the conflict would not have reached irrational proportions had other members of the faculty been consulted as judges and as executors of whatever decision was reached.

Many incidents of due process were characterized by lack of notification, lack of counsel, lack of a hearing *and* lack of separation of roles. The following incident is typical of these multiple violations:

It happen on a school day in the cafeteria when the teacher in charge grabbed a students books and told her to go to class. The girl hesitated for a moment by the way she was told by the teacher to go to class. So the teacher said it again for her to go to class. The student went for her books that the teacher had, and the teacher pushed her in the chest. The student tried forcing her books out of the teacher's hands and the teacher reported it to the office that the student had punched her and had pushed her.

Immediately, the student was expended from school. She didn't have the right to explain herself. She was just kicked out.

I feel this is wrong. The administration should have had the teacher and the student in the office to find out just what happened and why. I was there and to me the teacher was at fault. She shouldn't have yelled at the student telling her to get to the class. I believe that the teacher had some personal grudge against the student because she yelled at her and not at the rest of us who was there.

This incident describes the violation of all four aspects of due process. The student was not notified of any charges specifically related to her conduct; she was not given a chance for "the rest of us who was there" to come to her defense;

she was not given a fair hearing since "she didn't have the right to explain herself"; and she was punished by the same teacher who accused her in the first place. Even in this incident, however, there was some rudimentary due process. Taking the student to the principal's office was a step toward providing some separation between accuser, judge and executioner. Due process was honored when "The teacher reported it to the office." The school that attempts to provide due process has to be governed by more law than the school that ignores due process.

Summary

The four democratic rights, participation in decision-making, dissent, equality, and due process were put together by one student in this way:

Well the way I feel about school student government is a feeling each student has. We are supposed to be taught how our democracy works but we're never taught how to *work* in our society.
Because in our own school we don't have any say in what goes on.
Such as: the way students should dress in school. How can we get clubs and student involvement in clubs. Because education does not stop at 3:00. How can we deal with racial problems in a way which can benefit us by learning how to deal with people instead of the principal closing the school to dodge the issue. Or a teacher throwing a student out of class because he is too objective and asks too many questions. These are problems which can be handled by student government which can be responsible if given a chance. The students in high school are the ones who will be the moving force tomorrow.

5 Talking Angry VERBAL CONFLICT IN THE SCHOOL

THE CONFLICTS IN THIS chapter show how high school conflict aroused anger. They also show how students and school adults handled their own and each other's anger. Sometimes the anger was put into words—as in the case of angry confrontations of students and teachers. Sometimes it was put into action as a way of avoiding its expression in words—cutting classes, losing books, and defacing the restrooms. Several conflicts illustrate how some students and school adults can *act* angry but cannot express anger in words. The angry acts of these individuals appear to be beyond their control, compelled by underlying aggression that leaves them no choice of what they say or do. They become each other's helpless aggressors and victims.

How can we tell what people feel from what they write? Spoken language uses stress, pitch, and tone inflection to reveal the emotional states of speakers. Since these vocal cues are absent in written language, word selection and sentence structure are used to communicate emotional states. In this way written communication can be a basis for inferring the feelings of the writer (Wiener and Mehrabian, 1968). These linguistic conventions are the basis for our analyses of the students' written reports and for our inferences about their emotional states.

Furthermore, Davitz (1969) has shown that there is a cultural consensus about the emotional meaning that particular adjectives convey. The analysis of the incident involving the camp counselor and the two girls (pp. 107-108) applied Davitz' meanings. Davitz also divided adjectives used to convey emotional meaning into three major categories which we have labeled apathy, anger, and satisfaction.

Freud believed that the verbal expression of emotion could change behavior. He focused on the expression of erotic feelings that were "unmentionable" in his social milieu. This book has emphasized the expression of angry feelings because these are expressed so rarely in the school even though they are the emotions appropriate to conflict. Emotions one is unaware of control one's behavior. But when one puts these emotions into words one develops the awareness which restores control of behavior. The individual then controls behavior rather than emotions.

The conflicts show how school adults try to control student emotions by banning their verbal expression. However, by banning verbal expression of emotions, particularly anger, the school increases the likelihood that unverbalized emotion will control behavior. Emotions not expressed in words will still be expressed in deeds or misdeeds. The old proverb says, "Actions speak louder than words." The less awareness the students have of their own emotions, the less control they have of their own behavior. The less control the students have, the more control the school must impose. Therefore, by encouraging the expression of student anger, schools can help students learn to control themselves. The emotional reality of dissent or anger becomes the emotional reality of self-government.

Emotional expression, however, is not enough. Students must have choices of the behaviors which express their emotions. There have been many attempts at individual and group therapy within the school: individual psychotherapy, sensitivity groups, creativity and awareness training, and so on. These therapeutic settings encourage the expression of some emotions of which the students are aware and bring other emotions into new awareness. The practice of emotional exercises in the absence of real school conflict is little assurance that students will express anger in handling real conflict. The encouragement of expression and the development of awareness in schools that severely constrain student choices—particularly the civic choices of participation in decision-making and dissent —may exacerbate conflict and ultimately breed apathy. Administrators' fear of allowing the expression of anger stems from their uneasy knowledge that the expression of more feeling by students and teachers results in more control of their own behavior and less control by the school. The students' proposals for school change, for example, may prove to be more relevant and imaginative than those of the school officials. These changes may also require the school officials to change administrative policies and practices.

In the original research we distinguished between "bad" and "good" outcomes of conflicts—terminations by one party or resolutions by one or more parties. In 61 percent of the conflicts the student perceived the outcomes as bad. In only 9 percent did they perceive good outcomes. We also distinguished between outcomes which lowered or did not lower tension levels. In only 9 percent of the incidents did students perceive a lowered tension level. In 91 percent they perceived it as not lowered (see Appendix B, Table 10). Since discussion is a necessary part of negotiation, negotiation provides opportunity for the expression of anger and for articulating choices and, eventually, the channeling of anger into institutional change. If the schools provided more constructive channeling of anger, students would very likely have reported more "good" outcomes and reduced tension levels—in brief, more satisfaction.

This hypothesis was supported by a recent experiment in which both authors participated. In one high school students were polled about their preferred ways of handling problems in school. They chose direct negotiation for problems that arose between students, and those between teachers and students. They chose a committee as the best means for handling problems between students and administrators. Students' views of teachers as close enough to themselves to be able to settle questions directly in face to face negotiation suggest that failure to negotiate is less a matter of generation gap than one of power gap or contact gap. The teacher bears the brunt of the feelings generated by school problems since he is the real person with whom students wish to negotiate.

In the analysis of the following conflicts, we state that anger has been verbally expressed *within the conflict* only when it is spoken by at least one party to the other parties in the conflict. The verbal expression of anger to the interviewer alone is expression *outside the conflict* and could not affect what happened.

Avoidance of Angry Expression

First, consider conflicts in which there was the least expression of anger. In the incident below the student writer believes that the way officers were elected to student government would be changed if students expressed their anger:

Our G. O. (student government) is more or less an organization that is designed to help students to express their desires to the authorities in our school. I feel that the G.O. is under the hand of the teachers and that the kids are too weak to stand up for their rights. I think the problem lies in the leadership because the people who are elected are elected on a popularity basis and most of the time they lack effective leadership. Most students feel that the G.O. is not actually representing their interests. Thus, when a new way was devised to elect the G.O. the teachers objected because it would hinder their influence. I think that a lot more of the students should make their feelings known but everyone is under the big hand of the teachers. The teachers don't believe that we have qualifications to handle school matters—but first we have to get real leaders in it not mere puppets.

In this student's view fear of the teachers blocked the expression of anger. This fear of school authorities underlay apparent student apathy or weakness. The teachers blocked the expression of anger by choosing student leaders rather than allowing students to argue over their own choice of leaders. The kids are "too weak" in the sense that they lack the confidence to put their anger into words spoken to the teachers.

The fear of verbalizing anger can also be due to the simple mistrust of school adults by the students, as this student states:

As the school co-curricular council representative, I am responsible for legislation such as budget requests and approval of events. The problem we have is whether to be honest or not about where certain monies are being kept and that there is graft going on. Nobody hardly in that department knows where certain monies are being banked or why they are always asking for student body funds when they have $2,000 or so in the bank somewhere (in Switzerland). I want to be honest and get only what they really need. The physical education department thinks that it's contributing more than their share for the co-curriculum—which is not really true. They feel that they deserve the unanimous support from the student body which they do not recieve. They've been on my back for some time now. . . . I've not been going to gym unless I have to and once in a while I do cut gym class because Im tired of brainless people. (Some of them are pretty decent though.) *I wish that instead of avoiding the problem we could understand each other.* I understand them and am fair to them when I represent them, but they don't understand how a "nice kid" turned into an "anti-physical-ed hippie" overnight. Maybe if they weren't archaic and stupid, I wouldn't mind them. Phys Ed class here is absurd., all you do is dress and sit. No one knows how to teach. Going to class is a waste of time. They know it (teachers) too, but *they won't be honest enough to admit it.* They suffer in the long run. I don't even pity them, they don't deserve it. They have the potential to do better, but they just sit on their fat asses all day and take roll and send cut slips to kids who want to do something more challenging and relevant to their lives.

The writer's mistrust prevents her from letting the teacher know how angry she feels. She does put her anger into action by cutting class. This repeated avoidance of verbal confrontation with the teacher creates apathy in both school adult and student and leads to withdrawal from future conflicts.

The next incident, written by a student, also involves a non-school adult. However, it illustrates another way students can avoid the verbal expression of anger:

If I don't want to hassle with someone, I come up with an excuse
for something like I'm too stoned to fight or I don't want to waste
my time or something. I was down on the beach with my bike.
You're not supposed to be on the beach with a bike. A cop came
up on a horse and said what do you think your doing with that on
the beach. Riding it. He asked to see our license and the
registration for the bike. He said he was going to give me a car
ticket for being on the beach. And I talked my way out of that by
saying I did not know and kissing his ass. So I got off with just
being told to get off the beach.

By pleading ignorance rather than challenging an ordinance,
the biker avoided expressing his anger over a law he believed
was annoying and unnecessary. His fear of getting a ticket or
going to jail caused him to suppress his angry words. The
anger is conveyed by the sudden switch to obscene language—a
sudden eruption of his surface calm. Students plead ignorance
to avoid punishment and to avoid the expression of anger. The
suppression of his anger did not make it go away. It had to
be released in describing the incident.

In the next incident we see how the student writer deliberately evaded adult anger and caused apathy:

My parents are prejudiced. I have come into contact with many
underprivileged people, both White and Negro. One specific
occasion I felt that I should help a Negro friend who needed someone
to take care of her younger brothers and sisters, while she went
job hunting. In order to get out of the house I had to either lie
to my parents, or not help the girl. In making a decision I took
several factors into consideration. Number one, who would I
be hurting more? Being that the girl could get hold of no one else
and this was her only opportunity to look for this job, I overlooked
the lying and helped her.

As it turned out my parents never found out. I cannot put myself
in their situation completely. Knowing them as I do, they probably
would have been furious with me for what I'd done coupled
with the fact that I had lied. If it had been me, since I don't think
I would discourage my children from helping the underprivileged,
the incident may never have arisen.

The anticipation of possible conflicts with her parents prompted this student to lie rather than to face the anger of open confrontation. This kind of anger-avoidance can create growing alienation from adult authority figures. Here the writer dissipates anger by creating fantasies of raising children in a totally different way and thus forgives her parents for being prejudiced.

When school authorities constantly ignore student anger, they discourage the students' future attempts to put it into words. In the last incident the student has surrendered hope that her words would make any difference. In the following incident, described by a student, neither student nor teacher initially expressed anger:

The last fuss I got into was just a scant three weeks ago, or so. I was taking sociology for my civics requirement. The teacher, whom I'll call Mr. C., talked down to us, one thing I hate. I played along with his little games for exactly three days, after hearing his vows that "this class will be relevant" etc., etc, ad nauseum. So after the class one day, I very humbly and politely suggested that perhaps, maybe, please could we use another book to supplement the text. (The text-book was even more infantile than the teacher.) I named off a few books I'd read of sociological import, by Martin Luther King and others dealing in social problems. Then Mr. C. very calmly informed me that he will not change his teaching methods for anyone, and that I should find another teacher.

O.K. Fine. If he's going to be so unresponsive to such a constructive suggestion, *I didn't want to be in his class anyway.* So I go to my counselor and find out that *all* classes (not just sociology) that fill my requirement are very, very overcrowded and the only classes I could even maybe get into were, of course, the ones taught by Mr. C. It was also a hassle because I worked afternoons then, so I couldn't have taken any classes in the afternoon. I'd asked all the teachers if they'd in any way let me in their bulging classes, but to no avail. So I assumed that I'd have to stay in Mr. C.'s class. Wrong again. Next day, I walked in the class, Mr. C. grabbed the books from my hands, turned around and since then never let me back in his classroom, and always gives me a hard look if we pass in the hall.

Legally, I could have fought the issue with higher up administrators, but that would have done more harm than good.

The only solution left was for me to do "Solopacs," time consuming busy work reports on boring topics. They are a tremendous amount of work, more than any class would ever be, and they are atrocious. I must turn in one report every three weeks to recieve credit for graduation.

I think that it was grossly unfair to make me do these crummy reports against my own will. If they really were fair, the counselors could have devised something more suitable to me. But they just quoted rules. . . .

The "humble and polite" objection of the student to the text and the teacher's "calm" refusal to change the text are clear evidence of their avoidance of the expression of anger. Since the anger was there it erupted in the action of grabbing books and barring the student from class. The disaffected student changes from a hopeful activist to an impotent nag.

Partial Avoidance of Angry Expression

In the second set of incidents there is both expression and suppression of anger. In some cases there is only partial or vicarious verbal expression. In other cases anger is expressed by only some of the parties to the conflict.

The first incident illustrates how the teacher suppressed her own anger against a colleague:

I'm involved right now in a fuss with one of my master teachers. She is a rather conservative person and I'm another extreme. She has her methods of teaching which include a definite spelling, writing, and composition grade each week, definite "in-class" activities, definite rules, etc. This isn't my way. She is an excellent teacher and I respect her, but I don't like her. Why? Because there seems to be, (to me) a conflict of outlooks. I don't think that the classroom needs to be so structured to have success. Success comes in many different packages.

I'm not a structured person. She is. I can't do a thing about it
because she writes my recommendation. Instead, I burn up inside.
The fuss hasn't been resolved, just put aside for a while until
I'm on my own. Yet, it is a shame, that chance will never come
because there aren't any jobs, anywhere. . . .

Still, I can't change because it's taken so long to get here. People are
flexible, so it follows that the class should be very flexible. I don't
believe the students will be bored if the teacher doesn't have
a definite assignment and plan each day. I will just have to wait
for my chance to express this.

Thank you for this opportunity to write about something that has
been bothering me for a long time but even I didn't quite know
what it was 'till now.

This teacher presented to students an adult model in which
anger was suppressed. The teacher was able to express her
anger in writing but not in directly encountering her colleague.
Unable to face her conflict, she was unable to resolve it. Having
avoided direct expression of anger, the teacher appeared to displace it. For the vicarious satisfaction of her anger, this teacher
opened the door for students to direct their aggressive behavior
against her colleague. In other situations students expressed
displaced adult anger in actions directed against fellow students, non-school adults, and even themselves.

The following incident, written by a student, is an example
of the expression of anger by only some of the parties involved
in the conflict:

During the spring of 1970, I was involved in several moratoriums
about the Vietnam war. On one such day, it was decided to spread
out across the city, giving leaflets out and asking for a petition
that made a plea against Vietnam. A small group of about five
or six of us went to the Marina Safeway, which is located in a
very conservative area. It was very early in the morning, so the
elderly folks were out buying groceries. We were met with a
majority of statements like: "I don't want to even look or think
about such 'radical stuff'." A few agreed, signed the petition,
thought it was great and even tried reasoning with the previous
sort of shopper. The non-petition signing people upset us mostly
because they wouldn't even listen; their views, of course, were

disturbing, but the fact that they tuned us out was an exceedingly powerful blow. We would have much preferred that the opposition had at least talked to us. Of course there were a few arguers, which was good, at least they had views and were interested. One such man brought back a leaflet put out by U.C. medical school and raged that he'd never donate money to U.C. ever again. Then he proceeded to tell us where and how wrong we were, in a very irrational frame of mind. But he calmed down and listened for one or two moments, and this was great. But, here comes the ironic and sad part, another "hard hat", a lady, came out and ruffled him back up again and we had two irrational people to deal with. It was funny, she stood behind and told him what to say and he'd shout it out and he'd agree. Finally all was forsaken and both of our parties went our separate ways. Of course, we would have liked it to have been resolved by convincing them that we were right. But we would have settled for some open ears, and minds. The resolution would have been somewhat satisfying if we all could have talked.

Some adults expressed their anger but others did not. Those adults who turned away did not provide young people an opportunity to find constructive ways to express their anger. Those adults who took the time to argue were useful to the students in getting them to think about what they were doing. These students verbalized their anger, welcomed it in others, and used it to learn. Because they confronted the shoppers' anger, the outcome of the incident seems more satisfying than the outcomes of incidents in which spoken anger was avoided.

In some situations individuals failed to verbalize all the things they were angry about. In this incident the adult writer expressed her anger over a sudden change of plans but not over the lack of trust involved in her friend not telling her until the last minute about the change:

In December of last year another couple wanted to go to Las Vegas with us in the spring. Plans were formulated, airline tickets were purchased by the wife and motel reservations were made. All four of us were looking forward to the trip. Then my friend called about seven days prior to the deadline date to tell us that she could not keep the date. She said that an ex-roommate of hers was getting married and she was asked to be a bridesmaid. Would

my husband and I be very angry if she accepted the invitation?
I told her that I would not break up our friendship but I would be
angry at her for breaking up plans that were made
several months ago.

I am not sure she really was aware of how wrong she was in breaking
up these plans, but I do know she felt quite guilty in
my company for a long time.

I solved this conflict by letting her know I was angry about the
sudden change in plans, but on the other hand I didn't want to
break up our friendship. However, we have made no more
long range plans with them since.

The partial expression of anger led to only partial resolution
of the conflict. This partial resolution, in turn, led to a loss
of contact and the conversion of an intimate into a superficial
friendship—the interpersonal analogue of anger transformed
into apathy.

Now recall the incident (pp. 94-95) in which a teacher suppressed her own anger with a colleague while seeming to permit
open emotional expression in her students. It was suggested
that because she was not aware of her anger, she might induce
students to express *her* anger against particular adults. The
following incident provides more explicit evidence of how
adults can use young people for the vicarious expression of
adult anger:

I was directly criticized for allowing the children to express their
feelings; which entailed both hostility and pleasure. The teacher
that observed this open displeasure interpreted it as disrespect
and in presenting her views said that she felt sure that the children
were being "so sassy" and disrespectful. I do work with children
who have any number of problems and due to their acting out
behavior are often punished for expressing their real feelings.
Because I work in small groups and can spend more time with
individuals, I feel that this is an opportunity for them to deal
with real emotions.

Unfortunately, because I am a new teacher, I try consciously to
avoid open conflict and therefore thanked her for her concern,
stating that I did not mind hearing what they actually felt. Had

I felt more secure, possibly through experience, I would have
elaborated, but in this instance I chose a flight tactic. This situation
left neither of us enlightened, which was unfortunate. Hopefully,
in the future I will be better able to express *my* true feelings in
defense of my own philosophy. It is no accident that the children
are open. I encourage it and do hope that I can share
these beliefs, if this situation should arise again.

This teacher is able to write about the anger she felt toward
her colleague although she was unable to tell her colleague
about her feelings. She writes nothing about the anger she
may have felt toward the children. The fact that she encour-
ages the anger of children toward herself suggests that she
may be substituting their anger for her own. The incident
illustrates the necessity of allowing students and adults to speak
their anger when the problem involves both.

Open Expression of Anger

The open expression of anger by all parties in a confrontation had various results: (1) the anger converted to mutual
satisfaction; (2) the anger escalated into more anger; and (3)
the anger became apathy.

In the following incident, written by a student, both parties
expressed anger. The teacher then barred further expression
and transformed anger into apathy:

This was the fuss: One day, in English class, it was nice and sunny
outside. I wanted to sit on the floor and read in the sun, but
I was not allowed to. I was not disturbing anybody, nor was I
going to. I was dressed in a long peasant skirt and it was more
comfortable to sit on the floor than to sit in a stiff chair
at a small desk.

This is how the fuss was taken care of: I was told to sit in a chair.
I refused. The teacher kept hassling and, as a result, disturbed
the rest of the class. She then called the principal who came in
and threatened to kick me out of school, and also accused me
of trying to cause a riot. The matter was resolved, I went back to the
chair and refused to do anything for the rest of the day.

The failure of the teacher to allow the verbal expression of anger wasted time and energy. The student sat out the rest of the day, the principal had to visit the class, and the teacher nagged instead of teaching.

Unlike the teacher in the preceding incident who did not express her anger to anyone in the situation, the father in the next incident (told by his daughter) expresses anger in a command:

My father couldn't understand why I always met my boyfriend at a special place instead of having him pick me up. I told my father that Joe didn't have a car so I just met him at his house or near his house. Then he said that Joe could take the bus over here (our house) and pick me up and then take the bus back over to his house. This seemed ridiculous. I didn't mind going over to Joe's house, but my father did. Also we usually go to a park near Joe's house and that is why I go over there. It's kind of like a "hangout".

So my Dad told me that I could call Joe and tell him to pick me up. But I was stubborn and felt it was my business, and if I wanted to meet Joe, I would. So I told my father that I just wouldn't go out because I saw no reason why he should mind me going to see Joe. It was as though he only wanted to hassle me and I told him so.

So I just stayed in my room and about ten minutes later my Dad came in my room and told me to go out, that he didn't care if I went to meet Joe. And that was it. He hasn't hassled me any more about it.

Both daughter and father spoke their anger. Then the father decided to capitulate rather than negotiate. In this case anger is expressed but apparently not used to arrive at any negotiated resolution. The father's capitulation could decrease rather than increase the communication between father and daughter ("He hasn't hassled me any more").

In the last incident the expression of anger was not essentially constructive. In the following incident, told by a student, the expression of anger had destructive consequences:

When I first came into this school, my first core teacher would understand everyone's problems. At lunch time he would share his closet with the class so they could hang up their coats. And another closet for our books. When he left the class gave him a going away party. Then when our new core teacher entered our lives everything began to happen. She kept the two closets for herself. If someone talks back to her, she makes it sound like Homicide. She tells your parents that you hit her. She coaxes you to get mad and when she gets enough things on you she transfers you to another class. She tells you to fix the chairs after you had fixed it ten times. When we tell her it was the class before us she says you don't have to fix them I'll just lower your grade. She never listens to the students side of the story.

Anger seems to pervade this classroom, with one confrontation leading to another. It appears that the teacher punished the students for the expression of anger in a way that provoked more anger. Such behavior on the part of teachers can produce a cycle of guilt and punishment that makes the classroom emotionally intolerable.

Conflict descriptions showed many ways in which the direct verbal expression of anger was avoided. Anger was often displaced in ways that made its channeling into negotiable issues difficult: (1) sometimes angry rhetoric replaced action; (2) sometimes the anger was disguised by humor that pleaded helplessness; and (3) sometimes anger was intellectualized in ways that led to impotence. Consider now a conflict, described by a student, in which anger takes the form of rhetoric without action:

As a member of student government, I was mandated out of all my classes to complete an accreditation report, one of the responsibilities of our board. I had already become quite disillusioned with student "government" in general and the co-curriculum council in particular. On this particular day, I decided that I was a student first and representative second (at least this is how I am classified) so therefore I would attend the meeting only during my free mods. I felt quite strongly that my responsibilities to student government should be fulfilled during my free time or the forty minutes twice a week that I was allotted for the council meeting. When Super A (our adult advisor) inquired as to whether anyone

would have to leave, I stated my case. Feeling that I had
challenged his authority, he became very, very angry and said
I could either stay and shut up or resign and leave. I decided
I could do more by staying than by resigning, so I shut up . . .
for a while. The relationships between Super A and myself had
become openly hostile and culminated in an hour and a half talk,
his method of resolving conflict. He mouthed the usual platitudes
and rhetoric about my irresponsibility as an "officer", my ineptness
at resolving conflict and my general unworthiness. He asked me
to write down my priorities and then threw them out, saying they
were insufficient. I told him that I neither respected or trusted
him and that I felt he was taking his insecurities . . . his presumtous
authority. The conflict has never been resolved.

The student did manage to express his anger to the adult
advisor when he originally stated his case—to use his free time
for student government work. The school adult considered
this expression of anger a personal attack on his authority. He
managed to express his own considerable anger but in ways
that silenced the student. The student then appears to have
displaced his anger on to the personal relationship with the
advisor. In this way a conflict over official functions was
changed into a personality conflict. Displacement of anger
from the original issues on to personality prevents negotiation
of conflict. Personality is a non-negotiable "issue" in the sense
that parties to conflicts are usually neither able or willing to
concede parts of their personalities to resolve conflicts. The
displacement of anger on to "personality" is sometimes done
to avoid negotiation.

The next three conflict descriptions are about the same
incident, involving an English teacher and her class. In each
case anger was directly expressed by both teacher and students.
However, since the teacher seemed unwilling to negotiate, some
of the anger had to be displaced by the students. Each writer
describes a different form of displacement. In the following
description, the writer uses humor:

In this so called institution of higher learning we are faced with
a teacher who is nearly 65 years old. What she teaches is nothing
that will effect our lives. This contemporarily irrelevant material

is only half the story. She is quick to judge and what she feels
is the way she grades. In one incident she failed the whole class
because she felt they had plagerized on their book reviews.
We have complained to the great God for mercy but she has refused
claiming that old testament lesson—if I make you fear me you will
obey and love me. HELP!!! The leaders of this great institution
are powerless to do anything. The only justification for retiring
the old lady is if she taught what is immoral, but she is victorian and
we are back where we started from. So I repeat
HELP!!!!!!!!!

After failing to change the situation by talking to the teacher
and consulting with the principal and the law, the student discharged residual anger in the form of humor. Humor is a
socially acceptable way to express anger, especially in situations
where the possibilities for immediate change seem slim.

The second writer mentions the same attempts to resolve
the conflict: going to the teacher and consulting the administration. But he adds another: the intervention of parents who
may have responded to the first writer's cry for help:

Since the beginning of the year Miss L——'s English classes have
been handing in a book report every month. It has been common
practice that when these book reports were returned they were
nearly all failing or unacceptable. This was due to the fact that she
suspected us of using Monarch or Cliff Notes instead of reading
the required book. This was denied continually by the students
but she refused to discuss the matter and continued marking
the book reports in this arbitrary manner. Several students
organized a group to bring this to the attention of the administration
but nothing has been done. It has now come to the point that
individual parents are demanding conferences in which this
teacher give satisfactory proof of her accusations. To date this
problem is unsolved and it seems the only way a solution
can be found is if the administration investigated the situation
which is highly unlikely.

The anger is discharged by an intellectual analysis for which
the writer uses mostly the third person (i.e., "students" instead
of "we"). He finally suggests an "investigation" for resolving
the conflict. Intellectual analysis is also a socially acceptable

and even useful way to displace residual anger. Both humor and intellectual analysis cripple negotiation when they replace the goal-directed anger.

The third writer appears to grapple most compassionately and most seriously with the problem:

A clash between the rigid and old generation and the younger can produce conflicts. An old teacher of unmarried status tends to teach a course for 25-30 years. As known, everything changes, the human element, curriculum and teacher-student-parent relationship. And old teacher (63) has been teaching senior year English according to teaching methods of the 1940's. The difference lies in the fact that methods of teaching has changed as well as the teacher. Probably a rather gay woman in 1930 and a good teacher our dear Miss L has turned into an old and possibly senile nag, fond of teaching senior classes on a 5 or 6th grade level all the time convincing herself of her superior teachings. A few concerned students became involved to change her ways. A meeting was held at Dr. A's office (principal at X H. S.). The meeting began with Miss L placing her grade book in front of herself, condemning anyone who opened his mouth by rabbling up incompleted work in most cases completed but corrected by Miss L. Personally my work was in but along with the other "instigators" I was pushed back to the former position of a dumb mule having no right to talk on things over my head to understand. So should be added that Miss L is an unwilling woman, protected by the school system and old age. These factors were indirectly explained [understood] and the students had no right whatever to infringe upon her superior teaching methods. The affair was finally toned down by the school but parents are now working on it.

This student mentions no student expressing anger directly to the teacher in the classroom. The meeting in the principal's office allowed the teacher to express her anger but she apparently gave the students no chance to express theirs. Her anger was expressed by the act of posturing behind the grade book, by verbal intimidation of complaining students, and "rabbling" up the incompleted work. It appears that the anger, seriously felt by the students and unexpressed to the teacher and principal, was expressed to the parents.

Looking to adults, however, as we see in the following incident, written by a younger member of the school auxiliary, does not insure satisfactory use of anger:

For a number of years, this auxiliary unit, together with other such units in California, financially supported a trust fund created to aid qualified dental students in one of our state's three dental schools. The monies lent by the trust are to be returned at a later date. The local auxilliary, which each year worked to raise money to contribute to this fund, has never seen or even known the names of the recipients. In addition, it was learned that the university dental school (the school located nearest to our county and to which the great majority of our dentistry-oriented students in our area are directed) has never used any of the money in the fund. It must be mentioned at this point that the trust fund is a pet project of the elderly member and that she was one of the original founders.

Several younger members, including myself, began to feel that our annual efforts were simply nothing more than the maintainance of a bank account of little import to our own communities. We began to look for a "cause" within the realm of dentistry that could also be considered a community cause. It didn't take much investigating to learn that our own dental school was in great need of cash for its students use. The majority of students in this school come from low income families in our own area. Though these students are using various loan funds, there is still a great need for "free money" to supplement loaned funds. The prospect of financing 4-5 years of dental schooling on borrowed funds alone can be pretty discouraging to even the most talented students.

The fuss ensued when the younger members presented their findings and opinions to the group at the regular meeting. The older member resented the group working to raise funds for a purpose other than hers. After she threatened to withdraw all of her support from the group, I knew they were all going to go along with her. I had no more time because of the end of the school year, so we left it that she still gets to choose what we should do.

Like the students in the three preceding incidents, these adults were able to speak their anger but this expression did not result in negotiation. The anger turned to frustration ("they were going to go along with her") and this led to apathy ("I had no more time").

All the previous incidents illustrate how anger was displaced onto substitute targets; none showed angry confrontation leading to serious bargaining over the issues. We did find incidents in which the expression of anger in confrontations by all parties to conflicts was followed by negotiation. Writers describe the outcomes of these incidents as affording the conflicting parties some degree of satisfaction.

In the following incident, however, the negotiation resulted in anger rather than satisfaction. The student editor describes the incident in these words:

Early in January, a "minor" confrontation occurred between the more radical members of this school's Black Students Coalition and the Administration. Centered on key issues of a holiday for Dr. Martin Luther King's birthday, special club jackets (which had been denied) and on the subject of black history and culture, which, while supposedly taught in all classes, was not being taught by the older, more conservative teachers who treated the whole movement as a joke. This joke turned into a major walkout from classes on Wednesday. The 77 black students held a mass meeting in the south wing of the cafeteria which later moved to the lecture room. When accosted by Dr. ——, the principal, they shouted him down in a wave of violent language. As I am the editor of the high school paper, I was present in fact, I was the only white there. As co-chairman of the student Curriculum Committee, which is the most powerful student group next to the paper in the school, I was allowed to come in and listen. The problem apparently came about when the moderate leaders of the Coalition found their goals opposed by a radical "action-now" minority. The Administration, represented (following the principal's debacle) by Dr. B—— the Superintendent of Schools, finally sat down and listened. The results were—a) the Coalition was still forbidden to have jackets b) there would be a special assembly for Dr. King and c) "something" would be done about black history on the non-regents level. The "something" turned out to be a hastily thrown together "Black Culture" Course which was put together in three days over the dissent of the entire Social Studies department, the Student Curriculum Committee, and the paper. The Board was running scared—and were in effect coerced into this action by 5 or 6 black students who led the movement. What the board should have done is to direct the teachers who refused to teach black history to teach it and to continue integrating black history into the curriculum. They should have allowed the Coalition to have jackets. The only success came with the King assembly following which the blacks went home anyway.

The anger at the end may have resulted when the parties to the conflict failed to carry the negotiations far enough. The negotiation model in Chapter 10 makes the expression of anger by all sides a necessary first step, as shown in this incident. This does not make all issues immediately negotiable, since the issues provoking the most anger (jacket issue) must be negotiated later.

In this incident the teacher states that he asked the student for a direct expression of anger by assigning anger-provoking topics, but the student resisted:

In my art class I assigned each girl to make a collage on any theme which dealt with the more serious issues of today, such as pollution, discrimination, unemployment, violence and drugs. The idea of the project was to get the students to express themselves and their ideas in a visual manner. And to make them aware of how art as a tool can be impressive and persuading. Not to mention giving them, as a student, as an individual a chance to express themselves on something relevant today that affected them personally.

A student raised her hand and said she didn't see the importance of this sort of thing. She wanted to know why she had to do such a serious topic—and why she couldn't do one on Tom Jones.

I asked her viewpoints on certain subjects—such as the Vietnam War, pollution and discrimination. The student responded with dead seriousness—and showed she had given these issues some thought—or showed that these things did bother her. I pointed out how this was a chance to express her thoughts, her concerns on the issues—and in a way that would be much stronger than

any words—pictures. She turned in one of the best collages
in the class.

The teacher wanted a serious topic and the student wanted her
own choice of topic. He allowed her to express her anger about
having her choice and then about the various controversial
topics he mentioned. The conflict was resolved by his giving
her the time to express her anger and by her giving up her
original choice. This resolution enabled the student to express
anger in the collage. And the collage appeared to give satisfaction to both parties.

This incident reveals the basic emotional aspect of negotiation—the constructive and even creative use of anger. Here
the anger was channeled into an artistic product. Through
negotiation it can also be channeled into the creation of new
institutional forms.

Just learning to verbalize their anger seems to be the necessary first step for most adults who try to use negotiation to
resolve conflicts, particularly with students. The counselor in
the following incident describes how she learned to express
anger:

I worked at a group-oriented camp in Connecticut sponsored by
a Settlement House. One of my groups consisted of 13-15
year olds. All of them were Black and Puerto Rican. Millie and
Ernestine were members of this group. They were generally
critical and bitter, constantly challenging my role as their counselor
and dealt hostily with me as a symbol of the white (Jewish)
middle class.

Both Millie and Ernestine did not have fathers: Ernestine's
mother was an alcoholic and Millie was living with an aunt
who was very old and ill. Hence, they "let loose" at camp and
gained (the needed) recognition by disrupting the difficult
group and challenging their counselor.

My behavior toward these two girls in particular, up to this point,
was gentle, patient, understanding, but firm. Apparently, this
method of "breaking through" to them was not effective. One
day, they were especially restless and I suppose, eager to
"get my goat" once and for all, by mimicking me, calling me

unpleasant names and annoying me in trivial ways. It was at
this point that it was my turn to "let loose." After all, I was human
and had sensitive feelings, too. They thought I was merely an
authority figure. Ignoring them or individual conferences did not
help. I decided to try a new tactic: in front of the entire group,
I exploded in anger and told them off, criticizing their negative
behavior and demanding heatedly, "Who do you think *you* two are?"
Surprisingly, they did not counter attack; they remained still.
Another interesting reaction was that their "allies" seemed relieved
that I finally gave them a taste of their own medicine and had
the spunk to do so.

Neither Millie nor Ernestine posed a serious problem for me
after that encounter. I feel that they gained respect for me—
for fighting fire with fire, as they are used to doing. And this
new respect was mutual, and they gave me the chance to show it.
Millie cried when she bid me goodbye at the end of the
summer. Ernestine said goodbye grudgingly.

There were several signs of the counselor's anger before her
conscious expression of it. She had a need to "excuse" the two
girls because of their family background; she describes their
behavior as "bitter" and "critical" and "hostile" and "challenging"; she describes her own behavior as "gentle, patient, understanding, and firm"—adjectives which reveal the over-control
of her own anger. She engages in the anger game: I'll make
them even angrier by not letting them "get my goat." The counselor's super-control could make the girls angrier or make them
feel guilty about expressing their anger. Finally, when she does
express her anger she finds that the girls became less guilty
about their own anger and had less need to provoke her. At
that point the relationship appeared to be more satisfying.

When the angry sense of injustice is not contained, but
allowed expression in sometimes heated debates, the satisfying
results justify the pain of confrontation. For example, consider
this incident:

A situation like this came up in school a few months ago when
we were trying to decide where to go on our Senior Trip.
The ideal was to have everyone agree on where to go, and then
have the whole class be able to go. We had three choices

of where we could go: 1. Montreal—Expo, 2. Boston, 3. Washington
D.C. There was the normal problem of deciding which place
would be the most fun. But then another problem came to view.
Montreal was more expensive than the other two. Although
it was only a matter of about $10.00 plus money needed for
souveniers at Expo, there were many girls who felt they couldn't
carry that kind of expense. This was where the argument began.
The girls that couldn't afford Montreal, (without some sort
of struggle), and there were many, felt that it wasn't so much
where they went that mattered. It was the fact that we were
going as a class that was important. These girls felt that we
could have just as good a time at one of the less expensive places.
The girls that wanted to go to Montreal felt differently about it.
They felt that if they were going to spend that much money,
what was a little more. For that price they wanted to go
somewhere that they really wanted to see, not just anyplace.
Everyone always goes to Washington, and Boston would be
too boring. Isn't it better that most of the girls go, and have a
really great time, than everyone go and have a terrible time.
The other girls argued that we wouldn't have a terrible time.
Being typical girls, the argument went on for days. Finally
we just had to come down to a vote. Should we go to a place
that would be less fun, and have everyone go. Or should we go to
a place that was really supposed to be great and have three-fourths
of the girls go. The vote was that it would be Montreal.
Girls tried to get babysitting jobs for girls who were going
to have a struggle. Girls that couldn't get up the money didn't go.
I don't know of any other way the problem could have been
handled. There were two opposing sides of what was fair
and considerate.

The debate revealed a genuine conflict of interests between
two school factions. When the debate failed to settle the issue,
the students resorted to a formal vote. After the vote was
taken, the students who won chose to help the students who
lost. The channeling of anger into debate allowed for negotiation and a humane resolution of the conflict. Merely allowing
the expression of dissent, opposition, and anger, the school can
make decisions more equitable. Angry expression, however,
requires the short-run tolerance of inconvenience and pain.

Summary

The first set of incidents shows how individuals and groups kept their anger buried. The decision to avoid angry confrontation was usually made unilaterally. The repeated failure to express anger in words sometimes produced the appearance of apathy. The concealed anger was displaced on to other people and situations. The anger did not vanish but was expressed non-verbally in the sudden eruption of physical violence in students and school adults and assaults upon both people and property.

In the second set of incidents there was partial verbal expression of anger: some but not all the parties spoke their anger, only part of their anger was expressed, or it was vicariously expressed through the anger of others whose behavior they could control. In the third set there was rather full expression of anger by all parties to the conflict.

The expression of anger in either words or deeds was not always equally acceptable to all parties. More often, the suppression of anger in one party produced more anger in the other parties to the conflict. When all parties to the conflict were able to express their angry feelings in words and to use these words for negotiation, the resolution of the conflict often produced satisfaction.

The verbal expression of anger appears to be a major part of negotiation. By structuring the anger around specific issues, parties to conflicts can determine what issues need to and can be resolved. Anger conveys to allies and adversaries where commitments lie and which commitments must be respected or changed. When negotiation starts at the level of "angry commitment" parties to conflicts have the energy available and necessary for negotiated conflict resolutions. Even if the parties to conflict participate in the mechanics of presenting demands and bargaining, without the emotional involvement of anger, they may find it difficult to stick to the agreements they reach.

Anger must be contained as well as expressed in negotiation. Uncontained anger often takes the form of verbal threat and, as the next chapter shows, is more often a prelude to violence than to negotiation. The available conventions for expressing anger allow us to adjust to certain situational realities by binding the anger in terms of issues and conditions that we can change with reasonable amounts of effort and time. Not all anger one may feel nor all issues one may feel angry about can be handled in a single negotiation or at a single moment in time. Some anger can always be displaced, hopefully in ways that do not impede negotiations: for example, by humor, intellectualization, and silent reflection.

Negotiation requires emotional vulnerability. The consciously felt and verbally expressed anger is a source of both pain and anxiety. There is the pain of exposure to the anger of others. There is the anxiety of risk—the worry over alienating one or more parties to the conflict and of losing more than we gain or losing everything. This emotional vulnerability is the price we must often pay when conflict is resolved through negotiation as an alternative to violence and coercion.

6 Acting Angry VIOLENCE AND COERCION
IN THE SCHOOL

THIS CHAPTER ANALYZES incidents of violence, verbal and physical threats, and institutional force in order to see how conflicts went from negotiable issues to non-negotiable impasses. Later we will show how the understanding of the ways in which negotiation of conflicts went wrong enables us to follow a path of negotiation that leads to creative resolutions instead of escalation of conflict.

Violence is the physical rather than the verbal expression of anger. It can take the form of bodily assault in which individuals use their bodies or any available weapon. The incidents in this chapter show different forms of violence: violence directed by students against students, by students against adults, and by adults against students. We include in acts of violence the physical removal of students from the school by force or by suspension. Violence can be directed toward property, as in the case of school vandalism, as well as against people.

Physical threats (e.g., shaking one's fist) are actions that express the readiness to use force. In high school they usually lead to violence. Verbal threats also lead to violence unless uttered following the eruption of violence when they usually signal a de-escalation of conflict. Institutionalized force (e.g., students knowing that some acts may be punishable by the school) can increase violence when it suppresses the verbal expression of anger. In high school, institutionalized force takes the form of rules and codes that regulate student dress, conduct, movement, and activity and that carry the implicit threat of punishment.

Research on aggression (Feshbach, 1970) shows that the high school may have two options in dealing with student violence: it can impose its own external controls or it can help students develop their own internal controls. The developmental research indicates, as most students move from elementary to junior high school, that their aggression patterns change. First, they move from less aggression to more assertiveness. Aggression is action destructive of self, adults, other students, and school property. Assertiveness involves action that is useful in self-fulfillment. Second, they move from physical to verbal aggression. In elementary school students react with physical violence to verbal threats, insults, and physical attack. In junior high school they begin to distinguish between verbal and physical attack and engage in less physical aggression. School adults, the incidents suggest, in physically restraining students, even for the purpose of preventing students from hitting other students, may be perceived by the students as physically attacking them. Third, they move from dependence on parental models to dependence on teacher models of behavior. High school students use school adults as models (of angels and devils) in order to develop their own personalities (Jacobson, 1961). Students use parts of several teachers' behavior to internalize their own adult composite model. They also may fantasize the teacher is angry as a way of dealing with their own anger.

This research also shows that students may react differently to fantasized violence as presented in fiction, in movies, or on television. Most students can use the fantasies and accompanying verbalizations as a substitute for violence. For other students these act as stimuli rather than substitutes for violence.

Our original findings showed that there were 1,284 incidents which involved the use of violence by peers, by students against school authorities, and by school authorities against students.

That number was about 19 percent of the incidents reported. This is less than one-fifth of the incidents. When we consider, however, that force was defined as any actual use of physical force, coercion, or restraint, it is hard to understand the use of force in the resolution of one-fifth of the conflicts reported by high school students!

The findings are even more disturbing: school authorities used force in 716 incidents (about 11 percent) while students used force with other students in 376 incidents (about 5 percent) of the time. Against school authorities the students used force in 192 incidents (about 3 percent).

Students reported more violence in urban (22 percent of the incidents) than in suburban (16 percent) junior and senior high schools. Students reported more peer violence in junior (9 percent) than in senior (5 percent) high schools. Both of these findings are consistent with the studies described by Feshback (1970). It is, therefore, surprising that there is more adult use of force in senior (9 percent) than in junior high schools (4 percent).

A follow-up study (De Cecco, 1971) showed that teachers, when given explicit choices of negotiation vs. decision by authority or force, choose "negotiation" as a way of getting the student to "cooperate," and then, when the student resists, resort to force before they consider mediating the conflict with the help of third parties. This study also found that outside of school, teachers resort to force in dealing with children more often than they do in school.

Our original research showed that students believed they were victims of adult violence four or five more times than they are the perpetrators. Later research suggests that school officials and teachers often believe that they are more often the victims.

Violence

The incidents in this category involve the use of violence by adults and students. Sometimes the violence was in response to violence between students and sometimes violence was combined with verbal threats.

This principal is described as adding violence to student and teacher violence. The writer is a ninth-grade student recalling an incident that happened in the seventh grade:

I got into a fight in my math class and Tony punched me in
the stomach and when I went to hit him back the teacher came
and she hold me and Tony was slugging me so I broke loose
from the teacher and I started beating him up. The teacher said
if you dont stop I will write a referral and send me to
the vice principle. So I did stop and I went to my seat. I was mad
be cause she was holding me and she let Tony hit me.
So I went down to my seat and put my foot on the next chair.
She told me to get my feet off the chair and I did not. She told
me again, so I did. She said four me to come up to her desk
so I did. She root me a referal and I went up to the vice principle.
He told me if it was true that I broak loose from the teacher.
I told him it was true and he wanted to paddle me. So he found
my house and no body was home. So he paddled me. I toaled
him it wasn't fair be cause she was holding me and the boy was
punching me. He just toald me to go to class.

In this conflict we can see how both teacher and vice-principal added to the violence between the two students. The writer became enraged when the teacher held and exposed him to Tony's punches. When he broke loose to defend himself the teacher believed that he had been violent toward her. Failing to help him handle his rage, she immediately provoked another incident by forcing him to remove his feet from the chair. The vice-principal added to the violence with the paddling of the student because the student had broken loose from the teacher although the occasion for his being sent to the office was his refusal to remove his feet from the chair. It is often no easy matter for teachers to decide what to do when students physically assault each other. Whether it be shouting at the students to stop, separating the students by stepping between them, or getting the help of other students and teachers, any effort should be toward converting the physical to the verbal expression of anger. In this conflict, if the writer had the opportunity to verbally express his anger toward Tony and the teacher, his subsequent angry acts may have been unnecessary.

The following incident, described by a student, illustrates how violence between students was met by the threat of punishment by adults, described here as the "greater powers":

I can clearly remember an incident when two students had a disagreement which led to a small fist fight. The two young men who had the fist fight shook hands after and were prepared to forget it as a mishap. The teacher, in his attempt to make an example of one or both of the boys, sent pink slips down to the office of the dean. He in turn called the parents in, you can see already see how it is getting out of hand. Naturally each parent considers her offspring to be an angel. The issue with the dean of boys, the parents, and the teacher was who started the fight, determining the right and wrong of the two boys and the punishment. By the way, the boys were playing basketball together on the same team during lunch when they were interrupted by their teacher to come and attend the meeting of the upset parents, dean and teacher. When they were asked of the incident they both denied it and stated that they were the best of friends. At that point it was dropped which left the greater powers perplexed.

The intervention of each adult appeared to escalate the conflict. The teacher, instead of having the boys discuss the reasons for fighting, reported them to the dean. The dean, in turn, involved the boys' parents. In the conference with the adults the issues shifted. The original issue over which the boys fought was replaced by the issue of who was guilty and who should be punished. Since both boys shared some responsibility for a fight in which both had actively participated, adult attempts to focus blame perpetuated the conflict. The adults could have encouraged the boys to express anger verbally, focusing on issues to be negotiated. By the time they attempted negotiation, the boys had no anger left to motivate their effort.

This conflict, described by a teacher, is an example of violence between a school adult and a student, with the adult
initiating the violence:

Gail comes storming down the hall in school yelling that
some one has stolen her Parker pen. The language is unbearable.
A teacher stops her and starts to yell at her about her language.
They both yell at each other for a short period of time.
Students gather. The teacher grabs the student by the arm
to take her to the office. She resists calling the teacher names.
In fact she attempts to hit the teacher and finally does. Other
teachers join in and they take the girl to the office. The principal
hearing the story suspends the girl because of her language
and because she struck the teacher. Parents, teachers union,
civil rights leaders, etc., enter the situation until finally
she [the student] is reinstated.

The conflict started with the student's verbal expression of
anger over the loss of her pen. It was escalated to violence
when the teacher grabbed the student by the arm. The student
resisted with both name-calling and violence of her own. The
principal added to the violence by ordering the student's suspension. With the conversion of verbal to physical expressions
of anger more and more students and adults become involved
and the issues become murkier. Although the original issue was
the loss (or theft) of the girl's pen, the issue shifts first to
"unbearable" language and then to the student's physical attack
on the teacher. It later becomes a civil rights issue involving
non-school adults. The school adults, in this incident, may seem
to have failed to distinguish between "bad" language and physical acts of violence. The student may have believed that the
arm grabbing was an act of violence, although the teacher may
have meant only to restrain her language. No one seems to have
offered the girl help in finding her pen.

   In the following conflict the student describes adult (police)
violence against his sister and the use of verbal threat:

Right now a "crisis" is happening in our school. All of a sudden
the police just came into our school and now our school
is loaded with policemen, who, for absolutely no reason at all,

are insulting and mistreating the students. It seems that students
that have a free period during school have a big problem.
If they leave school, they are called cutting. If they stay in the
lobby they are kicked out of school, and if they stay out in front
of the school, they are eligible to be arrested for "loitering".
Yesterday, my sister was cursed at and shoved around by a
policeman for standing on the side of the school. Today the
students had a strike. I really wanted to go, but having a 7th period
I would have been called cutting and I can't afford to have
a bad record . . . The police have made us damn mad and
our hate will burst out of us soon.

The physical presence of police was seen by the student as a
non-verbalized threat of violence against students. Both parents and school officials see the presence of police in the school
as a way to avoid violence while the students see the police
as a physical threat against students. The common practice of
many schools to have police cars patrol the school areas at the
beginning and end of the school day makes students angry.
They perceive it as a non-verbal threat of punishment for acts
they have not committed.

The following incident, described by a student, shows the
use of violence against the school:

Well my problem is the lunch. Boy! Do they serve sloppy lunch.
Sometimes they gives you lefover. The people that serve the
lunch act like they cann't cook The children (pupils) started to
complaint about the lunch but they just didn't get anywhere.
Anyone in my family can cook better then the cooker. We tryed
to get better lunch but it just didn't work. We have the G.O.,
to go down there and tell them about there cooking but they just
didn't work! And you should go down there and see the lunch room,
It look like a hurrican have just went by. Go down there at
4 & 5 period. (Sloppy) This should teach the cooker that we
want better lunch! I think that the teacher should eat the lunch
that we get, and let us eat the lunch the teacher eat. And
let the teachers know how bad our lunch is. And maybe we might
get some better lunch. And let our principal eat the lunch too!

The writer implies that the mess and possible vandalism in the
cafeteria was the result of the failure of the cook and other

school adults to heed student complaints about the food. Since the verbal expression of anger produced no results, students turned to violence to express their anger. The school lunchroom, along with school restrooms, are favorite places for students to vent their anger against school adults and school as an institution. If students were asked about the food they liked and what spaces they needed and liked for their activities, much angry feeling about the physical environment could profitably be used in changing the school building.

This incident, described by a student, shows how the school adults can use parents to inflict violence on students:

One day I was in school and my friend put fire cracker under
the teachers seat. And the teacher fainted. The principal
came up to the class and said: Who put the fire cracker under
Mrs. Cranes seat. A whole lot of boys & girls started laughing
and the Principal took 4 girls & boys down to their office
and called their mother and they got in trouble. Their mother
came to school and beat them in front of the class and principal
and after all of that they went home and went to bed. Well,
their mother could have beat them in front of the class
& principal. Because that would be very embrass. Really George
put that fire cracker under the teachers seat. I didn't. And
I went home and out and played with my friends.

School adults evade the legal restrictions on adult violence in ways this incident illustrates. The public punishment is also a non-verbal threat to other students.

Here the school erred in two ways. It used violence as a way of punishing violence. It ignored due process and incited parents to punish innocent students. What the school may have taught in this incident is not the avoidance of the use of violence but the avoidance of getting caught for violent acts. It may also have taught students that violence is a legitimate way of dealing with violence. The public punishment was also the non-verbal threat to students of their being possible victims of random punishment.

The act of punishment in this incident, told by a teacher, involves the physical removal of the student from the school:

In the spring a student reported to the athletic director to claim his letter which he felt he had "earned" as a member of the tennis team which had won the league championship. The young man in question wore his hair a bit longer than his peers but not to the extreme that it was shoulder length. He had worn his hair this length all through the tennis season. The athletic director informed him that he would not receive his letter until he had his hair cut. The student remarked how no one had challenged his hair style while he was on the tennis court and his efforts had contributed to the team's championship. There was a series of verbal exchanges in which the student accused the director as posing as a despot and the language became very heated between them. The student was reported to the principal, was suspended for insolence to the teacher, and his mother brought to the school. The mother, oddly enough, welcomed the school's intervention because she had been unable to "do anything with her son." It seems that the director erred in making his denial of the letter on a type of ex post facto basis.

We see how the avoidance of the expression of anger led to that undesirable outcome. The first angry expression of the coach over the length of the student's hair provoked the student because it came only after he had won his letter. The student might have reacted differently if the coach had warned him earlier. Because the coach did not allow an open confrontation, when the student expressed anger over taking the letter away, the coach had him suspended. By suppressing the verbal expression of anger, the incident shows how school adults are forced to resort to extreme punishment.

Physical and Verbal Threats

It was difficult to find examples of incidents in which physical and verbal threat did not ultimately result in physical violence. Verbal threat may be interpreted as a signal for the physical violence that follows. The following incidents illustrate both physical and spoken threats. A physical threat is an action expressing the readiness to use force. A spoken threat is a statement of the same readiness to use force. In this incident, related by a teacher, the student strike is a physical threat:

Two incidents came up over the decision-making rights of the school's student government, the G.O. The first situation was where someone raised the question in a G.O. meeting of the appropriation of a sum of money to add to an amount that the local college was raising to get Eldridge Cleaver—Black Panther Minister of Information—to speak at the College. The appropriation was passed in the G.O. in two votes but after this the principal vetoed the move and said that such an appropriation was against the State law. The original idea had been brought up by a black student to get this black leader to speak. The school had a strike over this issue and after many long meetings with the Board of Education, it was found that it would have been perfectly legal for the G.O. to give the money to Cleaver. The problem originally had been that Cleaver was a candidate for the Presidency and it was against state law for a public school to donate money to a political cause or person. A problem that was raised by the incident is who has the ultimate power in the school or is there some balance of power between the student body (represented by the G.O.—an elected, supposedly representative body) and the administration (represented by the principal). The immediate (or seemingly to the administration), threatening problem was the strike where the situation turned into a black-white struggle for power in the school. The black students led rallies in the main corridor in the school where the whole issue of racism or discrimination in the school system was discussed. Cleaver did speak at the College, but the appropriated money was not needed.

The Cleaver issue got lost in the shuffle, but it was the spark that has caused a total re-evaluation of the school by at·least the semi-involved and the involved segments of the student body and many teachers.

Anger was first expressed in the G.O. by the debate over the speaking invitation. The principal's opposition to the G.O. action, occurring entirely outside this debate, angered the G.O. majority and provoked the strike. The strike, a physical threat of violence, escalated racial tensions and increased threats of violence. The conflict de-escalated only when it was known that the speaker would appear.

The following incident, described by a student, illustrates the use of verbal threat of force in BRO (Black Radicals Onward) demands and the intimidation during the roll-call:

The General Organization (student government) at New
Rochelle School is composed of elected representatives from
the student body and the officers which are chosen in a school-wide
election. Early in the year there was a protest initiated by
black students—some G.O. members, some not. The demands of
the Black Radicals Onward (the name of the black organization)
included: 1—a course in Zwahili, 2—more black history, 3—more
black literature, 4—more black guidance counselors, etc. The
demands of the BRO were to be discussed at a meeting of the
G.O. The President of the G.O. opened the meeting and proceeded
to go down the list of items on the agenda. The demand of
the BRO was the third or fourth item on the agenda. Before the
other items could be discussed, the leaders of the BRO moved
to the platform and without being recognized by the President
who was using parliamentary procedure forcibly took possession
of the microphone and proceeded to dominate the meeting.
The meeting broke into chaos and the BRO walked out in protest.
The problem which arose, of course, was one of "tyranny of
the minority". The only recognized authority was intimidated
as were the members of the G.O. The problem was handled or
there was an attempt to handle it on the part of the president.
When he realized that he had no choice, he then laid aside
the agenda and allowed the BRO to present their demands.
How effective this method was is doubtful as there was a great
deal of chaos and open intimidation of some of the representatives.
In the course of the meeting, a vote was taken on some of
the demands. It was a role-call vote and this is where
the intimidation took place.

The incident illustrates the use of collective threat. The threats are made by a group of students against other students. This incident also shows on one hand how verbal threat can disrupt democratic decision-making. On the other hand it shows how the verbal expression of anger may have prevented violence.

The following incident, described by a student, is filled
with verbal threats and violence:

[W]hen I was 15, one day while walking in the corridors going
to class I crossed the Senior Garden. I was pushed and then
punched, then when I was finally pushed out I was seized by
the school officials and taken to the office. While I was in the
office, the principal scolded me for crossing the garden and
threatened to suspend me. I also threatened the Senior that pushed
me. The Principal threatened that if I shold lay a hand on the
student I would be expelled. He could have at least interrogated
the other student but instead he release him almost immediately.

The act of walking across the Senior Garden was responded to
with violence by the senior who attacked the writer. The
writer was then subjected to further violence by school officials who "seized" him. An exchange of verbal threats followed
the violence. Because the threats followed the violence, they
seemed to save face while de-escalating conflict. In other
incidents, verbal threats preceded violence and seemed to
escalate the conflict to violence. When teachers are intervening
in student fights they may find that a final exchange of threats
is a way to cool down the fighters.

A teacher name I had gave me a grade on a test of 68 and
said that you do it over and you will get a better grade. So I
did it over. This took place in the begin of the Marking period
so I had done it over, but I had came late to school all that marking
period 20 min. each day. Late, but had a excuse for all the time
I came late and I missed some test but she let me make them up
so I had a advage of 80 but she said that I miss 4 test.
Then at the end of the marking period she said that I was going
to fail because I was come to school late and that the 68 was a
85 and she gave me the same 68 grade and promise me to fail.

The non-academic problem was tardiness and missing four
tests. Instead of the teacher verbally expressing anger over
these matters, she uses the verbal threat of failing the student
in his academic work. There is ample evidence, however, even
in this unbiased account by the student himself, that the teacher
faced an exasperating situation.

Institutionalized Force

Force can be exercised without verbal threat or physical violence. Institutionalized force carries an implicit threat of punishment. In the high school institutionalized force takes the form of rules and codes that regulate student dress, conduct, movement, and activity. The exact nature and purpose of the rules may be confusing to both teachers and students but the certainty of punishment for rule infraction remains.

In the following incident a student describes how he believed the school dean exercised force by controlling the students' leaving and entering the school building:

Last year, at the beginning of the year, when I had just come
to this school, I cut school one morning for what I thought
was a good reason. I wanted to visit Urban School, which is
a private school, somewhat freer than the public schools. At the
time I was considering going to such a school. I went with a friend
without telling anyone or asking permission. When we returned
to school the boy's dean was standing guard, as was his habit,
waiting to catch anyone who had broken the closed-campus rule.
He caught us. It also turned out that my friend's mother had
called the school to make sure that she was all right. This was
a habit of her mother's, she did it most days but my friend
had not taken it into account. . . . Anyway, we went down to
the girl's dean and, being inexperienced in the art of cutting,
we admitted every class we had cut and thereby caused ourselves
to have to serve detention for all the classes, whether the teacher
had given a cut slip or note. This fuss was resolved by our
serving detention. I would would like to have seen the fuss
resolved by the dean admitting that high school students have
every right to go to class or not, as they choose, and the
principal repealing the closed-campus rule, as ours is the only
high school in the city with such a rule.

The "closed-campus" rule restricted student movement to the school building and grounds. There was also the rule for attending classes. The writer discovers that the punishment for breaking either rule was detention. But she also implies that there are ways of evading the rules ("the art of cutting") and thereby evading punishment. The expression of anger over rules that restrict freedom of movement is displaced on to efforts to evade and subvert rules—a way students use to avoid institutionalized force. To the extent that the students consciously left the school and planned the visit without the permission of school and mother, they seem to deliberately provoke an angry reaction. One way in which students displace anger is by getting school adults angry at them and forcing the school to punish them.

In the following incident, described by the student, the dress code is the institutionalized threat:

About two months ago the students in our school got into
an argument with the "establishment". This argument was about
the dress code at this school. Boys were wearing tennis shoes,
made of canvas, and heavy work boots which are not permitted.
We got into a heated argument about why we could not wear
the forementioned objects. We could see no reason why girls
could not wear panchos even if they went good with the uniform,
but the principal said we couldn't because it was considered
outdoor wearing apparel. She also stated the fact that the heaters
were always on and there was no reason for us to be wearing them,
but people always have the windows open. In the end, the
boys were not permitted to wear canvas tennis shoes or heavy
boots, but they can wear leather tennis, and girls were not
permitted to wear clogs or panchos and had to wear blouses
that go with the skirt. I can see girls can't wear clogs because
they ruin the floor, but I can't see why the girls can't wear panchos
even if they do match the skirt.

The writer depicts the struggle with institutionalized force as the students' argument with the school "establishment." Her argument is not against dress codes or even uniforms. The issue is no particular item of dress but who decides what the dress will be. She is willing to go along with reasonable restrictions (e.g., not wearing the clogs) if she can help decide what is reasonable.

The next two incidents deal with censorship of the school newspaper by school officials. The first incident was described by a teacher:

Two years ago, a student who was the editor of the school
newspaper wrote an editorial in which he accused the teachers
of having no interest in their students. He cited as proof the
low level of student achievement in the school. On hearing about
the article the principal forbade publication of the article
and lectured the student responsible on the evils of irresponsibility.
In protest, all the student members of the newspaper staff
resigned. Several days later the censored article was distributed
to students on the street as they were coming to school.
The responsible student was then suspended by the principal.
At the same time the principal learned that the offending article
had been printed at the home of the newspaper's faculty adviser
who was then relieved of that assignment. Shortly after,
the student sued the principal for violating his civil rights.
He was upheld in court and his suspension rescinded.

The reality of institutionalized force was made clear in the student's suspension and in the removal of the teacher as advisor. The newspaper article was an expression of the writer's and staff's dissent, apparently viewed by the principal as "irresponsibility." The principal's attempt to force them not to publish incited the students to defy his order and act unilaterally. The article's distribution, therefore, could be viewed as defiance, thereby justifying the punishment of teacher and students. That the force exercised by the principal was "illegal" (even though "institutional," since he acted in his official capacity) was established by the court ruling. By charging "irresponsibility," the principal failed to confront the students on the issue of teacher interest in students and thereby involve both students and teachers in negotiations that would join efforts to add pleasure to school learning.

The following incident, also described by a teacher, involved censorship of both newspaper and research findings:

A group of journalism majors at high school met on their own
to make a survey of seniors and high juniors using James S.
Coleman's research questions as who the school heroes were, what

the peer friendship group was, did teachers affect their choices or decisions in a number of areas and so on. When the results of the carefully taken survey were published in the school newspaper the students found censorship, ostensibly administrative, cut out the results of some interesting findings. The students were furious and went to the principal in a group. Adults possibly connected with the censorship disclaimed knowledge. The issue was, unfortunately, not settled and aired to student satisfaction.

The censored version of the findings that appeared in the student paper was an institutionalized act against the dissemination of research findings. Since the purpose of the school includes the dissemination of knowledge, the official use of force to alter a research report provides a poor model of academic integrity.

There is institutionalized threat in vague, unformulated rules and rules that allow arbitrary decisions by school adults. A student describes this incident:

I needed only two courses to graduate, but, being a student, I thought I had the right to take a full set of courses for the year. Since they were not required, my desire to take extra courses were proof of my sincerity to benefit from them. The extra courses would help me get into a good college. The principal deceived me as to what procedure I should follow to obtain permission by telling me and my parents that I should write to the board of education for approval. For some reason, I received no reply from the guidance department of the board's decision. My mother, a teacher in the district, saw Mr. N at a meeting and was informed that the board approved of my taking extra courses. In a meeting the following day with me and my mother (and the principal) we were told that only the principal had the right to approve the extra courses and that he didn't think I would be able to catch up with all the work I had missed while waiting for the Board's reply, but he finally permitted me to take an extra Spanish II course (of which I made up the missed work in less than two weeks) necessary to get into the type of college I wanted. When asked why he did not let me take a full set of courses he explained that he wanted to get all the 19 year olds out of high school. This was an odd explanation because of the fact

that I was going to be 18 when I graduate and he was informed
of this many times. I would like to know what the procedure
is for getting extra courses—from an honorable source.

The student describes several sources of school coercion: (1)
the rule that students cannot take more courses than they
need for graduation—an extremely survival notion of learning;
(2) the necessity to obtain the permission of the board of
education; (3) the principal's sole right to approve the extra
courses; and (4) the principal's policy to force graduation.
In order to implement his graduation policy, it appears that
the principal changed the rules without students' advice or
knowledge. In this way he avoided an angry confrontation
with students and parents who would dissent from his policy.
The avoidance of the anger of debate can lead to vague and
essentially unenforceable rules that eventually lead to widespread anger and apathy. The administrative procedure for
forcing graduation was seen as coercive because rules were
changed without the students' advice or knowledge. Information about the change may have made it appear less coercive
to the students, even though the price of giving this information may have been their verbal expression of anger.

In the next incident, told by a teacher, the majority of the
teachers add their authority to that of the administration and
the teacher has only the option of compliance:

Our faculty, in a whirlwind and exasperating meeting, decided
that a teacher may ring his classroom buzzer at any time he wished
to extricate a problem child by immediately taking the student
to the vice-principal. After such an office call the teacher
who has a preparation hour would have to handle the classroom
in the absence of the subject area teacher. Such, in brief summary,
was the action initiated by the administration to solve discipline
behavior in the classroom: the idea is that bad behavior meets
immediate action. The faculty approved the proposal ten minutes
after six p.m. in a prolonged session with the exception of a few.
Then the system was initiated. As a result, I am called upon
almost every day to give up my prep period to a teacher [for]
whom I have no great admiration and who, I believe, is a "cop out,"
a "dud." The injustice is one is freed while the other is enslaved

to a "messy" class with recourse and having protested and dissented against the plan's innovation. Such an innovation infringes upon my time by supposing democratic rule. The plan should have had an experimental trial and pro-con debate or at least the assignment of those willing to attempt a workable plan.

As we have seen in these incidents, the use of institutional force is an effort to avoid confrontation and anger. Even though the dissenting teachers did not have a chance to present opposing arguments, they were forced to conform to the new buzzer system.

Summary

Alternative action to appropriate verbal expressions of anger are the following: violence, physical and verbal threats, and institutional force. Violence includes the physical removal or barring of the student from school by force or suspension. Physical and verbal threats can lead to violence. After the eruption of violence, however, they can serve to de-escalate violence by replacing it with angry verbal expression. Institutional force is used by the school to establish external control of student behavior. It is often used as a substitute for helping students develop their own inner controls. Institutional force presents the school to students as a model of the suppression of knowledge rather than one of knowledge dissemination. There is school coercion involved in students and teachers not knowing current procedures and thereby having their plans upset. The adverse effects of institutional coercion are felt by teachers and parents as well as students.

The last two chapters have dealt with the emotional aspects of school conflict. The conflict descriptions have shown how the verbal expression of anger by all parties to the conflict, structured in terms of specific issues, can lead to negotiation. Physical expressions of anger or threats of punishment and coercion, on the other hand, frequently escalate conflict and prevent negotiation. The next two chapters will show how particular cognitive abilities can help handle the anger that conflict arouses.

7 The Good and Bad Guys INTERPERSONAL CONFLICT

IN THE SCHOOL

THE LAST TWO CHAPTERS showed how the verbal expression of anger could be a first step in the negotiation of conflict
and how acts of violence, threats, and institutional force could
stalemate negotiations. The present chapter discusses the cognitive abilities necessary for successful negotiation. In addition,
this chapter will present a system of classification that should
be useful for the understanding and resolution of school conflicts by school adults, parents, and students.

In order to negotiate, one must know who is involved in the
conflict. Each party needs to know who is on its own side
and who is not. If there are others on its side, it can use their
collective help and strength. If the party is really alone, it can
evaluate the adequacy of its power to fight alone. It can then
decide whether the conflict is worth the effort it will take to
carry on the negotiations. In this way, one can avoid trying
to get people not involved in the conflict to fight one's own
battles under the mistaken notion that they are also their
battles. One can also avoid getting involved in other people's
battles when one has nothing at stake in them.

The advantage of knowing who is on the other side is that
one knows with whom to negotiate. One can estimate their
single or collective strength. If there is only one adversary one
can avoid adding to the number of adversaries by involving

those who have no stake in the conflict. For example, sometimes the teacher will punish a whole class for the misdeeds of one student or a student will get angry with all teachers because of his treatment by one teacher. If there is a group of adversaries and we negotiate with some members and not with others, those left out may not accept the settlement as their own. If there are several other sides, one can involve members of each in order to increase the number of parties that will be satisfied by whatever agreement is finally reached in the negotiations. The more parties satisfied with the agreement, the more people there will be with a stake in upholding and protecting it.

Nor are our adversaries always our peers. Successful resolution of conflict requires us to recognize when we are dealing with peers and non-peers. This recognition is important for several differences it makes in negotiation: (1) the conventions for expressing anger; (2) the issues that structure the anger; (3) the issues that are negotiable and non-negotiable; and (4) the appropriate and available concessions.

Negotiating with peers may call for direct and colorful expressions of anger on both sides. By contrast, negotiating with authorities may require tactful deference to positions of status in order to avoid alienating them. The issues that structure the anger may involve higher status groups which have the power to make the concessions and changes one wants. In Chapter 9 there are detailed examples of negotiations in which understanding of who is involved determines the results of negotiation efforts.

Negotiation requires the ability to understand other people's points of view, be they one's allies or one's opponents. It requires that one see other people's multiple roles so that one can distinguish between situations in which they are on one side and issues in which their interests may line up with quite a different group. It requires a continuous flexible reorientation to other people's roles in different situations.

The general ability to view conflicts between people from the perspectives of other individuals involved is known as *decentering*. There are two aspects of the ability to decenter.

One is *coordination*—the perception of the common interests of the parties to conflicts. Another is *differentiation*—the distinguishing of the diverse interests and statuses that separate the parties to conflicts.

Our evidence for determining the writers' ability to decenter is limited to their descriptions of incidents. Although our classification system is based on a developmental theory of role-taking ability (Inhelder and Piaget, 1958), our evidence for the absence or presence of this ability in our writers is limited to their descriptions of solitary incidents. Therefore, what we classify as coordinated and differentiated is not the ability of the writer to decenter but the writer's *description* of the incident. Writers who produced uncoordinated and undifferentiated descriptions may have been able to decenter but chose not to. Descriptions are also influenced by situations they described. For example, the fact that a writer depicts himself as one individual pitted against another individual of equal status is not necessarily evidence of his inability to decenter conflicts. It may be and often is a very realistic description of the only parties to the conflict. But if he depicts himself as a member of a group, we can say he *has* coordination and therefore *is* able to decenter. Our analysis in this chapter always distinguishes between ability and performance. If we asked a group of students to ice skate and half of them skated around and did figure 8s, we would say that those who did skate had the *ability*. We would not know whether those who did not skate were unable or chose not to skate. Similarly those who *did* decenter are said to be able to. Those who did not may or may not be able to. Yet, the presence of more decentered description in senior than in junior high school leads to the conclusion that decentering reflects cognitive growth.

The descriptions of incidents in this chapter will show both coordination and uncoordination and differentiation and undifferentiation. These incidents are presented under two headings: (1) under one heading we analyze incidents to show the various ways in which writers described the first party to the conflict (the good guys); (2) under the other heading we analyze incidents to show the various ways in which writers described the other side or the second party to the conflict (the bad guys).

First, consider the various ways in which the writers depict the first party. Writers present either coordinated or uncoordinated descriptions of the first party. Uncoordinated descriptions use singular pronouns (I, he, she) to represent the first party. Coordinated descriptions use plural pronouns (we, they) to represent the first party (see Figure 1).

Being able to see a conflict in terms of "we" rather than in terms of "I" is an indication of social development in high school students in two ways. First, it shows a more realistic appraisal of the structure and purposes of high schools. Second, it shows that the person describing the conflict is more likely to be effective in resolving conflict by negotiation.

1. High schools really are organized by society to serve classes and categories of people rather than any one particular person. The ability to see high school conflict in terms of group rather than individual issues is an indication of understanding that reality (regardless of whether the student could express such understanding in the abstract).

2. Social effectiveness can be indicated by describing conflict in terms of "we" rather than "I" because it leads naturally into undertaking collective action. People who are not aware that others share the same grievances they experience feel isolated, powerless and are too hopeless to even try for change. Feeling alone is often associated with hypersensitivity to real or fancied insults which makes it difficult to see the issues or to negotiate realistically. If they were aware that others felt as they did and enlisted their aid, they might be effective in changing both their own situation and those of their allies. To see conflict in terms of a collective "we" can thus be more effective than seeing it in terms of a solitary "I" because it facilitates negotiation. Yet, awareness of group needs may pose more dilemmas for students than they would have if they were interested only in their individual needs.

Writers present either differentiated or undifferentiated descriptions of the first party. Undifferentiated descriptions use first-person pronouns (I, we) to represent the first party. Differentiated descriptions use third-person pronouns (he, they).

Seeing a conflict in terms of "he" rather than "I" can show social effectiveness because it allows someone else to be the center of the drama while the writer is in a peripheral role. To write of "we" in a conflict *may* indicate that others are important only insofar as their positions strengthen one's own. To write of "he" or "they" is to subordinate one's own interests at least for the time being. The individual can participate as an ally, mediator or neutral observer in another's conflict. One can then enlist others to return the favor by participating in one's own conflict. It thus increases one's chances of bargaining successfully. The point of view also allows each student wider scope for participating in a greater number of issues rather than just those in which he can see himself as "the star of the show."

Descriptions of the first party, therefore, could fall into one of four categories. Each category points to the presence or absence of coordination and differentiation in the descriptions. The four categories are: (1) uncoordinated and undifferentiated descriptions in which the writer describes himself as alone; (2) coordinated but undifferentiated descriptions in which the writer describes a group (we) as participant-observer; (3) uncoordinated but differentiated descriptions in which the writer describes another individual (he, she); and (4) coordinated and differentiated descriptions in which the writer describes a group (they) as non-participant-observer.

Figure 1 shows the four categories of descriptions of the first party based on the evidence they presented for the two aspects of decentering—coordination and differentiation.

Now consider the various ways in which writers describe the adversary or second party. Descriptions fall into one of four categories: (1) uncoordinated and undifferentiated descriptions of an individual peer (e.g., a student); (2) coordinated but undifferentiated descriptions of a group of peers (e.g., students); (3) uncoordinated but differentiated descriptions of an individual of higher status than the writer (e.g., a teacher, a principal, etc.); and (4) coordinated and differen-

FIGURE 1   Decentering: Classification of descriptions by
the first party to a conflict

	Uncoordinated Descriptions INDIVIDUAL	Coordinated Descriptions GROUP
Undifferentiated Descriptions FIRST-PERSON	*I* am the only "good guy"	*We* are the "good guys"
Differentiated Descriptions THIRD-PERSON	*He* or *she* is the only "good guy"	*They* are the "good guys"

tiated descriptions of a group of higher status people (e.g., teachers, principals, the school adults, etc.).

Figure 2 shows the four categories of descriptions of the second party based on the evidence they presented for the two aspects of decentering—coordination and differentiation.

Figures 1 and 2 show that the meaning of coordination shifts a little as we move from the first party to the second party. In the case of the first party, coordination refers to the writer's identification of common interests—the coordination of interests with a group. In the case of the second party coordination refers to the writer's description of the second party as individuals or groups. The description is classified as uncoordinated if the second party is described as a single person. It is coordinated if the second party is described as an institution ("the school") or group.

The meaning of differentiation also shifts a little. In the case of the first party, differentiation refers to writing from the perspectives of a party to the conflict which does not include the writer. In the case of the second party, differentiation refers to separation of statuses, particularly adult from student status. In the original study we referred to this latter type of differentiation as "relative status" (see Appendix B, pp. 245-263).

The coding rule was to designate as the "good guy" or "good guys" the first individual or group described by the writer.

In our study (see Appendix B, Table 5), the incidents showed more coordination than differentiation in the description of the first party. As for coordination, about one-half the incidents were described in the uncoordinated terms of "I" or "he." The other half were described in the coordinated terms of "we" or "they." About two-thirds of the incidents were described in the undifferentiated terms of "I" or "we." Only one-third were described in the differentiated terms of "he" or "they."

The second party was described as an individual by about half the writers. This is almost the same proportion that described the first party as an individual. Thus, coordination appears to be about equally frequent for the first and second

FIGURE 2   Decentering: Classification of descriptions by
the second party to a conflict

	Uncoordinated Descriptions INDIVIDUAL	Coordinated Descriptions GROUP
Undifferentiated Descriptions PEERS	*"Bad guy" is a student*	*"Bad guys" are other students*
Differentiated Descriptions ADULTS	*"Bad guy" is a teacher, a principal, etc.*	*"Bad guys" are teachers, principals, the school, etc.*

party. Coordination seems to be a characteristic of the description no matter which side of the conflict is being described.

The second party to the conflict was differentiated from the writer in 80 percent of the descriptions while the first was differentiated from the writer in only about 30 percent. Thus in many cases the writer appears to have described adversaries as more different from oneself than allies—a reasonable view of the world. There was more differentiation than coordination in the descriptions of the second party.

There are significant differences in coordination and differentiation shown in the description of junior and senior high school writers. More junior than senior high students described incidents in the uncoordinated terms of "I" or "he." Junior high writers showed less differentiation of the second party than did senior high writers. They described more conflicts with individuals than senior high students described. Thus, descriptions of incidents by junior high students showed less evidence of decentering than those of senior high students.

ADVERSARIES: THE PARTY OF THE FIRST PART

In all the incidents in this section we will examine how writers described the first party to conflicts. First we will look at incidents in which the writer participated. In some of these incidents the writers depict themselves as individuals; in others as members of a group. Second we will examine incidents in which the writer was a non-participant observer.

The Participant Observer: The Writer as Individual

In the following incident the writer describes herself as alone in a situation other students depicted as a collective experience:

I have Spanish during the second period, and usually my Spanish
teacher and I don't get along very well. Most of the time
I cut her class because I passed Spanish 5 and 6 last year

but didn't pass the Spanish Regents.* So one morning when I
attend class, she waits until the lesson is started and then stops
the whole lesson just to tell me that if I don't stop cutting,
she would fail me so fast my head would spin. I felt this was
an injustice towards me on her part. She should've called me aside
either before or after class and then we could've possibly
come to some agreement, but because of this, we, or rather
myself, can't stand the sight of her.

The writer sees the problem as simply one between herself and
her individual teacher. This is not selfishness in the sense of
inflated self-importance, but merely the attitude of seeing
situations from her individual point of view with no particular
effort to relate her problems to the situations faced by other
people in her class.

   Another student appears even less aware of the collective
nature of this experience:

My blood in my foot stop circulating and I first ask the teacher
could I walk around and she said no—So she kept on speaking
so I tried to make the blood circulate by hitting, patting down
on the floor, etc. The teacher yelled to the high heavens
and started telling me all this jive. And I had this metal bar
I ring the bell with and it fell on the floor loud. And she said leave
it there, this is the same teacher, So she kept on talking and
I picked it up and this same teacher said the same old jive,
but someone could've gotten hurt.

The student displayed no awareness of classroom requirements
for order or quiet. There is no evidence that he appreciated
the point of view of any of the other students sitting in that
class. It appears that he sees the classroom only as an adjunct
to his own needs.

   In the next incident there is still only one good guy (the
student writer) but now he has a particular teacher who he sees
as only interested in him:

* A statewide examination in New York required for credit
in some subjects.

During my freshman year in high school I had a math teacher
who was what I consider nasty. The first day of school I felt
that as soon as he laid eyes on me he disliked me. He made me
sit on the first seat, next to his desk. Every day when I walked in,
he used to start giving me wisecracks. Because of this, I found
myself in a state of nerves everytime I walked into the room.
I found that I developed a mental block. So all I did was walk
in and sit down and I wasn't able to learn anything at all.
He notice this and so he would stop teaching the class and started
asking me questions which I couldn't answer. Finally I couldn't
take it anymore so I stopped going to the class and failed it. I
spoke to the grade guide, but she didn't help any. This teacher
let personal feelings affect his teaching. I was too dumb not to
do more, so I paid for it by repeating the subject.

He draws no parallel between his troubles with the teacher and
what other students in the class might have experienced.

The student in the following incident joins a group but continues to view himself as alone:

The student Council in my high school is virtually the
administration's rubber stamp, concerning itself with such vital
issues as graduating class colors and admission prices for basketball
games. It has no real power in anything concerning disciplinary
action or school policy towards students and the community
(minor examples: speakers for auditorium programs, hair, dress,
censorship in the school newspaper of perfectly straight news
and opinions, etc). After a few people, (including myself) were
told to trim their sideburns above their earlobes, everyone felt
"persecuted" & decided to make somewhat of an issue of it.
A few people with liberal radical leanings had been waiting
for such an opportune moment & formed the Freedom Union,
an appellation later changed to Student Freedom Union, because
of the original organization's initials. In short, my choice was
joining the SFU or not. I did, not without doubts as to its
relevance, possible effectiveness, the shallow motivation behind
its formation, or the possibility of strengthening the Student Council.
AFTERMATH: The hair demands by the administration faded
into oblivion.

He maintains an impersonal aloofness from the larger group,
keeps his distance by emphasizing his fears and doubts about

it, and winds up still focused on his own original complaint
against the school administration.

When the student does see himself as isolated, his effective
functioning can be hampered:

The problem which I have trouble with is censorship in the school.
I am on the executive committee of our school newspaper and
I have found that some articles which are proofread by the
principal are never entered into the paper. I have taken this
problem up with our advisor and the answer I get from them is
that it didn't meet with the approval of the board. I then went
to the principal himself and I was told that it wasn't very good,
but I was told that it was a fine article and had facts about
our school and/or community. There wasn't much I could do
except bring my complaint to my advisors. I always thought that
freedom of the press was in our constitution, but the school
disregards this item. I keep on writing articles which are critical
but true and are always torn up. I keep on looking for a solution
but the school board has more power over any student body.
I keep hoping for a solution so that our community
will face up to the truth.

This description shows how the hypersensitivity associated
with feeling alone would make it very difficult to see the issues
and to negotiate realistically.

The student below clearly articulates his perception of his
own isolation:

At a convention I attended all the people were broken up into
discussion groups to talk about any topic which they chose.
I was put into a group with kids who were younger and very
much more immature than me and I couldn't discuss the problems
that were troubling me with them because they hadn't experienced
these problems yet. I decided I would, on my own, switch to
another group which had older people in it. I joined this group
and was soon engrossed in a very lively conversation. One
of the leaders came over to the group and saw me in the wrong
group and told me I had to change to my original group.
She had meanwhile interrupted a very good discussion and
destroyed any trains of thought people had had. I argued with
her and told her that the other group was too immature and I was

very engrossed in this conversation. She insisted that I leave
and return to my original group. I just sat and waited for her
to leave and she finally did. After she left, I called over
one of the other leaders and explained to him what had happened.
He also said that I should return to my original group. I still
wanted to stay with the second group, but returned to my
original group. After I returned, the people in the original group
turned sullen and refused to talk about anything, while people
from the group I had left were so disgusted with the action of
the leaders that they lost all interest in the conversations. Instead
of interrupting the group and yelling at me, the leader could have
quietly called me aside and spoken to me separately.

While the student may be faulted for not informing the leaders
of his intention before changing to another group, the action
of the leaders seems to have isolated him from any group. It
appears that the decision of the authority figure prevented
students from forming group attachments. This incident
ironically occurred in an alternative school. It is important
to note that just moving from the school building, or even from
the school as an institution, is not enough to guarantee that
the relationships between people will change in a way that will
make them more aware of common interests. Nor will these
external changes necessarily give them the perspective to see
others as having some of their problems and encourage them
to join others to make changes.

The Participant Observer: The Writer and His Group

The following student perceives the class conflict from
both a single point of view ("*I* belong") and from the group
point of view ("*we* have a problem"):

I belong to a special gym class, for which they chose me, called
Senior Leaders. Besides being our regular gym class, we are
also required to do a period of service in other gym classes.
The teacher, or faculty advisor prefers to consider the class a
"club" with "spirit". She calls it democratic, (we have elected
officers) but I always have to laugh to myself because at meetings,
whatever she says goes.

We had a problem because the teacher was getting anonymous letters because they object to the way teams are picked (democratically, but the worst players are embarrassed to be picked last). A council was set up to handle problems. I am a member of the council.

This is the problem—we were discussing the "lack of spirit" and reasons for it. The teacher wasn't there. It was mentioned that many kids were annoyed at the way the teacher noticeably picks on this one girl. As a council, we decided to point this out to her. That same day, she was talking and not everyone was paying attention, this girl being one of them. The teacher picked on this same girl. "Judy, am I picking on you now?"

We had made the situation worse. We had made the wrong decision. This teacher was not the one to tell this to.

The incident nicely illustrates the maturity of those who think of social problems in terms of "we." If the writer had seen the incident from a solitary point of view, it would be described as confrontation between a teacher and a student.

Imposed group membership may force a student to act as if he were a group member but, as we see in the incident below, does not necessarily change his perceptions of his isolation from the group:

In our school during the time of the death of *Reverend Doc* Martin Luther King, something extremely interesting happened to myself and I am sure others just like me.

At this time our school (the leaders of our school, including many teachers) were involved in a kind of protest to police department. The protest involved *Police Brutality,* which was not actually true.

Many students, teachers, Radicals, etc. formed a parade to the police department protesting this. (I might say that I marched also.)

I did not really believe in what was going on, but without thinking, only reacting, I marched for something which I really did not believe in.

The point I am trying to make is that I was persuaded (in a way forced into a strange position) undemocratically to participate in something which I really did not believe in.

(Point of interest, my school is made up of over 50%
black students.)

While he does call the school "our school" and does recognize
that there were "other students just like me," he reverts to
the solitary "I" position when he thinks he is being forced to
march.

In the following situation we have the first clear example
of a student writer who includes himself as a group member—
using "we" and "our" instead of "I" and "my":

Our school is 30% Black. There are two main groups in our
school; the academically talented and the regular classes.
The academically talented are supposed to have a higher I.Q.,
so they are resented by the regulars. The regulars are predominantly
Black and the academically talented are all white, but for
the one Black boy and the one black girl that are in the
academically talented classes. The problem is this: recently, the
academically talented were all put on one lunch shift. This puts
the whites and the blacks apart and the academically talented
and the regulars apart. We have instituted a student council,
which does not seem to be working. Meanwhile, the races and
the groups are getting farther and farther apart.

The student who described this incident clearly understood that
the first party is a group. This individual's concern for the
group interests enables him to be an effective member and
helps the group to achieve formal status as a student council,
though not to achieve its goals.

In the following incident, the writer also perceived himself as a group member. Since this group is so cumbersome, he
refers to the need for subgroups to achieve the group goals:

At my high school we recently staged a protest about the
school diciplinary policy. Approximately 700 students (over half
the school) sat in the auditorium for three days and didn't go
to classes. The issues involved a review of the school's disciplinarry
policy and the charges that there was racial discrimination in
the enforcement of the existing rules. The administration agreed
to meet with a small committee of students but this presented

a problem. There had been repeated charges among the students that a certain few kids were running the school. The Student Council was almost non-existent because students felt it was always ruled by a certain few. There had been the problem of cliques in the school and we, us, the student body, finally felt that we were moving closer to mutual understanding. We decided that it would only divide us if we had to appoint committees. We told the administration that the 700 students were the committee. This presented a problem. We realized that it was illogical to have a 700 man committee and accomplish anything, but it would be hypocritical for us to appoint a committee since we had emphasized that we are together and that the large 700 man committee would represent us. Eventually we had to agree to a smaller committee.

Because of his sense of group solidarity (note the use of "we," "us," and "student body"), he faces a difficult school dilemma: the need for mutual understanding with the whole group (i.e., 700 students) and the greater effectiveness of small group, face-to-face interaction. Yet he is aware that there is the danger that the small group will become another clique, running the school for its own interests.

The same problem of subgroups appears in this student's incident:

Here at H—— we have a black society mostly of black girls and an Afro-American history course which many girls from each grade attend. In these two groups many issues have been repeatedly discussed over the past six months. A few days ago, black girls of the black society wrote out and mimeographed a petition of demands addressed to Dr. M. They discussed that they wanted compulsory courses in minority history into our curriculum, minority culture aspects to be included in literature, art, music, dance, history and cooking courses. They discussed that they thought Puerto Rican Spanish should be taught and accepted in our schools rather than Castillian Spanish. For the courses on black, oriental and Puerto Rican history and culture, they wanted preferably teachers of the specific race. It was also implied that the white teachers shouldn't teach these courses because they were racist.

Now my reaction to this petition is that the demands for black, oriental and Puerto Rican studies included (in the courses currently offered) but not separate is just. However, can students of less experience than the administrators and teachers make demands? And can they expect co-operation if they demand? This is a conflict in democracy. Every member has rights to voice and vote. But are we equals in school? There is a contract made when the state supports schools. We get education and the education tries to be helpful to us. A contract of cooperation has been made. Because supposedly we all have the same ends in mind, a good education for all children in our society.

The writer talks of herself as a member of the school group, the group of students which is a subgroup in the school, the group of non-white students which is a subgroup of the larger group of students. She poses the very difficult question of equality in status between these groups. Is one racial group of students equal to another? Are students equal to teachers? She relates these questions to the membership of all these groups in the larger democratic society of which the school is only one part. She sees the conflict as within subgroups of a larger "we" group.

The Non-Participant Observer: Another Person as First Party

In the next incident the writer sees the other person's interests as the central issue:

One problem which aroused conflict in my mind and in my family came about as a result of the New York City teachers strike. My stepfather is a teacher and has been for many years and I know he works very hard. The situations involved in the strike caused him to feel a sense of conflict and there is still conflict between my brother and stepfather because of the ideas involved. (The only reason I'm not actively involved in the dispute is that I'm quiet and constantly changing my opinion from one side to the other.) The new programs would have meant to my stepfather that he would have less opportunities and his "competition" would be people who do not have the training and

experience for which he had worked very hard. In order to
express his opinions and in hopes of achieveing security, he went
on strike. He is at the same time compromising himself as a
teacher who has a responsibility to his students. I don't know
what is right or what should have been done and this causes
me worry. Now with the new law regarding strikes of public
employees another strike would be (even more) illegal. This
doesn't really bother me as much as the feeling that whatever
he does he is fighting against himself.

She could see the alternatives her stepfather had and the
effects these choices would have on him rather than on her.
Though she expresses her personal point of view, it is kept
distinct from that of her stepfather. He is central in her description.

The next incident shows the ability of a writer to take the
point of view of a fellow student even though the writer has
something at stake:

This July I took a course in beginning Italian. In my class
was a boy who was going to be a senior in college and who
needed the credit from this course and the intermediate Italian
course he hoped to take in August in order to graduate from
college. I expect he needed to graduate and get a job rather
badly since he was married and had a baby to support. He had
no particular background and so, since the course was quite
difficult, he did rather badly, though he worked at least 6-8 hours
a night and was very alert, bright and interested. He even
came in Saturday mornings by the end of the month, however,
he hadn't passed a single test, nor the final. The teacher was
faced with quite a problem. This boy needed at least a C– to
get credit for the course, at least a C in order to get scholarship
aid for August which he needed to enable him to take the course
which he again needed for credit. I don't know what decision
was finally made by the teacher, though I think he wanted to
pass him. If he did, the teacher would be putting himself in a
tight situation. For someone might check the test records and
find out that the boy had never gotten more than a D.
Technically he didn't deserve any more. If he passed him,
he would however not be hurting anyone. For this boy was

obviously capable of dealing with work after a year more at college and he also needed very badly to get out of college after a year. Since he was taking the Italian just for credit, he would not be needing to use it in the future. I personally would have passed him even though the rules would have had him failed.

This writer can see not only the point of view of his fellow student, but also that of the teacher. He sees that the teacher faced the dilemma of giving a student, who was working at night and who needed the scholarship aid, a disqualifying grade or of arbitrarily lowering his grading standards. He clearly states the teacher's dilemma and choices even though he knows that these are not his own choices. He maintains this objectivity even though he knows that he may be graded on higher standards than the working student.

The next writer is able to describe four different points of view—those of three student groups and the student candidate for the presidency of the student government:

A student in my school wanted to run for president of the G.O. but he couldn't meet the qualifications. He had failed too many courses and the screening committee wouldn't accept his petition. He was a member of the Student Action committee, a school club which strived to achieve certain goals like the destruction of obsolete and archaic institutions and ideas in society or at least in the schools. They took up this cause and demanded that the constitution of our school be thrown out and a new one be written. This split the school into three factions, one for the rewriting, the backers of the G.O. who wanted to keep the constitution, and those who didn't care. Unfortunately, the majority of the school didn't care and after enough pressure the Student Action Committee won and the principal threw the constitution out and set up a constitutional committee to write a new and more democratic one.

I agreed that the constitution was archaic and that it should be replaced and I got myself on the committee. We've spent almost a year working on it and the rough draft is finally done. It is a much more democratic document, but I'm afraid that the student body, because of its apathy may not ratify it and if they do this apathy will make it ineffectual and it won't work.

Some of the language is rhetorical, i.e., "obsolete and archaic," and the writer devotes one paragraph to the expression of his own views. The incident, however, differs from previous ones in that the writer distinguishes between several groups of good guys. This is a level of the ability of an observer to take several points of view in the same conflict.

The Non-Participant Observer: They Are the First Party

In this set of incidents the observer presents another group as the first party.

In the following incident, the young male student presents the girls as the group of good guys:

The event which I will write about is sort of a minor point, but it was the only thing I can think of that happened in my life that was new. It happened in my school in Eastchester. The girls decided to wear pants to school in winter and the rest of the year. The administration is quite conservative and wouldn't allow it at first. One day, a lot of girls wore pants to school. The administration didn't like it, but no girls were sent home. The event was nothing really important but it shows what a semi-organized group can do. The girls could have gone along passively and not stood up, but they didn't. There was a choice the principal could have made also. He could have said that no girls could wear pants. I think he realized that the girls would wear them anyway. I think the girls were right and more dissent should be in the school.

While he was aware that, as a boy, he was not a member of that group, he was also aware that the girls belonged to a larger student group of which he was a member.

The next student was able to see the point of view of a group of which he was clearly not a part. He even managed to take the viewpoint of teachers in his school:

The teachers of the biology department wanted to offer a new and well specified course in sex education. All the said subject's teachers were for it, but the school board, or should I say the

head of the school board, wouldn't allow the motion to be made
to discuss the said topic. To explain my views first I must say
this. It's shown every day in this country that there is not
a democracy with real democracy. The School Board could at least
have heard from these teachers, not only out of courtesy, at
least of democracy. The decision of the school board left a deep
impression on the students of the school. And again I refer
to here, "Is this democracy within our democracy?

This student views what happened to the biology teachers in
terms of what could happen to him. He considers the status
of citizens in a democracy and objects to the perversion of the
democratic process. He feels that he and "they" (teachers)
have a common stake in due process.

Both of the above incidents have had a kind of lop-sided
good-guys versus bad-guys quality. The writers clearly expressed the viewpoint of only one group. The next incident
shows that the student is able to describe the viewpoint of the
people who disagree with him:

In our school newspaper everyone objects because they claim
the school is run by the editors of the newspaper. The people
in school say that the newspaper is biassed, uninteresting and the
issues are too short. Yet the students never bother to submit
articles or to write letters to the editors or make suggestions.
The editors are faced with two choices. They can run the paper
theirselves (most would prefer not to do this because its
too much work.) The other choice is to go encourage friens
and kids on the staff to write for the paper. This way more students
get involved and interested in the paper—yet at the same time
the students get the variety they want. But usually the editors
lose faith in their staff because they take the attitude that
if I don't do it, it won't get done, or my staff should come to *me*.
The students—who the paper is written for—do nothing but sit
on their apathy and indifference.

It is not clear whether the editors or the other students are
the good guys. Both points of view are expressed with some
supporting arguments. The final statement about student apathy
makes it seem that the writer has more sympathy with the edi-

tors than with those students who complain about them. Still, the difficulty of deciding whether the student point of view expressed at the beginning or the editor's point of view expressed at the end represents the good guys is strong evidence that the writer could represent both points of view.

The incidents described up to now have all involved people with whom the student was directly involved. The "they" groups were immediately present, tangible, easily recognized sets of people. In the next incident the writer sees "highly selective colleges" as the central party:

When highly selective colleges choose which applicants to accept, there is often a conflict between two students who are equally qualified but from different backgrounds. Since students from slum schools, usually black, Puerto Rican or Mexican, do not recieve equal educational opportunities, when they do well in school and recieve high Board scores they are accepted by the most highly selective colleges almost immediately. A middle class white student, with perhaps a suburban high school diploma, might have recieved higher scores, or be more qualified, but might not be accepted at that college.

Since the slum school student has obviously had to overcome more obstacles than the suburban student, his achievement is greater and he deserves to attend a selective college. However, his immediate acceptance might also be seen as window-dressing and there might even be competition between colleges over how many Watts or Harlem students they can snare. The suburban student has to compete with many other students who have had the opportunities he has had and are equally qualified. His chances to are much more uncertain, even though he may deserve to attend that college. Ideally, students should be selected irrespective of color, but that appears impossible when colleges are committed to accepting students of many different backgrounds, and when compensations to students who have been deprived of other things seem necessary.

It cannot be wrong to give the black student as much as possible, because so much as been taken away from him, but the white student who had to compete with so many other white students inevitably suffers. The white students cannot protest and the black student is entitled to get as much as he can. As of now, the black student is favored.

As heated an issue as this has been, the girl describes it without once personalizing the issues.

In the next incident, the good guy is a large group composed of college students and administrators:

Although I was not involved, my cousin told me of an incident which I think illustrates the point. She goes to College. Recently, there has been some difficulty over their policy of Afro-American studies for black students only, with the consent of the other people. Recently, the government decided to take away the school's money because they are maintaining sergationist policies and they ordered them to change. So, the government is going against the will of the students and the administration of the college, both of which were satisfied with the existing situation. It is their opinion (I think) that if they allow this situation of reversed segregation, then other colleges, mainly in the South, will allow their traditional policies of segregation to continue, and they will expect the government's aid. In this respect, the government is right. But the situation that exists at Antioch is one that the students wanted, fought for and are at present satisfied with. If they are not complaining, why should the government interfere? According to my cousin, this situation had died down, so I would assume that the government, which seems pretty scared of campus unrest, has backed down. However, this may lead to difficulties in other schools.

The group is described as an even more distant "they." As the writer makes clear, he is not personally affected by the decision "they" make. He perceives college students and administrators as a unified "they." Since he is not personally involved, his description of the incident reads like newspaper reporting, with both sides fairly presented. People on either side of the issue could agree that the writer gave supporting evidence for both sides. The bargaining step of negotiation to be discussed in Chapter 9 is aided by such understanding.

ADVERSARIES: THE SECOND PARTY TO THE CONFLICT

Any conflict has at least two sides: "good guys" and "bad guys." Writers viewed "bad guys" in different ways: (1) as individuals or groups (uncoordinated or coordinated) and (2) as peers or non-peers (undifferentiated or differentiated).

Peer Individual or Peer Group

The following incident illustrates how one writer described the bad guys as a solitary peer:

It happened in school. My brother was sitting down eating his lunch
and this guy was swinging around a sack with some ice-cream
in it and my brother told him to be cool and not to hit him
with it so the guy got all bad and threw it at him. My brother
grabbed him by the neck, knocked him down and hit him.
All of my brother's friends were there and they were all down
to help my brother fight. My brother was stopped from hitting him
any more. Problems began to develop when they called in
my Mother, this problem was kept in control and they suspended
him and my brother four days.

The peers, in this incident, are the writer's brother and the
boy who attacked him. The writer's brother appears to be the
good guy and the boy who started the fight the bad guy.

The writer in this incident about marijuana does not clearly
distinguish between two possible individual bad guys, both of
whom are peers:

In our town in school there was a boy who wanted to buy a pound
of marijuna. He didn't know where to get the grass. But I
know where to get the pound. In fact, I know where I could
get 50 lbs. from my friend in New York City. This boy had
$150. for a lb. I could get it for $100. so I cut the $50. for myself.
I arranged it for my friend for me to cut $50. Then I took
this boy to the city. He gave my friend $150 and [he] told him
to wait in front of the apartment while my friend goes upstairs.

My friend took the money and went up to somebody's house
where he said he could get the grass and runs down the fire-escape
with $100. I had the $50. and was waiting in the car with the boy.
We waited for an hour. We realized we were beat. We came
back to town and I told him I could get his money back.
But I never did pay him back. I also kept the money. I got a
beating, bleeding and everything. He never bothered me again.

The writer even fails to distinguish between his own interests
and those of his peers.

Consider an incident in which the bad guy is a peer group:

It happen in group that I have where we play music. And some
one is not always with them, or when they are they interrupt
the others. And some don't want even to cooperate with the group,
like when we have to buy some music or books that we need
for the group, somebody of the group say I am not going to
cooperate or give any money for the group because the instrument
I play does not need any music to read. In other way,
if you play some kind of instrument where you don't have
to read music to play in you can make the music out of the sound
of the piece that they are playing with. And I think that
everybody have to cooperate with the group because that is why
we have a group. All the people playing in the group
should listen to the one who is in charge of the group or the one
that they have put to make the decisions. I think that if
I put money for the group I to play, I need the music, even if
the other does not need music he should put the money too,
because that's why we are a group, help each other because if
it has not been for that way, we wouldn't have made up the group
and the one in charge of the group or the boss like we have
rules if any of us does not keep the rules he will be punish,
sometimes we have trouble with one of our group because
he does not care too much about being one of the group. This is
the way I think about my group and what I think should
be done about it.

Although it is a peer conflict, the writer appeals to authority
for its resolution.

In the following incident, the bad guy could be either an
individual peer or a group of peers:

In, of all places, a school men's room, I ran into a little scuffle
with some colored boys. They were pitching pennies, and in
my way, so I said, "Hey boys, do you want to move? I need
to do something." Whereupon one of them, apparently looking
for trouble, said something to the effect that I shouldn't tell
him (them) what to do. That started an argument which he
neither relinquished nor regretted. Along the way, he said he
was black, that I'm white, and that I was wrong, out of place, etc.
Wanting to leave as best I could, I waded among the three boys
and left with them right behind me. I turned my back and
started to leve when, I later learned) one of them raised his fist
to me. But a passerby, black and a friend of mine, stopped him
from doing so and told him to "lay off him" (me). Before this,
however, I told them to shut up several times because
I certainly did not want to fight and also wanted my lunch.
I had gone in the restroom with a white friend, who stood helplessly
by, watching the entire incident. He later informed me
of the later events which I did not see.

I don't know who started it: it could have been me or him. I knew
one of the three colored boys. I used to play softball with him
and later learned the name of another. I probably could have
apologized to them in the men's room, but I had my pride, too!

In the marijuana incident the writer seemed confused about
who was the individual bad guy, whereas this writer seems to
vacillate between viewing the individual (the boy who hit
him) or the peer group ("the three colored boys") as the bad
guys.
     Sometimes both the good guys and bad guys are described
as members of peer groups:

This past year a new idea concerning the yearbook published
annually was put into effect. It changed from what used to be
just a report of what had happened during into something
with a personal touch. Something that would be part of this
graduating class and the school. Different decisions had to be
made concerning the cover, style and so on. One of the thoughts
that came up was to have the pages in a box instead of a book
that would have been bound. It was stated that it would make
the layouts easier to do and add versatility to what you could have
done. Arguments were given both for and against this new idea.

The fairest thing that to do would have been to take a vote
to decide what would have been done. A vote was taken and the
idea of the box won a majority of votes. Although this would
usually mean that this would have won, it didn't. As a result of
the opposing side being so against the new idea, it was dropped.
The old idea of the book was kept because it seemed that
this side felt a stronger ideal about the book and would have ended
up hating the final work as a result. On the other hand, even though
the majority vote was in favor of the new book, they would not
have disagreed as strongly, if their idea was not accepted. The main
problem in the final decision was to follow the democratic
process, that majority rules, or follow what would have been a
more obvious good. I think it was handled in a good way for
a small group. It could not be done in a larger group
or state of affairs.

The bad guy appears to be a small clique within the larger
group. They appear to be making the important decisions.
Voting for them was a way of winning what they had no intention of surrendering. The writer appears to wrestle with a
conflict created in him when a group of peers, playing an elitist
role, behave as authority figures rather than peers.

Adult Individuals or Groups

Many more of our writers described incidents that dealt
with conflicts between students and non-peers, such as teachers,
counselors, principals, and so on. The following incident is a
clear example of a description in which the bad guy is an adult:

I'm a senior and my English IV grades will count a lot on my
acceptance or rejection at the college of my choice. This year
my English teacher has been a constant torment. Failing grades
for a majority of her 74 English regents students. One day
after about 12 weeks of this 72 of the 74 students got book reviews
back with the grade F. This prompted another student and I
to write a letter of protest of questioning to the editor of the
school paper. The letter was "liberated" from the editor's desk
by the paper's advisor and given to the teacher in question.

We were called in and spoke about our grievances and the teacher
in question talked in circles and the administration bought
every word. We had a second meeting after 4 weeks of time
had gone by, we promised to back off if she could change a few
things, book review form, her jokes, oh, yes, she reads a joke
a day before she starts to teach, etc. Nothing was done. We
backed off and now the parents are trying to do something.
This woman is 63 years old by the way. Solution retire her.
I am going to sign my name because I sign my name to the letter
we wrote and I sign my name to everything either to take
credit or blame for it.

The writer does not describe the adult who stole the letter as
bad guy even though the behavior of that person is a serious
breach of his democratic rights.

The following bad guy is described as an adult. The status
of age is again the issue:

If you are under 16 and go to the movies but are also over 12
you still have to pay an adult price. However you do not get
the privileges of paying this price. When I went to a movie
something concerning this situation happened to me. I was 14
so I paid two dollars and sat in the children's section.
In this theater they have a witch as a matron. She hates
young people. So at six o'clock when the movie was not even
half over, this old biddy comes running around hitting everyone
in my section with a flashlight and telling them they had
to get out. Now this is alright for kids who only paid 75¢ but when
you pay two dollars you would like to be able to see the movie.
Besides, this practice of throwing us out at 6 was not stated
anywhere by the theater so how were we to know. I refused to
leave so this walking corpse hit me again. I felt like hitting
her back but instead I left and went home to write a letter to
the manager. I never received an answer. I wouldn't have
minded leaving at six if I had been told before I went in. Then
I would have gone earlier. I felt that my rights were violated
not only because I was under 16 but because this nut was hitting
me with her flashlight. I don't think it was her fault that we
had to leave because she was just doing her job but she had a
lethal weapon in that flashlight. If I had been the manager I would
have put up a sign that all people under 16 have to leave at 6.

They could have also explained to me why they had this policy but they probably didn't think that it was worthwhile explaining something to a kid. Maybe I should have lied about my age. But it wasn't worth it. I just wasn't respected in fact few people respect kids my age now.

The writer describes the villain in this piece as the individual authority figure and not the theater management. The description lacks decentering.

The bad guy was sometimes the principal, a person with even more authority than the teacher:

The principal was unfair to me one day. She was coming down the hall and a boy was bothering me in a very vulgar way. I called him a name. She said: "You shouldn't do this," and told me to come with her. I came but this was highly unfair why didn't she take him instead? If I have a gun, I would have shot him! He tried to take advantage of me, and I got all the blah mouth because I tried to defend myself! This occurred in the school on the fourth floor. The whole class was there and saw what happened. She did not know how to handle this problem otherwise she would have talked to us both finding out who was the troublemaker. Of course, the boy started it by touching me where he shouldn't have. I would of slapped him, but she was coming instead full of anger I called him a name.

The writer makes it clear that she resents the principal's intervention in her private love-hate battle with her peer. She expresses her wish to handle the situation by keeping it on a peer-to-peer level and by slapping the boy herself.

In this incident the authority figure (the student acting as teacher) complains about her "subordinates"—the students:

Our school started a modern dance group. Being the only one in the group that has had any experience, I was appointed the teacher. The song that was picked was too fast and long for the first try. Another song was selected but no one had any ideas, so I proceeded to show some steps. Some girls then acted up and refused to do them and said they were too hard. A bickering of words went back and forth and they said they never would do it again and refused to try. A dance group cannot be conducted without discipline and the will to try.

The solution . . . What a joke! I left. My reason, as I stated
before, they refuse to even try to contribute anything of value.

Her role as teacher shaped her perceptions of her fellow students so that she does not describe them as peers. This incident
suggests that role more than age separates students and teachers.

In the next three incidents the good guys are described
as being in conflict with an institution rather than a group of
individuals. In the first incident, the student describes the
conflict as between "the students" and "the principal." The
principal is not personified. He described the police as another institutional force intruding into an internal conflict between students and their school:

The dilemma that I was faced with occurred in May of last year
at this school. The students had made a list of demands and
had presented it to the principal. These demands included
Afro-American history as a major subject, better eating facilities,
better gym facilities, black books in the library, more black
teachers, firing Dean of Girls, remove all non-teaching assistance
(NTA) and other demands totalling 22.

If these demands were not met, the student body had scheduled
to have a walkout. We had the support of other black
high schools in the neighborhood. I was faced with the decision
of walking out or remaining in school and attending class.
My mine was made up for me when the Chief of Police
sent his men out to the school. I felt this was an uncalled for
move on the part of the police. So I joined the walkout.

The writer made his decision to strike when he found out that
the police entered the school. Students used petitions and
strikes whenever they perceived the conflict was with the
whole institution.

In the second incident the writer describes the parties to the
conflict as a group of students (The Concerned Students Union)
and the faculty:

Unawareness in the areas of political movements, student apathy
towards contemporary problems and poor race relations
all played a part in the establishment of a student group at

my school known as The Concerned Students Union. The group was started by two male students who promptly asked for an advisor and called a meeting at which 20 some other students attended. Quickly, the group set its objectives as the following: to create a better school, improve student-teacher relationships, and support the rights of all oppressed students. No sooner than these objectives were made public was the group branded as "a bunch of leftist radicals" by prominent faculty members. Cries were heard that this group intended to take over the operation of the school and incite mass student unrest and possible insurrection.

When members of the group approached faculty members with the question "Why did you consider us radical?", the answer was a simple. "You are trying to gain control of things and you better cut it out." This writer was in fact branded by three members of the faculty as a "left wing fanatic" because he dared to suggest a meeting between a teacher going on tenure alone and her students who were frustrated by her acts. Later this writer was led to believe that school authorities had his name on a list as a subversive because he "violated his patriotism" and instead adhered to amendment one by not saluting the flag. This case has come to the CSU, but hasn't been worked on because membership was dwindled due to the faculty spread of rumor and lie.

The writer describes the faculty as labeling his group as outsiders—not part of the student body. He states that this labeling prevented his group from functioning within the school.

In the third incident dealing with the institution as the bad guy, the writer appreciates two points of view: (1) that of the administration and (2) that of the group of students:

Here a few months ago a group of students staged a student educational assembly period, which was to liberate the students from the faltering administration. This was only a discussion period. The administration deemed the meetings illegal; they announced all students illegally absent from class and would take action. The whole question of right and wrong arises because the administration was right in claiming the assemblies illegal, but the students were very much distressed by policies of the school. I think that there must be some shades of right and wrong to understand the problem.

Because this writer sees this as an institutional conflict his language becomes high-flown: "deemed the meetings illegal," "faltering administration," and "distressed by policies." Despite the humorous aspect of the language, the writer describes a real conflict.

The last three incidents show how the means used by the students are determined not only by the issues but also by their perception of who are the parties to the conflict. In the first incident the writer decided to strike when he perceived the intrusion of an outside party even though the issues were always institutional. The strike was seen as appropriate because this was a conflict with an institution. In the second incident the students formed an institution (The Concerned Students Union) to deal with a conflict with the school as an institution. In the third incident the students used student assembly to deal with the policies of the school. If these conflicts had been perceived as interpersonal rather than institutional, the students would have used other means of dealing with them.

SUMMARY

Parties to conflicts can be described as "good guys" or "bad guys." The writer can describe each conflict as having one good guy or a group of good guys. The good guy, that is, can be seen as individual or group.

The individual good guy may be seen as oneself or as another person. If the good guy is seen as a group, the group can be the writer's own group or other people's group.

The bad guy can also be described as an individual or a group. Another view of the bad guy is in terms of status. Whether individual or group, the bad guy can be described as having equal or unequal status.

Coordination is the perception of the common interests of the parties to the conflicts. Differentiation is the perception of the diverse interests and statuses that separate the parties to the conflicts. Coordination and differentiation make up the ability to decenter—to see issues from other points of view.

There are distinct advantages in school conflict situations for students and school adults who have and use the ability to decenter. They can perceive their common interests with those with whom they could unite to make changes. They can perceive other people's interests and choices when these are distinct from their own. They can avoid getting mad only because others are promoting their own interests rather than helping them. They can perceive their adversaries more realistically. They can distinguish between a personal and institutional adversary. They can avoid fighting individuals when they should be fighting institutions. And they can fight the antagonist with whom they are in conflict—not someone else.

The inability to decenter seriously impedes negotiation as a means of conflict resolution. In the incident, for example, in which the student complains about the lack of student interest in the school paper, the writer does not see that other students had interests different than his own. If he did, he could accept their non-participation or open the paper to their needs and interests. Similarly, the matron in the theater could have found some common interest with the students if she did not see young people only as children who must be punished. The experience of commonality can also help young people cross age and status barriers and see that adults are like themselves. Then the students, as in the case of the old English teacher, would see the teacher as having a common interest with them in making the class enjoyable. The jokes she brought to class were *her* effort to revive the class. *Their* effort would have to extend beyond criticism of the jokes and the teacher. An appreciation of common interests would also have helped the students in this conflict see that their real conflict was with the teacher who harmed them by misusing the letter they wrote to the editor.

Negotiation requires a realistic assessment of common and opposed interests and the need to sacrifice some of the latter in order to build on the former. But the balancing of gains and losses can occur best when individuals can view their conflicts from all their varying perspectives.

8 It Takes Time

To VIEW SCHOOL CONFLICT from various dimensions of time enables participants to improve their chances for analyzing and resolving conflict. The appropriate anchoring in time of the events in a conflict enables participants to locate issues that have aroused anger and the range of practical options they have, given the limitations of time, for resolving the conflict. As parties to conflicts struggle to negotiate, they broaden and deepen their understanding of how they and other parties are conceiving and using time.

There is a body of theory and research that links various conceptions of time to adolescent development. Lewin (1939) stated that larger units of time become more salient as we move from childhood to adolescence. Children think in terms of days, weeks, and months but adolescents begin to think in terms of years. This change makes adolescents able to envision remote as well as immediate goals so that they can make plans to bridge between present ability and future attainments. The ability to think in terms of longer time spans is one dimension of abstract thinking.

In dealing with school conflict, adolescents are able to perceive the long-term effects of different conflict resolutions. Although they still tend to grab at immediate, global solutions, they are developing the capacity to defer resolution until all parties to the conflict can tell their sides. Conflict resolution takes time and adolescents are developing an increasing capacity to put in the larger amounts of time required for stable resolutions.

Larger amounts of time can be comprehended in terms of larger units of measurement. These larger units of measurement provide a better perception of duration—a broader background of events against which the adolescent can perceive foreground events. When there is little background (or perception of duration) the foreground events almost entirely dominate attention. Nor do all adolescents of the same age reach the larger time perspective. The findings of Sebald (1968) and Kagan and Kogan (1970) suggest that conflict analysis and resolution, as described here, will not have equally successful results with all adolescents.

Meerloo (1966) believes that there is a relationship between a stable biological rhythm and awareness of external events. A stable rhythm of heart beats, breathing, sleeping, waking, hunger and so on, is required to provide the individual with a sense of duration against which he can conceive and weigh foreground events. Adolescent biological changes may thus upset smooth internal rhythms and distort time perspectives. We found that distorted perspectives can become a source of conflict with school adults who see the adolescent student as unaware of history, too caught up with the present to understand the past.

Research indicates that description of time is related to verbalization of emotional states: when affect is positive (e.g., an enjoyable ski trip) the time is described as too short and when the affect is negative (e.g., waiting on the lunch line) then time is described as too long.

Psychoanalytic theory has added to our understanding of time. Freud (S.E., Vol. 7, p. 119) stated that since the individual's ideal models are timeless, they clash with the demands of reality. Freud also referred to the timelessness of infantile wishes. Arlow and Brenner (1964, p. 100) presented clinical evidence for time distortion. They concluded that:

Such feelings as time seeming to stand still or that a very long
period seems to have been lived through in what was actually a
very short space of time, the feeling that one is a child again,
the feeling of having experienced a particular situation at an earlier
time, etc., are phenomena which result from intrapsychic conflict.

Intrapsychic conflicts first crystallize during early childhood.
These conflicts recur in adolescence, as discussed in Chapter
10. At that time, they happen in school rather than in the
family. Arlow and Brenner (1964, p. 100) explain the relationship of these conflicts to the child's sense of time:

For the first several years of life the child has no concept of time
or an inadequate one. Those phenomena (dreams, symptoms)
which in large measure derive from infantile sources often
reflect the little child's inadequate sense of time.

Children's concepts of time develop from about the ages of
five to ten. When they reach adolescence the conflicts they
have in school are distorted by unconscious intrusions of the
old childhood conflicts. Students must learn to bring their
more cognitively developed sense of time to bear on present
school conflicts. This realism is made more difficult by the intrusion of the timelessness of their earlier conflicts.

The dimensions of time that provide the child with a
realistic sense of time have been described by Piaget and
Inhelder (1969). Our analysis of the time dimensions described
in the incidents was based on these distinctions. Three independent time dimensions can be applied to each incident. Like
dimensions in space, all three must be used for a writer to completely describe the time of an event. Each dimension is a
continuum—like a ruler—from obscure time to clear time description.

Temporal dimensions are related to negotiation. First,
knowledge of these dimensions is necessary for successful
negotiations. Negotiators must be able to think of experience
as discrete events and to set events in sequences that relate
causes to effects. They also need to differentiate between
foreground conflicts and the enduring aspects of background
conflicts. Finally they need clock and calendar dating of con-

flicts to establish the sequence of events with which they are dealing and to compare the different sequences as conceived by various parties to conflicts. In this way parties develop a realistic sense of the time span needed to effect change.

Second, the negotiation process, by forcing parties to use time concepts, deepens their understanding of the three dimensions of time. In any particular negotiation, time plays a specific role. A variety of experiences develops higher-order concepts (Bruner, Goodnow, and Austin, 1956). We are extending this general principle of concept-formation to the development of the concept of time.

To introduce the analysis of the incidents we will first define the three important dimensions of time and then describe their theoretical relationship to adolescent development.

In order to deal with conflicts effectively, the participants must be able to view time in three different ways: (1) By *sequencing* time they separate events and fit them into a series. (2) By *duration* they describe the background action that gives the foreground events special significance. (3) By *measuring* time they use the clock and the calendar to date events.

Here are examples of the sequencing, duration, and measuring of time. The riddle, "Which came first, the chicken or the egg?" states the problem of *sequencing*—determining which event came first.

Duration is required to solve the following riddle:

As I was going to St. Ives
I met a man with seven wives
Every wife had seven sacks
And every sack had seven cats
And every cat had seven kits
Kits, cats, sacks and wives
How many were going to St. Ives?

The answer is one because only "I" was going to St. Ives. To solve this riddle the listener must note the difference in verb forms: "was going," marking the interval; "I met a man," marking an event; and "were going," marking the interval.

The *measuring* of time is illustrated in this nursery rhyme:

> A diller, a dollar
> A ten o'clock scholar
> What makes you come so soon
> You used to come at twelve o'clock
> And now you come at noon.

The riddle solution depends on the listener noting the identity of "twelve o'clock" and "noon." The joke is that the scholar has not changed the time at all.

By sequencing, the writer both separates and orders events. By separating events he can describe all the events occurring. By ordering events, he can describe what came first, second, third, and so on. By sequencing, therefore, the writer can establish the causal connection of events occurring later with those occurring earlier in time. He can be sure that events occurring later could not cause earlier events.

There is a difference between a clearly stated sequence marked, for example, by *then, later, after that,* and an implied sequence lacking clear markers. The incidents described without a clear sequence of events often used *and* or *but* to link events rather than more differentiated sequence markers such as *first, second, third* or *before, then* and *next.*

Duration enables the writer to describe the background action that gives continuity to foreground events. In describing this continuity the writer can use verb and adverb forms: *was going; while;* and *as I was going.* All these forms mark the time between events—what we have called background action or events. By describing both background and foreground events the writer has a second way (sequencing is the first) to establish causal connections between events. By describing background action the writer's options for resolving conflict in foreground events become clearer. The description can either proliferate or eliminate acceptable options.

By measuring time (with clock and calendar) the writer can differentiate similar events happening at different times. Clock and calendar time are also important in the negotiation process. Talking about issues cannot go on forever. The time available for emotional statements and common statements of issues must be proportional to the time available for bargaining.

Sequencing: He Started It

The first set of descriptions show how students perceived sequences of events in the incidents they described. There are examples of all three aspects of sequencing: (1) separating events; (2) ordering events; and (3) determining their cause-effect relationships. Three types of grammatical structures indicate how writers sequence events: adverbs, adverbial phrases, and verb tense.

The first incident occurred on the school athletic field. The student vividly describes a series of events:

I was playing handball with a friend. The first one out of the game would get hit with the ball. I was the first one out so I let him hit me with the ball. Then we played another game and he was the first one out. He didn't want me to hit him, so I hit him anyway he went and told his brother. His brother came up to me and said Why did you hit my brother. I said, "I hit him because he lost the game. So his brother said how would you like me to hit you with the ball. I said, "go ahead he went to get the ball and threw it at me he hit me on the arm. I got mad pushed him he pushed me back I punched him in his face & knocked him down when I jumped on him on the floor his brother jumped on my back I grabbed him and threw him on the one on the floor they laid there crying. Then a man stopped me. He sat me down and tole me to cool off. When he picked them both up. The big one charged at me I got up hit him in his eye it turned colors I hit him in his nose and his stomach he fell to the floor crying like he was dieing. I went home.

It happen in the center I go to on 104th Street and Columbus Ave. He did but I make up the game when his little brother said that he throws harder than me. Know one else was there. no problems came up.

That action-packed incident took place in the span of a single afternoon. The student used a number of devices to describe the events. He signals the end of the first round of the "game" and the beginning of the second with "Then." He uses a separate past-tense verb to put each action in its proper order. He describes as simultaneous action the interventions of the younger brother in his tussle with the older brother ("when I jumped on the floor, his brother jumped on my back"). The writer indicates the next stage by another time adverbial ("Then a man"). The older brother's final charge is treated as a separate event, indicated by "When he picked." The description is vivid because of time adverbials used to distinguish each event. The order in which the writer describes the events is also the order in which he perceives their occurrence. The sequence of events is important in sorting causes and effects and in getting causes linked to their proper effects.

This writer, a student, uses different verbal forms but still provides clear sequencing:

It started about a year ago. My boyfriend had started to become involved with drugs. It wasn't the "hard stuff", it was the light stuff, pot. He said he got a good high and it made him happy to be high. He figured if something makes you happy, it's all right to do it. We fought many times about that. It ended up in partial break-ups, but, fortunately, they didn't last long.

He went to college the following year. I knew that he would be able to get anything he wanted, so I figured the best thing to do was hope for the best. He constantly wrote that he had "smoked" with his friends. He also started taking ups & downs, ups to keep him awake all night, and downs to put him to sleep. When he said he had "tripped", I got quite upset and I made him promise that he woudn't take anything more than ups or downs. Eventually the promise was broken, he had started on speed.

At about that time, my cousin was also constantly smoking pot. My mind started to wonder what it was like. I became curious. To turn on with my boyfriend could be great. Because I knew that you couldn't get a good high the first time, I decided to take pot once with my cousin. Then, when my boyfriend came home, we could get high together, and have a better feeling (like in sex) I tried it once—called my boyfriend. His reaction was just as upsetting as mine was to his. He was being so hypocritical, and I was getting pissed off—after all, I did it for him. (& myself also, I guess) We made a pact—he wouldn't take anything and neither would I. I was sort of mad, but I accepted it.

Well, I saw my boyfriend last week-end. He became very sentimental and emotional. Then, he broke down and told me the truth about why he had me stop smoking. He had lied to me—to everyone—he never touched the stuff in his life. He only told people so he could be accepted. I looked at him, but it was true even though I almost couldn't believe it.

The writer sequences events by using these phrases: "a year ago," "the following year," "at about that time," and "last week-end." She also separates events by using timed verbs. She deals with longer time spans than the younger writers of previous incidents. By making their pact to abstain from drugs, the writer and her boyfriend negotiated an agreement regulating their future behavior on the basis of past conflicts. The final confession of innocence shows how negotiation led both parties to a more realistic understanding of past events.

The last two writers described a series of separate events by using various ordering terms to set off each event from the others. The next incident, by a student, has no sequencing:

This is about my brother Fred. He is always picking on us always. One time I was downstairs with my friend the all of a sudden he came down and told me to go up but I didn't want to my mother didn't tell me to come up or anything, he was just showing off just because he's with his friend. But I always win because I tell my father ha ha ha.

The lack of both separating and ordering is indicated by the writer's repeated use of "always." Because he provides no clear sequence, it is difficult to make inferences about causal connections between events. The writer's reaction to the brother's action comes in the passive "I don't want to." It is not described as a separate and later action. A clear sequencing, such as the following, immediately suggests ways in which the conflict can be resolved: (1) my brother teases me; (2) then I tell my father; (3) then my father yells at my brother; and (4) then he gets even by teasing me. The writer could suggest set-

ting up a schedule of times when each boy had the exclusive
right to have his friends in to visit or setting up parts of the
house available to each.

Sometimes the student writer only partially sequences the
events described:

In school, in our Spanish class our teacher Miss A. tells us to
take off our coats every day. Once a girl in our class refused
to take off her coat and the teacher sent her out of the class and
locked the door. I don't think she was right to deprive this
girl of her Spanish lesson because she wouldn't take off her coat.
But then a school rule is taking off your coat in the classroom.

The writer mentions only two events: the student's refusing to
take off her coat and the teacher's expelling her from class.
The events are separated by "and" but ordered. This sequencing
is still clearer than that of the preceding incident. Extending
the sequence into the future clarifies available options that
could be chosen on the basis of events they could lead to. Negotiations between teacher and students could have suggested
such possible consequences as these: (1) the principal might
stop the class; (2) the whole class might discuss the coat with
the administrator; and (3) all students might lose time from
the Spanish lesson.

The next writer provides only partial sequencing. The lack
of event separation produces a global, single event:

There is a specific chemistry teacher who teaches poorly (not only
according to my standards but all the students agree) It's not
that this teacher lacks the knowledge of her subject, but she
has tremendous difficulty putting it across. We have told parents,
guidance counselors, etc, but they all say "Oh, you're crazy."
This is a problem of no equal voice. They (the establishment)
should at least lend an ear to our gripes.

He indicates the first event in a possible series with "We have
told parents." There the sequencing ends. The use of the present tense ("they all say") fails to separate past, present, and
future events. This use of the present may express the writer's
sense that the same action has gone on in the past and present

and will continue into the future. Sequencing that extended into the future could have prevented the stalemate of these negotiations. Future effects of keeping this teacher could have been pointed out, as in these examples: (1) students might fail final exams because they did not understand the material; (2) they might be unprepared for college chemistry courses; or (3) they might complain to the board of education about inadequate instruction with the board, in time, censuring the guidance counselors and school officials. Such an array of future events might have convinced adults to keep the negotiations open.

The student writer of the following incident also uses "and" and "but" to separate and order events but achieves a somewhat clearer sequencing:

This particular event happened in our English class. We had broken up into groups of four or five kids to read poetry. The teacher said that each group should decide on one poem that each kid in the group would read to the whole class. In my group we picked three poems that everyone liked but when we took a vote to decide the one we would read, four voted for one poem and the other girl for another. This one girl just didn't care that much for the poem we decided on and she wanted to read another one. I can understand her not liking the poem because I know there are some poems that I just don't like and after reading the poem a couple of times I decided that I didn't like it as much as some of the other poems myself. Well, we read this poem anyway and we told this one girl that she should read the poem like she didn't like it. (In other words, reading it like she felt like reading it.) She agreed and we read the poem. After all five girls had read the class discussed the different readings and it came up that one girl didn't like this poem. The teacher then asked the girl which poem she would have preferred to read. She told him one of the other two poems that were in the original list of three. Then the teacher did what I thought was the fair thing to do, that was he made all five girls read the poem that the one girl thought was best. I think this was the only fair thing to do. He could have said that it was too bad for that girl and that the majority picked the one poem and the majority rules but he didn't.

Note the use of these phrases to sequence the events: (1) "when we took a vote," (2) "after reading the poem," (3) "we told this one girl that she should," (4) "after all five girls," (5) "the teacher then asked," (6) "then the teacher did," (7) "he could have said . . . but he didn't." The writer failed in some of the sequencing: (1) She does not state whether the groups were formed before or after the selection of the poems; (2) she does not say whether each group was to read in chorus or in sequence; (3) she does not tell how often she read the poem before or after it was read in class.

Had the sequence of these events been made explicit, negotiators could better know and consider available options. If groups were formed after the poems were chosen, each student could select a poem and join the group reading that poem. If they read in chorus, all would have to read the same poem, but if they read in sequence, they might choose different poems. If the writer read the poem before it was read in class, she might have been able to evaluate it more carefully than if she had to choose it on the spot. Once the options were clear, bargaining could have been facilitated.

In summary, sequencing was defined as having three components: the separation of events from each other, ordering events, and determining causal relationships between events. The incidents showed that separation can be indicated by timed verbs and adverbials. The use of adverbials (e.g., "always") that convey global time shows that the writer is not separating events. The incidents showed that ordering can be indicated by enumerating events, by adverbial phrases, or by use of conjunctions and disjunctions. The incidents showed that causal relationships could be indicated by words such as "so," "anyway," "could have," "would have," that indicate cause and effect.

Duration: How Long, O Lord?

The previous set of incidents shows how writers separated and ordered events in time. Events also occur with a background of ongoing action. Background action can extend over past, present, and future. There are two ways for writ-

ers to use duration: (1) by distinguishing background and foreground events and (2) by causally relating the two sets of
events. Duration in both past and future is illustrated in this
incident:

Recently a story was related to me which really affected me.
A close friend of mine attends the school in my neighborhood.
He is *not* a good student, but has the intelligence to be one.
He has a high aptitude in the area of mechanics, physics, etc.,
but has no will. He took a course in mechanical drawing—
a subject he really would have enjoyed and was of interest to him.
In mechanical drawing one has to copy mechanical things—
(e.g. screw, radios)—to scale and label them.

It was the assignment, one day, for them to copy something (it's
irrelevant what it was) and this guy really tried his hardest,
put all his effort into doing it. When he thought it was perfect,
he handed it in. (Expecting a good mark—which for him
doesn't happen too often.) He was obviously proud of what he
had done—but this was immediately destroyed when he recieved
a "red paper" from the teacher. By red I mean the teacher
made so many x's it looked red. For minor things, such as a
line being a wee bit heavier at one point—or something equally
trivial. Now on seeing this, the boy's will was destroyed.
After this he didn't even bother to try. What right did this teacher
have to destroy him?

I can easily see that it was the teacher's duty to correct the paper
& teach the student correct techniques, but why so ruthlessly?
This teacher honestly destroyed his will to work—for no valid
reason. (As I see it.) Why couldn't this DUMB teacher
explain to the boy his minor errors? so he could correct them—
or even—why couldn't she use a pencil to mark the papers?

In the first paragraph the writer describes the background
action of the incident. By using "one day" at the beginning
of the second paragraph, she distinguishes background from
foreground action. The last paragraph shows that the writer
saw that past events could have future effects. On the basis
of present events, the writer predicts an ongoing background
action. Had the effect on the student's motivation become clear

to the teacher in the course of negotiation, both the student's future motivation and the teacher's future effectiveness might have been enhanced.

Sometimes the writer (a student) describes the foreground action (involving the explosives and the cop) and the background action as both in the past:

On a summer day two years ago me and my friends had some firecrackers and ashcans [a type of firecracker]. I had five ashcans, a Roman candlestick and an M-eighty. An M-eighty is something like dynamite. I did not blow any because I was scared to light matches or even touch them and I was afraid of the large sound that they made, and once when I bit one I was filled with fright to let it go. One of my (supposed to be) friends bit my hand because they were shouting "Drop it. Drop it." (We were in the park.) Anyway, back to that day. We went blasting, having a nice time when a cop on a horse came so my friends pretended that they didn't know me and said that I was blowing them. And one of them slipped an ashcan into my jacket's pocket. So the horse cop said thank you to them and told me to get on the back of his horse. I cried and said, "No, no. They were lyeing. They were lyeing." I got so mad that when the cop put me on the back of his horse, I yelled back to them. "Fagits, I'll get even with you." But the cop slapped me and said "Where you're going, you won't be able to get even with him for a couple of years." Than I got scared as he ride on to the police station I jumped off and ran into the traffic, ran into the projects, called my mother and told her that I was at my friend's house, but I was really at the corner telephone booth. I never hung around these kids again and the cop didn't take me down so I got even with all. 2 hours later, (I think) I went home and went to my room and went to sleep.

By the use of "a summer day two years ago," the writer flashes back to the past. By "once when I bit one" he goes back to an even earlier event. He signals his return to the foreground action with "Anyway, back to that day." His fear of future punishment was so great that he called his mother to put potential pursuers off the trail. He sank into exhaustion as soon as he felt sure he was no longer being pursued. The future, at the time of the event, which is also now the past, is represented by "I never hung around these kids again."

The intense conflict left this boy unable to remember how long an interval had passed before he went back home. The incident vividly illustrates the assertion that conflict can cause a regression in thinking about time (cf. Arlow and Brenner, 1964). Even if the individual shows a sophisticated time conception in one situation he may not show it in another. Had the policeman listened to both sides, the youngsters might have realized that none of them wanted the responsibility for setting off firecrackers. Instead of threats of revenge and loss of friendship, negotiation could have led to more rational behavior. The policeman might have led the boys to see future consequences of setting off firecrackers and the boys could have made explicit to the policeman the past causes of their current behavior.

The student describes the next incident without using duration:

The place was on a school classroom. A girl had a book about people's horoscopes. I asked her to let me see it. So I started glancing through the book. Then I gave it back to her and I said I did not believe it. So she said she didn't care. So I said I didn't care either and I said to her "Let me see that book again," and she said "No I am not going to let you see my book, since you do not believe in it you shouldn't be interested in it. The whole classroom was there, but almost no one was listening or paying attention to the argument. Our teacher was absent and there was a substitute. The room looked absurd with the chairs scrambled all over the room. Hardly anybody noticed the argument until we started yelling at each other, and I thought to myself "All this argument just because of a disagreement of one person. Somehow I felt that I had started it." Then I exploded with anger and I said "All right you little midget. Shut up. I'm sick and tire of your bad breath." and I crumbled up the book and through it in her face. I also added "Why don't you get someone bigger like your godamn boy friend." at that same moment her boy friend came in and said "You better get off her if you don't want me to bust your lip. I got up and said "do it". "You fuckin ass, you can't even reach my face. At that time another problem came up.

This incident is unrelated to any enduring action that could be understood as causes for the events described. There is no reference to anything that happened on a previous or later day. The lack of reference to the future seems to leave the writer unsatisfied. He ends his account with the curious statement: "At that time another problem came up." The writer clearly sets the incident in one time frame. Rather than describing future consequences, he ends with an implicit denial that the event had any consequences. If the writer really wanted the girl's attention, he might have considered the long-term effects of his teasing and not have allowed conflict to escalate and to alienate them.

The last two student writers described incidents with a past and future. The next student writer mentions neither. He describes no connection between background and foreground events:

Well it happen in the park when we were playing a team.
A boy from the team refused to leave the field and a man from our team the manager went over to the field talk to him about leaving the field. He told the boy that he would like him to leave the field because he might get hit by the ball and he is responsible for anything that happens with intruders. So the boy said to leave him alone and at that moment the manager got mad and push the boy off the field. The boy went over and took a bat and swung with it all around the place so a friend of the manager jump in took away the bat and gave it to the manager but the manager refuse to take the bat. The manager came up to the boy and said he better not do that again because he said that if he does it again he is going to smack the boy down.

No background events are described. There are, however, references to possible future consequences: "he might get hit by the ball" and "if he does it again he is going to smack the boy down." Since he reports only what the manager states, we cannot be sure that the writer himself perceived future consequences.

To understand these events, one would need to know if the rules were habitually flouted (duration) or if this was an isolated incident (a foreground event). It would be helpful to know whether the boy was usually stubborn or reacting to some special event. The manager might have constantly harped on the rules or he was realistically reacting to a dangerous situation. A clear statement that distinguished background conditions and foreground events could have made the issues much clearer.

By contrast, the background and foreground are clearly distinguished by the writer of the following incident:

One of my teachers is discriminating against me in class. There are these two guys, they are always making noise or doing something to describe the teacher and the teacher does nothing to them. The teacher is a person whom one can get along with pretty well, but he is a little *whacky*. As I was saying before those two other persons are always making trouble before or they are imitating the teacher and get away with it.

Now for the good part. Whenever I make some kind of wisecrack he yells at me or has me staying out of class. Sometimes I say something funny and my peers begin to laugh so the teacher gets annoyed with me and again he yells.

One time we were in class and I was feeling groovy. I had been making wisecracks all period long and there was one boy who was sitting in the back of the room. He kept on laughing. The teacher finally threw him out of class. He did not get in trouble, but I did because he told the teacher that I was making him laugh.

I think that the teacher is being unfair to me.

>   Can you help?
>   Thank you!   ·
>   "WORRIED"

The problem has not yet been handled but I don't think it ever will! To make a long story short: The teacher picks on ME!

The first two paragraphs show the writer's awareness of the background events. The remaining lines are a description of the foreground events. The writer fails, however, to describe any causal connection between wisecracking and expulsion from class. His failure to connect these events may also be his failure to see how his humor is connected to his feelings of anger toward the teacher. The process of negotiation could confront the writer with casual connections so that he could structure the anger he felt toward the teacher. He would build on his understanding of the conflict in the process of resolving it.

In summary, duration was defined as the background action that gives foreground events special significance. The following components of duration were illustrated by the incidents: past and future, ongoing past action contrasted with a past foreground event, and the time between the past action and the present description of the events, which was in the future at the time of the event.

Measuring: Clocks and Calendars

The first set of incidents in this chapter illustrated sequencing of events. The second set showed how enduring action extended over present, past, and future. The third set shows how the writers measured time. In the following incident the writer uses both clock and calendar time:

The other day I told my mother if I could go to Coney Island
with my friend and my friends mother and father and so
she said yes and we left out of my house at *1:00* and we went
to Coney Island and got on rides ate over there so than
we came home at 11 o'clock at night and my mother got mad and
said I couldn't go to Coney Island no more because I come
too late and you have to go to bed early for school and she said
that maybe in the summer I could go to the beach and come late
but not during May and June because I come late and I
have to be read for school. And so I told her that I won't come
late any more and she said that its too late because she gave me
a chance and since I came late she thinks I may come late again.

Clock time is emphasized by underlining [printed herein in italics] and by specifying clock time. By connecting clock time with calendar time the writer was able to see how the conflict could be resolved. At different times of the year (calendar time), the clock times have different meanings. Here, time is both the content of the issue and an important aspect of its form. All parties need to understand the dual uses of time to negotiate the issues.

In the previous incident the writer describes both clock and calendar time. In the next incident, the student writer provides neither:

[P]eople in the school complain about there being policemen in the school and that J—— don't need policemen. I think we need policeman in the school because one day after school these boys waiting for the bus to go home and then the bus came and they went in and took and ladies pocketbook and ran out of the bus and the policeman caught them and if it wasn't for the school police they would never have caught them.

There is no reference to calendar time. The issue of having policemen in the school during school hours is confused with the other issues: (1) the school neighborhood having a policeman after school and (2) the school neighborhood having a policeman during school hours. To separate these issues, it would be necessary to know whether the purse-snatching took place in the presence of a school guard *as* students were leaving the school (e.g., at 3:15) or several hours later (e.g., at 5:15) in the presence of a city policeman. Just as the use of precise times sharpened the description of the Coney Island incident, the failure to use precise time blurred the issues here.

In the first incident, the measuring of time was done according to clock and calendar. In the second, neither clock nor calendar time was mentioned. The next incident, by a student, illustrates the use of calendar but not clock time:

Well I want to discuss the problem of getting a job. The Board of Health issues working papers at the age of 14 and 15 the lowest. And Everytime I go and look for a job you have to be 16. And then your stuck because when you do become 16 you have to have your 14 and 15 working papers to get the 16 year old ones. And by that time of two years waiting from 14 to 16 you might have lost. And if you did you might have to wait at least a month for the new ones. So I think we should be allowed to work

between 14 and 15 years of age. This all occured
during my age of 14.

Here the writer is complaining about a gap between two calendar times: his actual age and the required age. He wants
them to be the same. If he had dated the incident, he would be
clearer about how to resolve the problem. If he is fourteen
the problem has a different solution than if he is sixteen. He
focuses sharply on the distinction between the official age requirements of the city agency and the employers. He may have
learned all of this when he was fourteen, but not all of it could
have happened to him when he was fourteen. The month's wait
at sixteen had to happen after he was fourteen. Thus, understanding calendar time is crucial to understanding and resolving the conflict.

The next incident also focuses on time regulations. Here the
student writer gives clock times, but not calendar time:

In the Summer I went to camp and when I was ther there was a
cabin there the food was kept and at 8 the cook went in the cabin
and made breakfast and dinner and lunch and when you
go to that camp you would have to pay $350 for two weeks and
$850 for a month. And I went to camp for two weeks and a boy
I know went for a month. Me and the boy got to be good
friends and James and I became Junior Life Guard. And from
10 a.m. to 1 p.m. But the cook did not know James and I was
life guard and at 1 p.m. me and James went to eat and the cook
told us no more food so we did not eat. 11 p.m. in the night
James and me got real hungry and James said lets sneak into
the cabin so me and James went down the hill to the cabin and
broke in but the cook was in the cabin and we got caught and
went to the head man and James said it was my idea and he said
I broke in the cabin. And we went to bed the next morning.
James said I had to pay $850 a month and my mother would
kill me so I told the man I had broke in the cabin and got sent home.

The writer makes the clock times very clear. He accurately
describes the cook's schedule. Although he describes clock
time, he did not use it in negotiating a lunch time with the
cook and consequently lost his camping opportunity.

The student writer of the next incident used the most precise calendar time—month, day, and year:

One day on May 6, 1969 this girl told the school that I had made
her get a heart attack. And so on May 7, 1969, I was walking
by her class to get to mine. She came and pushed me and
I hit her back. And we start fighting and a teacher stepped
between us and he got hit in the stomach and he said that I did it.

And every time we go to math somebody throws paper and chairs
all around the room and we have to clean it up. This school is
so cheap and rotten these teachers have to go that's why
next year I am going to another school that's better than this one
and they don't want to teach us.

By dating them, the writer makes it evident that he understands the events of the second day as the consequence of the first date.

Measuring by clock and calendar time is prominent in the next incident. In the previous incident one day's events are described as the cause of the next day's events but there is no specific causal connection. Negotiation of this conflict would force all parties to consider whether the school was making good use of student and teacher time.

The following incident focuses and relates the issues in the negotiation to clock time and the days of the week. The student does not give the previous calendar time of the event as in the preceding incident. Instead, he uses the degree of precision appropriate for the issues.

This incident takes place on a Friday night about 9:00 and we
were trying to figure out where to go the following Saturday.
We had decided to go to the beach but the decision was now
to decide which one. In my group there are approximately 31
people and the majority of them boys. In my group there were
15 who wanted to go to Rockaway where we thought it would be
fun to be with all the other kids who flock to the rich sands of
108 [Street] and later to proceed to Playland. We were determined
to go. What we didn't realize is that the other crowd who had
one more then us wanted to go to Breezy Point to surf also because
four people had houses there and it would be easy to go

swimming then change because otherwise we would go home in our soaken bathing suits. Both ideas sounded good but I figured it out that if four people had houses why should they be so eager to see them as they will be seeing them all summer. The other group had something to say also he replied. All this year all you do is talk about the beach and how much fun it would be to surf and if you go to Rockaway all you would do is get drunk. "And what is wrong with drinking?" replied all 30 kids. "Nothing, nothing!" he shouted in a range. There was complete silence and it was now 9:45. Time for everyone to leave so as to be home on time and yet it was still unsettled. "Whose ever going with me meet at 8 tomorrow at #11 [Bus] I said. Everyone just nodded and soon after that I heard "Meet me at 7:45 at #11 and we'll leave at 8" By then I knew I had loss a strong hand always seems to win!! All 31 including me went at 7:45 and to my surprise there were no waves!!! Surf wasn't up.

The writer, in his mention of several precise and specific clock times, seems to be very aware of time as a pressing limit. He uses two questionable time references in his first sentence. This past incident is introduced by the present tense ("This incident takes place"). The next day is described as the "following Saturday." In the next to last sentence a similar awkwardness in time placement occurs ("I knew I had loss"), where the verb is in the present tense. The writer's understanding of the incident is similarly very precise within the limits of the meeting and closely tied to its concrete events. He doesn't describe any ongoing or prior action that would point to the causes of the conflict. The argument that "they" presented for having a place to change out of the wet bathing suits shows foresight. So does the argument "We" presented for having many other kids with whom to have fun at Rockaway. The debate made clear to the writer the alternatives and their probable future outcomes. Yet, the negotiation was constrained by time and perhaps also the possibility of his reaching a fuller understanding of the issues. Just as he begins to articulate "Their" point of view, he says "There was complete silence and it was now 9:45." Rather than pursue the alternatives, the group was forced to make a decision, with the writer's collaboration. He felt the decision favored those with the greater force. He concludes with a wry comment that sounds a little bit like "I told you so." "They" won and the group did go surfing, only to find no surf.

In summary, the incidents showed the following uses of clock and calendar time. Clock time was the content of the issue and an aspect of negotiation in the amount of time available for bargaining. Calendar time was also the content of the issue and an aspect of negotiation because it could be used to clarify issues.

Summary

Using the time concepts of sequencing, duration, and measurement, we have tried to show how a student's description of a conflict reflects his perspective of time. A student's time perspective, if it includes the full use of each time concept, anchors issues in a specific time context and creates options for conflict resolution that may otherwise be overlooked.

Consider, first, how sequencing is related to conflict resolution. The effects of obscure sequencing were illustrated in the description of the poetry reading incident. The writer conveyed little sense of causal connections. She did not indicate whether the groups or the poems were selected first. If the groups were selected first, students could have negotiated among themselves the original set of three poems. If the poems were selected first, they could have negotiated the groupings.

The resolution of this conflict depended on available options: can the students read the poem in chorus or can they take turns, one student following another? If they must read in chorus it was worth the time to reach consensus in selecting a single poem. If they can take turns, then they did not have to agree on a single poem. Later in her description, the writer's clear sequencing leads to resolution. The description is clearest at the point the writer explicitly orders events: "After all five girls read." From that point the actions of both teacher and students seem reasonable and are causally related.

In the incident involving a conflict between the writer and his brother, obscure sequencing fails to produce resolution options. A clear sequencing, such as the following, immediately suggests options: (1) my brother teases me; (2) then I tell my father; (3) then my father yells at my brother; and (4) then he gets even by teasing me. Sequencing can reveal how to change the order of events by our own actions.

Conflict resolution is also related to duration. By describing background action the writer's options for resolving conflict in foreground events become clearer. The description can either proliferate or eliminate acceptable options. Recall the incident in which the teacher used red ink to mark up the student's drawings. The corrections had a destructive meaning for the student because he had done very little class work. A little work appears less meager against a background of no work than against one of energetic work. A teacher whose sense of duration extended into the future could entertain the option of encouraging gradual improvement over making exacting evaluation. The writer may have had a greater sense of duration than the teacher since he refers to both past and future.

In the description of the wisecracking student, the clear distinction between background and foreground events suggests options for conflict resolution that the writer never described. If he saw that his continual disruption of the classroom was the reason for his expulsion, then he would understand why he and not the other student was thrown out. The options for resolving the conflict for the two students are different because of their different perception of background action.

Conflict resolution is also related to the measurement of time. In the surfing incident, for example, the writer recognizes that so much time had been used in stating the issues that there was no time left for bargaining. This, in turn, led to an arbitrary decision. Because they did not weigh the consequences of prolonged debate, they never considered the possibility that the surf would be down.

Accounts with little or no sequencing, duration, and measuring often express global anger while accounts with clear time operations express specific anger directed toward specified objects. When the directed anger combines with clear time description, the issues and the options for resolving conflicts are also clearer. The next chapter, showing how to resolve conflicts by negotiation, indicates how clarity about its options helps each party to make concessions.

9 People Talking NEGOTIATION IN THE SCHOOL

THIS CHAPTER DISCUSSES how to resolve school conflicts. It tells how to strike bargains by using the various ways of examining conflict discussed in the previous chapters. It will present a model of negotiation that is a synthesis of our theory and data. The model was formulated for the practical purpose of handling school conflict.

This model of conflict resolution uses negotiation. The negotiation process is divided into three stages: (1) the statement of issues by each side made with direct, verbal expression of anger; (2) agreement by all sides on a common statement of issues—they agree to disagree; and (3) bargaining in which each side makes concessions.

This chapter asserts that the constructive way to deal with conflict is to negotiate rather than suppress or avoid it. The previous chapters have explained how to analyze conflict. This chapter shows how the various analyses are used in negotiation.

Each chapter is related to the negotiation model. Chapter 2, dealing with survival teaching and learning, relates to the first step in the model. In the absence of choice, negotiable issues are not crystallized. Chapters 3 and 4, concerning civic choice and status, relate to the second step in the model. They provide the larger political framework within which agreement can be reached on common statements of issues. Chapters 5 and 6, having to do with the expression of anger in word or action, pertain to the first step in the model. When anger is expressed in words conflict becomes negotiable. When it is expressed in action conflict can only be escalated or suppressed. In both cases there is a discharge of energy—in one case potentially constructive and in the other potentially destructive.

Chapter 7, on interpersonal conflict, pertains to steps one and two of the model. In step one, the interpersonal analysis helps determine the number of different sides and who comprises each side. In step two it helps separate negotiable from non-negotiable issues. Chapter 8, on the temporal dimensions of conflict, pertains to step three of the model. Knowledge of time dimensions facilitates bargaining by distinguishing cause and effect, assigning values to options on the basis of their long-term or short-term effects, and assigning realistic time limits to the negotiation process. The present chapter relates particularly to step three—striking a bargain.

Theory and Findings

Coser (1956) has distinguished between constructive and destructive conflict. Constructive conflict integrates individuals into groups and integrates groups into the community. Morton Deutsch (1969, p. 19) describes productive conflict:

It prevents stagnation, it stimulates interest and curiosity, it is the medium through which problems can be aired and solutions arrived at; it is the root of personal and social change. Conflict is often the process of testing and assessing oneself and, as such, may be highly enjoyable as one experiences the pleasure of full and active use of one's capacities.

There are several modes of conflict resolution. Mack and Snyder (1957) mention the following: arbitration, mediation, negotiation, inquiry, legislation, judicial settlement, informal consensus through discussion, the market, violence or force, authoritative command, and varieties of voting procedures.

They define modes as sets of rules for handling resolution or accommodation. Different rules produce different results in different situations. Rules themselves become conflict issues.

Blake and Mouton (1970) advocate direct negotiation. Direct resolution of differences is a way for parties to conflicts to deal and possibly eliminate real or imagined social injustices. Negotiation, they believe, will enable men to resolve their own differences by committed agreement to identify and implement their own solutions. They distinguish between "compromise" and real "problem-solving": in compromise disagreement is avoided. One agrees to be agreeable even if it means sacrificing sound action. One settles for what one can get rather than getting what is sound in the light of the best available data. In the problem-solving approach, disagreement is valued because it reflects the parties' conviction about what is right. Emotions that prevent agreement based on logic and data are directly dealt with by the individuals involved in the disagreement. Although time-consuming, it permits parties to disagree, work through disagreements in the light of facts, and finally to understand each other. In the long run, this method is time-conserving.

Deutsch (1969, p. 21) also distinguishes between capitulation and authentic cooperation and their motivational consequences:

Neither undue smugness nor satisfaction with things as they are nor a sense of helplessness, terror, or rage are likely to lead to an optimal motivation to recognize and face a problem or conflict. Nor will a passive readiness to acquiesce to the demands of the environment; nor will the willingness to fit oneself into the environment no matter how poorly it fits oneself. Optimal motivation, rather, presupposes an alert readiness to be dissatisfied with things as they are and freedom to confront one's environment without excessive fear, combines with a confidence in one's capacities to persist in the face of obstacles.

Soreno and Mortenson (1969) found that pairs of experimental subjects who were slightly involved reached agreement more often than pairs consisting of highly involved subjects.

Accumulated anger and rage may impede negotiation while moderate and channeled anger energizes it.

There have been some studies of high school conflict. Chesler and BenDor (1972) found, among other results, that school negotiation had three characteristics: (1) it surfaced real issues for real negotiations; (2) it required open responses and hard work; and (3) it required that everyone be prepared to change. Frank (1973), in his review of research on classroom conflict, described the following classroom situations as occasions for teacher-student negotiations: (1) sharing choices of objectives, curricula, learning activities, evaluation, and norms of classroom behavior; (2) developing a humanistic over a custodial orientation toward pupil control; and (3) developing an interactive student-teacher feedback system that is non-competitive. He (p. 309) concludes:

Educators can make it [education in social conflict] happen by
starting now to teach about social conflict in their classes and
by learning effective strategies for conflict management both for
their own use in the classroom and for use in developing a sequence
of "conflict resolution through communication" as an
integral part of the curriculum.

In our study the students perceived little choice of behavior (see Appendix B, Table 8). They perceived that negotiation was tried in only about 17 percent, while they saw decisions imposed by authority in 55 percent of their conflicts. Only 18 percent perceived one or more choices for resolving their conflicts. Eighty-one percent saw no alternative to the resolution adopted. Eighteen percent of the incidents reported by suburban high school students were attempts to resolve conflict by negotiation, while 14 percent of the incidents reported by the urban high school students included negotiation. Negotiation occurred more often in junior than senior high school. In junior high school it was not surprising to find that conflicts were more often with peers.

Emotional Statements: Laying It on the Line

Incidents in Chapters 5 and 6 illustrated how anger can be expressed in words or acts. Emotional statements of issues are the means of structuring the anger by directing it toward issues that can be negotiated. Each of the parties in the following conflict, described by a student, made emotional statements for its side:

Last year money had been collected from the Senior Class to pay for a prom. The place has been selected and the major problem then was what type of band should we have. Suggestions came from all sides. The prom committee consisted of black, Puerto Rican, and white students. The Black students demanded that we have a Rock and Roll Band also. (Each having his own band in mind). Some of the teachers who planned to attend wanted a Band that could play fox trots and waltzes. The committee immediately eliminated the teachers suggestion on the grounds that the students were paying for the prom and it was a prom for them not the teachers. After a heated discussion on the relative merits of each type of Band, the committee came to a decision. It was decided that although there were many White and Puerto Rican Students attending the Prom the vast majority would be Black Students so a Rock & Roll Band would please the majority, but because the interest of the other students could not be ignored, one prerequisite the band must have was it should also be able to play Latin music as well as a few slower type Rock & Roll numbers as everyone would be happy. This was done and everyone (except the teachers) enjoyed the music. How else could it have been handled—since the Black Students were in a majority and hired a band to please themselves alone.

The writer describes face-to-face confrontation in which all sides made emotional statements. The various sides were the black, Puerto Rican and white students and the teachers. He writes that "suggestions came from all sides" and "After a heated discussion on the relative merits." Since most of the parties to the conflict were of the same status, anger was easily expressed, issues were stated, and concessions were made.

As in the following incident, described by an assistant principal, the parties sometimes failed to voice their anger:

Mrs. "Smith," the parent, questioned *very strongly* the authority of
the school and specifically how could her son be placed in such
a low ability level group. She demanded with vigor that
"Bruce" be placed in one of the "higher groups" in all areas.
How we handled the problem—First, during almost a two-hour
conversation (debate?) with Mrs. Smith, we tried to explain
the basic philosophy behind the type of grouping we had. As the
boy was "new to us" from one of our own elementary schools
we could only generalize on why he was given his original placement.
We told her we would make a full investigation of the boy's
background within a week and have her in for a conference so
we with the parent could make a decision together. The mother
said she would not accept this and said she would go to the
superintendent if the child was not changed at once! We refused
(really in a nice way) and told her if she wished to consult
with the superintendent it was fine with us. In the meantime
we said we would still study the case and would be happy
to meet with her as we suggested.

When the assistant principal said he "would be happy to meet
with her," he was not expressing the anger one might expect
in confrontation. His failure to make an angry statement may
explain why the parent left the office to appeal to a higher
authority. This incident shows how the suppression of anger
may obstruct negotiation.

The following incident, written by a department head,
shows how a student petition can serve as an angry statement
of the student side of an issue. The petition was also the
occasion for an angry statement made by the principal:

In the fall the new principal announced to the faculty that he was
introducing mid-year examinations. This raised immediate furor
from most faculty members as being a step backward in the
educational progress. At the same time, the principal began to
issue a series of preparatory warnings about the planned of SDS
agitators to move into the high schools of Nassau County. . . .
With this climate in mind the following took place: One morning
all the students arrived in school to find placed in their lockers

and on the bulletin boards unsigned notices urging students to protest the institution of mid-year exams. Flyers called for the signing of petitions and for students to seek a voice in school affairs.

The principal given the preconditioned apprehension toward SDS (the "agitators") immediately assumed this to be a signal for their arrival. After a full day's investigation the students responsible for the acts were located and they were summarily called to the principal's office. For a full day he closeted himself with the students and then called all their parents in. All students involved were threatened with expulsion or suspension for engaging in acts contrary to state law. Students involved were accused of being part of an SDS conspiracy designed to undermine the operation of the school.

The incident incited much student reaction many of whom rallied to the cause behind their fellows. Signs calling for "free speech" appeared in many quarters of the school. Articles both for and against were exchanged in the school newspaper and bulletins were sent from the principal to the teachers and also from the students to the teachers. After a tense week the tensions seemed to subside. No demonstrations or protests resulted. The extent of the damage, however, can never be really assessed.

There is evidence of anger in the description: "furor from most faculty," "a series of preparatory warnings," and "notices urging students to protest." Since the faculty failed to make public or direct emotional statements with students and principal listening, they were never approached by the principal. The department head who wrote this incident describes the principal as the "bad guy." The principal, according to this writer, saw the student petitioners as the bad guys. The students' use of a petition suggests that they viewed the principal as the representative of the school as an institution. Since the parties to the conflict could not agree on who the adversaries were, it was difficult to structure the anger around particular issues.

Parents, as we see in the following conflict, described by a teacher, may sometimes have needed to make angry statements that are heard by all parties to the conflict:

One day last Spring many students arrived at school highly agitated. Rumor swiftly spread through the school. Apparently, the police had beaten up three of our students the night before. Obviously class could not be conducted and the entire school went to the gym to discuss the issue later that morning. Some young people had burned some stores the night before, many had watched, the police arrived to restore order and had beaten up the three students because they had not moved away when told to do so. The students were Black and the police white. Anti-white feeling was strong. Some teachers pleaded for unity of action and most students rallied behind them. Parents arrived and told pitiful stories of the beatings and riled the students. The police chief arrived to answer questions and promised an investigation, and asked the students to take no action. The students wanted to question the officers involved, but the chief refused.

The administration requested that the students take no action. A parent spoke again and said she was going to leave and march to the station with anyone who would go. The students were ready to go. The administration did not sanction the march and tried to stop it.

The teachers got the students to agree to march after school and said they wanted to march too. The administration was relieved and agreeable to the after-school march although they never officially endorsed it. After school about 90% of the faculty and 75% of the students marched two miles to the police station and a committee presented grievances to the police.

Angry statements were made and heard by almost all the parties to the conflict: parents, students, teachers, and school officials. The police chief tried to express anger for the police officers accused of the attack but this was insufficient because the expression was not direct. The march on the police station was the confrontation with the accused police officers that the parents sought in order to exchange direct emotional statements of issues.

In the following incident a teacher tells how a principal avoided an angry confrontation with the community:

As a teacher interested in the drug abuse program in ——, I tried to have a meeting after school with students from my junior high meeting with ex-drug users (anti-drugs now). The principal was skeptical and said I could not use the auditorium, but he

finally agreed to let us use my room as long as it was after school
and well supervised. Over 200 students showed up, teachers
and parents. One woman from the newspaper who thought more
things like this should be going on wrote a great article.

We almost lost the opportunity because the principal was afraid
the community might not understand what was going on and
that drugs are really not a school-related thing; like we should mind
our own business. The principal finally gave in because he
trusted me and the students I was working with. I would like
to see these rap sessions carried on and expanded—not keeping
school matters only to math, science, and English, etc.

There is no clear evidence that principal or teacher made angry
statements of their own sides of the issues.

In summary, the incidents in this section showed the differences in effect when anger was and was not expressed.
Negotiation could proceed when anger was expressed. It was
impeded when one or more parties failed to express anger.
It was also necessary to link the anger to the issues. When not
linked to issues the anger was misdirected and impeded negotiation. These findings are consistent with Deutsch's (1969)
theory about "optimal" levels of anger necessary for negotiated
resolutions and the Chesler and BenDor (1972) finding that
conflict and negotiation surfaced real issues.

Common Statements: Getting It Together or Agreeing to Disagree

The previous section showed how parties to school
conflicts needed to make frank statements about their grievances
and positions. Each party should do this as the first step in
negotiation. Once the issues are laid on the table the next
step is to agree to common statements of issues. The writer, a
teacher, of the following incident shows how this step is taken:

The parents of one student angrily requested a conference of myself,
department chairman, and principal in relation to the course
information on the previous day. The father was all excited on my
teaching communism, the weakness of democracy and even

"teaching" communism to the students. Despite explaining the situation and events, aims and objectives fully to him, he still adamantly insisted on action against me or "like that" to rectify this evident un-American teaching of history.

All three of us tried, unsuccessfully, to convince him that our objectives in the course [were] the exact opposite of what he thought. Our goal was independent thinking; thought evaluation and comparative analysis technique, as well as understanding propaganda, from any side. The "argument" then shifted to curriculum control and content, with the parents favoring parental consent of a course, etc. The three of us sought to bring out the fallacies here; non-familiarity with education, teaching, etc. that would involve parental "control." We discussed education in relation to progress, changes necessary and to better understand or fight something (communism or ignorance) we had to deal with it, "teach" it and know it first.

Finally, with the great aid of the principal and department chairman, the parents gave in a little and stated that they would wait to evaluate it (the course and me) at the end of the 8 wk course period, in relation to the boy's reaction (in whom I trusted fully, and who inadvertently began it—he disagreed with his dad, also).

It could have been sticky—my job on the line, the right of teachers in class, free speech in relation to understanding "new things,"— threatening or otherwise. Decision-making and curriculum content aspects of education could have been endangered without the opposite outcome.

There are at least two parties to this conflict. The student and his parents are one party and the teacher the other party. The department chairman and principal could have acted as mediators by avoiding taking sides. It appears, however, that they allied themselves with the teacher and thereby joined the first party to the conflict (the teacher). Only the parents, chiefly the father, seems to have verbally expressed anger. The school adults avoided anger by shifting the argument to broad curricular issues the parents were not knowledgeable enough to discuss. Initially there were many issues raised in the emotional statements of both parties, parent and school adults. For the father the issue was whether or not the teacher should keep his job. The teacher, department chairman, and principal believed the issue was professional control of the curriculum and free speech for discussing new topics. Both parties finally agreed to one issue: the evaluation of the particular course in terms of the student's reaction. This agreement on the issue facilitated negotiation.

The interest in the following incident lies in the conflict within the teacher's union. This analysis views the conflict as internal to the union and as having three parties: union officers, the majority membership, and the dissenters. This teacher describes a failure of parties to reach agreement on common statements of issues:

The incident is one involving the body of an association and the officers or ruling group (duly elected). The incident concerns negotiations of contracts between the school board and the teachers' representatives, this ruling group from the association. At several consecutive meetings, the majority of the association rules to accept only certain limitations of salary, benefits, etc., in relation to the contract. The actual negotiators agreed to abide by the majority's wishes and returned to the bargaining table. Returning at the next meeting, these negotiators, composed of association officers and volunteers, declared an agreeable contract had been reached in accordance with the members' wishes. However, upon passing out copies of, and orally explaining the new contract proposal, it was found to contain many things that the membership had previously voted down or declared below the minimum requirements. Several dissenting voices were raised and pointed out these inconsistencies to previous majority wishes which were contained in association meeting minutes and policy decisions. The negotiating and ruling units decried these points of order and proceeded to extoll certain virtues of the new contract while "sugar-coating" the points that were originally deemed unacceptable by the majority. These "ruling and elected officials" then proceeded to "ramrod" the new contract, which they considered acceptable, through, for a close vote of acceptance. Two further things need to be pointed out— membership at the last meeting was slight compared to previous ones; the negotiators had been bargaining for four months and membership attitude was of a militant (strike, etc.) nature, in relation to a contract failure. The final contract was not a bad one, but neither was it considered a good one by the majority who previously had made their wishes known.

The conflict is between the wishes and ruling of the majority, versus the officials elected by it. The officials felt that further negotiations, refusal, etc., would lead to a worsening situation and relations between teachers, community and school board. The majority members felt that their wishes were ignored and rights neglected by acceptance of a poor contract. The democratic wishes of the majority had been sacrificed by a ruling minority to insure the overall "welfare" of the majority in the issues above. Rather than sacrifice "professionalism and teacher models of society," and turn to some action which would result in their loss, they went beyond the democratic wishes of the majority to achieve and maintain certain principles and ideas they believed more important to all, than gain short-sighted gains.

Therefore, in negotiations between the District School Board and the Teachers Association, the negotiators had seen the value of sacrificing the direct wishes of the majority (more materialistic short-sighted views—without thoughts or consequences) in relation to insuring what they saw more importantly—maintenance of the teacher as a teacher, as a professional and as a model for the community. If they had followed the original wishes, very militant attitudes would have resulted and surfaced causing several results—strike, loss of community respect, prestige, loss of professional aura, and the rising of "radical" (possibly minority) groups which would sway the association and majority (as radical minorities have done before) to do actions that would result in losing far more than it ever hoped to gain. In the final analysis, the only truly long-range, beneficial decision for all had been made—in direct contrast to one possible decision that could have "destroyed" the majority, or at least many of its unconscious beliefs and ideals.

It appears that two sides verbally expressed anger—the dissenting minority voices and the "decrying" majority. It is less clear that the union officials *verbally* expressed anger. There is even a fourth party, the school board. With so many parties involved, the negotiations became difficult and prolonged and common issues difficult to agree to. For the majority the issues were money and benefits. For the dissenters the issues were "professionalism" and teacher as model citizen. For the officers the issue was one of tactics. The officers feared that further conflict with the school board "would lead to a worsening situation." Since there are several issues, parties would have to agree to a common statement of at least one issue. Because no common statement could be reached, negotiation within the union did not progress to bargaining.

The first set of incidents showed how all the parties could make direct emotional statements about their grievances. The second set showed how all parties could agree or disagree on a common statement of issues.

Striking a Bargain

A common statement of issues can lead to a discussion of possible concessions to be made by all sides. This writer describes how one student and one teacher were able to strike a bargain:

A student—one of twelve—interrupted me, his 10th grade world history teacher, and said more or less the following: "What right do you have to stand up there and tell me about world history. You are not teaching world history—you're teaching white history! How can you know what I think or feel? What you have to say is not important to me or my life so why don't you take your white crap and keep it? I'm 17 and have known and felt things which you never will and I know what I want and I know that what you have to teach me I want no part of."

My response was this: first I said, "thank you Larry for your comments. Now that you have spoken, may I say a few words? I think much of what you have said is right. I don't know what you think or feel, though I try. Though I am 25, there are many things you have known and felt which I can't. Why am I standing up here? Simply because I have more knowledge of history than you. Why do I teach "white history"? Because the school system teaches African and Asian history in a different year. I don't think that is right but if I covered African and Asian

history as well as European history, we wouldn't have time
to do either well. But I like your idea and this is what I will do:
I spent three years teaching in Africa and I have many books and
slides and art works from there. I have many books about
the black man in America and many studies of Asia. Because
the two of us think that it is important to study these areas,
would you like to work with me and take these areas and study
them so that you can present them to the class? I will give you
one day a week to be the teacher for the important things
you think I have left out. Then you may present things as you
see and feel. Or you may choose students to help you.
Agreed?" Student agrees.

"But, first, what does the rest of the class feel?" By a vote of ten to
two the class agreed to do this. We worked on this project until
we felt that we had exhausted the neglected areas and student
interest waned. (The student was older and more mature than
the others. The class was dull normal 80 to 98 IQ in a
flexible program. The experiment worked rather well and
interest was great on the day when this student or another (Italian
or Puerto Rican) wants to present areas of interest to them.

How else could the problem have been handled? Student could
have been sent to Dean for disrupting class. I feel this would have
destroyed the framework of the class and would have had
extremely negative results.

It is quite clear that the student verbally expressed anger. It is
less clear that the teacher did except for his defense of his
position. But the teacher accepted the student's anger by
stating his own side of the issues. The issue they agreed to
argue was the ethnic content of the history course. Both sides
made concessions. The teacher conceded the time devoted to
other subject matter—"one day a week"—for the student to make
his presentation. The student conceded the time for the
remainder of the week. Both sides also gained. The student
gained interest and participation in the class and the teacher
gained the cooperation of the complaining student and the
involvement of most other students.

One teacher described how he struck a bargain with the
whole class:

A recent incident involved a World history class. 8 students complained we were moving too rapidly. Also they felt they had trouble finding answers in the book. There were various suggestions as to how to deal with this problem. They wanted to do homework in class and I vetoed it, explaining that we could not cover the term's work in this fashion. Several suggestions were made (all student initiated) and it was agreed, by hand vote, that we review each homework assignment at the beginning of each period, do homework in class during the last 10 minutes and raise questions. Devote one day periodically (student decided) as a "catch-up" or review for test day. Everyone seemed satisfied.

Had I not agreed to listen to student objections, I could have formulated my own approach to the problem, one which might have filled their needs, or could have ignored the problem. Having them voice their gripes created a more wholesome atmosphere in the class. They felt a part of the decision-making process, as indeed they were. Also, they felt responsible for making decisions which would benefit the whole class.

Anger over the homework was expressed by both sides—the complaining students and the resisting teacher. Also, where "homework" was to be done was the issue they agreed to argue about. The issue again involved the use of time—in this case the allotment of time for a certain classroom procedure. In the bargaining the students gave up the demand to do *all* their homework in class. The teacher gave up ten minutes at the end of class. Both teacher and students gained part of their original demands. They also gained the experience of negotiation.

Occasionally the school officials act as mediators and provide opportunities for the parties directly involved to take the steps that lead to bargaining:

Place: My office as assistant principal. Who initiated: Parent Why: because of an incident in a class. No one else present when parent came in. Problem raised—mother threw daughter's white blouse across my desk and screamed for me to look at chalk marks about the breast area. Mother said one of male teachers "touched her daughter" with his hand as other students were standing about. Problem handled—After about 20 minutes of

trying to reason with mother she calmed down so we could talk
and get to specifics. Mother seemed (after calming down)
like a logical thinker who wanted to get to the root of the problem
and see to it that nothing like this would happen again.
I was able to convince her to trust me and give me a couple of days
to investigate—I assured her while she was waiting there would
not be the slightest trouble like this [with] any [other] student—
that the teacher would be constantly supervised—the mother agreed.

Steps I took—(1) conferred with the principal—we decided
to have one of our women guidance persons speak to the girl.
(2) the principal and myself would speak to the teacher.
Results—(1) Daughter thought nothing of the incident—explained it
happened but was an accident—she did not relate it to parents—
but while fooling around with some of her friends at home,
the mother heard of the incident and "blew the whole thing up"
(2) We spoke to the teacher—he was rather surprised because he
never thought of the incident—it did happen as a dozen or so
students were "pushing" through his classroom door after class—
but an accident.

Next steps (Note: all of this happened in one day except the incident
itself)—(1) We conferred with the guidance person (2) We
called in the mother—she was able to come at once. (3) Principal,
myself, guidance person, conferred with parent and explained
our findings (4) We called in the teacher and had him speak
to the parents in our presence. (5) We then called in the girl—
the girl related the same thing to her mother as she did to the
guidance person. (6) Mother seemed to understand—was angry
at herself and her daughter—she apologized.

The parties to the conflict appear to be the mother, the daughter,
and the teacher. The chief mediator was the assistant principal.
It is clear that the mother expressed anger in both words and
action (throwing the blouse across the desk). The teacher may
have verbally expressed anger as "surprise" and the daughter
in her statement about her mother exaggerating the incident.
The mediator gave each side a chance to describe the conflict
from its own point of view. In this way each side had a chance
to structure its anger around a central issue—what actually had
happened in the classroom. After these steps were taken it
was possible to bring the three parties together. The careful

way in which the school officials proceeded probably saved the teacher's job. Eventually all parties to the conflict, including the girl, were able to make emotional statements, agree to the issue, and finally strike a bargain.

Although the following incident did not occur in school, it is an example of a student's attempt to act as mediator:

In our house sometimes we start talking about the problems in it, how we could keep order and how things could be set. Once my cousins came to our house so my little sister started to run around with them. My mother can't stand people runing because it gives her a headache. Because I don't like to see my mother like that, I help her. I start scolding her and give her a warning, and then my father scolds me because I'm screaming, but he doesn't know what's going on. I tell my mother so she gives me some advice, but it doesn't work. We said we were going to send her back to Puerto Rico but she doesn't want. We tried many things like scaring her but nothing. She does this all the time. It's like she's showing off or something. Right now we don't know what to do.

The efforts of this adolescent to mediate the conflict between his younger sister and his parents appear to involve him as a party to the conflict. The parents and the little sister seem to operate in isolated worlds. The conflict originated between the mother and the little sister. The writer's intervention as mediator did not facilitate direct negotiation between these two parties. The writer wound up acting on behalf of one party (his mother) and expecting all the concessions from the other (his sister).

Avoiding Negotiation

In some incidents there was only capitulation to the demands of one side. Here, in an incident described by a student, the school board capitulated to student demands:

From the beginning of the school system in my community, on the high school level especially, there have been certain required courses for all students. These courses are (1) World History

and (2) American History. Recently (last May) on the decision
of the entire junior and high school student body, a group
of elected student delegates wrote and presented to our board
of education a request for the "integrating" of African and
Afro-American history into the current history courses. The board,
however, stalled and took its time in making facilities and
arrangements for such a change. Thus—this December the *entire*
student body had a sort-of "sit-in" in the school auditorium
protesting the laxness of the board of education. In this "sit-in"
many black and white grievances and opinions were expressed,
thus uniting the student body not only as students, but as people.

Democratically speaking, everyone got a chance to air his views
through student moderators on stage. Of course, there was
disagreement and friction, but we became united through
understanding. Understanding in communication and in thought,
was the key to the whole problem—and after an entire week
of sitting in the auditorium, the administration and the board
of education finally comprehended that we, as a student body wanted
something that we were determined to get. As of now we have
an Afro-Asian history course and an African language course
(Swahili) on a half semester basis. Next year, we have the promise
of the incorporation (on a large scale basis) of black history
into the formally white or better known as World and American
history, as well as the history and language. Not being, basically,
a violent person I found however that I had no qualms about
outrightly protesting the school board. Many times I felt
nervous when a black or white person said something derogatory
about the other race, but on the whole, I understood my position
and the position of others. As a black person, I was determined
to try my best to get the history courses, so that others could
understand *my* history and *my* worthwhile contributions
as a black person.

The two parties to this conflict are the students and school
officials, particularly the school board. The students clearly
expressed anger as dissent against the content of the history
course. It is less clear that school officials expressed anger even
though the issue seemed clear. The absence of emotional
response in the officials suggests that they never made a
commitment to negotiate. After the common statement of the

issue—the institution of black studies—there was no attempt at bargaining. In the absence of bargaining the school board could only reject or accept student demands. What was lost was the opportunity for adults and students to negotiate with each other and to develop a common sense of responsibility for the school.

The authorities in the previous incident were the school board. In the following incident, written by a school librarian, the authority within the school avoided bargaining:

As a new school librarian I followed the policy of the previous
librarian and charged fines of five cents a school day for books
that were not returned to the library on time. If a student
was absent he was only expected to return his book on the day
he returned to school. . . . The money collected from fines
was deposited in the general school district fund. A parent challenged
the legality and advisability of collecting fines on overdue books.
The school was able to substantiate its stand legally, but
I did wonder about the advisability of the fine system. In an
effort to be democratic, I took the problem to the student council.
I explained the history of the fine system in our school, the
reason for the fines, the difficulty in collecting them, etc., and
asked the student council for alternative methods to accomplish
the same things. . . . The student council came up with
dreadful punishments for offenders—such things as hours of
detention, increasing fines, swats, etc. When I discussed with
the students the difficulties of their plans, they could not come
up with anything else. I left the counsel to discuss the
situation by itself and asked them to report back to me. After
two weeks discussion and committee work the student council
sent me their decision—"Let Mrs. —— decide." They didn't want
to have a part in the decision-making process!

The conflict originally had four parties: the students with overdue books, the parent, the student council, and the librarian. Only the parent seemed to verbally express anger but she was excluded from negotiations. The librarian never expressed anger and the student council displaces its anger by imposing severe fines on fellow students. The librarian stated her side of the issue but did not wait to hear the students' side. When she "left the council to discuss the situation by itself" on two occasions, she provided the students a model for abdicating responsibility. This model excluded bargaining between student and librarian. The students imitated the model first by re-instituting the old system of fines and second by deferring to the authority of the school librarian. This incident shows how the experience of incomplete negotiation affects student behavior.

In the following incident, described by a teacher, the principal decides what issue will be negotiated by the teachers:

This type of incident took place at the very first faculty meeting just before the opening of school in September. It started as soon as the principal asked the teachers to decide on procedures of such routine matters as yard rules, hall rules, general behavior and expectations. It became immediately evident that the faculty was split on how these items should be handled. The old-timers at the school (half of the group) wished to continue using the rules that had previously existed and proved worthwhile before. (Incidentally, the principal had been at this school as assistant principal.) The new teachers to the school favored an easy, relaxed, swingy atmosphere with as few rules as possible. They preferred no lines, talking in the halls and even voiced opinions against such a traumatic thing as saluting the flag. Some of the old-timers were accused of being narrow-minded and dictatorial (Achtung! was one pet phrase used.) although they expressed that their feelings were that school rules should be somewhat stiff at first but not inflexible and never subject to change even if the children demonstrated that a slackening of restrictions might be in order. . . . In my humble opinion, the problems were handled poorly. Many could have been completely avoided if at the beginning rules and expectations had been outlined for us by the administration to be changed as the need or opportunity arose. Outside help was brought in— Dr. (Head-Shrink) and 1-man staff. Two perfectly good evenings were wasted with these jokers with little or anything being accomplished. Unfortunately, bickering has gone for more than half of the school year.

Finally, through the student council, some of the problems concerning procedures are being resolved and strangely enough they have

asked for such things as class line, more order in the building, etc.
I very strongly believe in change, but change as an outgrowth
of experience and not just for the sake of change. Modifications
and/or innovation should take place on a constant developmental
basis through such processes as refinement and accrued knowledge.

This incident illustrates why there could not be bargaining.
The principal selects the issue (i.e., the enforcement of school
rules) to be decided. Although he makes no statement of his
position, he asks the faculty to state its position. He gets the
teachers to take the responsibility for making a decision that he
wanted made. Because step two, the common statement of
issues, preceded step one, angry statements by each side, the
principal risks nothing in the bargaining. Step three, requiring
concessions on all sides, could not therefore be taken.

Sometimes the language of negotiation (e.g., "contract" and
"agreement"), as reported by the guidance counselor, is used
but no negotiating steps are really taken:

The problem occurred when four girls were brought into the
counseling office when found smoking behind one of the school
buildings. Myself and four girls were in a soundproof counseling
room, seated, and discussed reasons for school rules related
to smoking, which was listed in the disciplinary code under
discretionary suspension. I asked the group to make a verbal
contract, being: those who would voluntarily give up smoking
at the school could leave (the room) and students not making
the agreement would accept a day's suspension. To my knowledge
the three girls did not smoke at school that year. I feel that
they felt the responsibility to abide by their own decision, where(as)
the one accepting the suspension felt she had paid in her way
and was free to make future decisions about smoking
under no previous obligation.

The parties to the conflict are, first, the counselor and, second,
the girls. Their meeting has the appearance but not the substance of bargaining. First, there is discussion in a soundproof
room where the counselor states her side of the conflict. The
description does not convey any anger. The students' side is
not reported at all. Second, the parties to the conflict could

not agree to a common statement of issues because they had failed to state their original positions. Third, there was no bargaining—the students could only obey or disobey the smoking rule.

In summary, the latter incidents have provided examples of successful bargaining and mediation, of incomplete negotiation, and of pseudo-negotiation in which one party made no concessions.

Guidelines on the Mediation of School Conflict

In a recent seminar on the resolution of school conflict graduate students occupying positions as teachers, counselors, and principals acted as individual mediators. They attempted to get parties to genuine school conflicts to engage in face-to-face negotiations. Based on their experience the seminar members formulated these guidelines for individual mediators of school conflict:

1. Mediators must be acceptable to all parties. If they offer their services directly to one party then they should also do this with the other parties to the conflict. If a mediator is asked by one party to mediate, then that party or the mediator must contact the other parties to obtain agreement on the use of his services. In the latter case, the first party should decide whether the mediator or the party initiating the request makes the contact with the other parties.

2. The mediator should not be a party to the conflict. He should be able to listen to each party's side of the conflict and understand the issues from the perspectives of all parties. After hearing the issues he may decide that he should join one party as ally. Not everyone can mediate every school conflict. Sometimes the involvement of particular parties or the raising of particular issues compels mediators to take sides. At that point they become parties to conflicts.

3. In offering their services as mediators, they may face conflicts over the use of mediation and negotiation as alterna-

tives to coercion and avoidance as ways of dealing or not dealing with school conflict. These issues over ways of handling and avoiding conflict must be raised and negotiated like other conflict issues. The result of successful negotiation will be the establishment of a mediational process acceptable to both mediators and the parties to the conflict. For the mediator to avoid his own conflicts or to try to impose a negotiation model on resisting parties would seriously weaken his credibility and effectiveness.

4. To reduce the initial rage and fear of parties in conflict, it is sometimes useful for the mediator to listen to each party tell its side without the other parties present. By focusing questions on specific incidents and issues, the mediator can help each party channel its anger into negotiable issues and avoid the displacement of anger that may alienate the other parties. The private interview also provides the mediator with knowledge of the issues as seen by each party that he can use during direct negotiations.

5. The primary purpose of mediation is to get the parties to directly negotiate. After hearing and helping each side formulate the issues, the mediator should help them decide when they are ready to directly negotiate. When parties remain isolated, they may ask the mediator to provide indirect communication between parties about what each party sees as the issues.

6. Whether or not the mediator participates in the direct negotiations should be decided by all parties to the conflict. If one or more parties object to his presence then his participation becomes an issue that should be debated and negotiated like other issues. Low status parties may want the presence of the mediator when they deal with high status parties (e.g., students with teachers, teachers with school officials) as a way of equalizing power. This may be especially true when the mediator is a high status person (e.g., principal, department head, colleague). Parties of equal status may decide to negotiate without the presence of the mediator.

7. When the mediator occupies an official role which carries authority to impose resolutions of conflict, he must tell each party that he is entering their conflict as mediator and not as authority figure. By listening to all sides the official should convey that no party is going to get treated unilaterally (with either rewards or punishment) and that the resolution of the conflict should come from the parties themselves.

8. There are several things a mediator can do to help parties reach agreement on common issues. He can support each party as it directs its anger toward particular issues, encourage it to anchor the issues in actual and specific incidents, and help it link issues to facts and events. Sometimes the mediator can help by enumerating issues so that parties can discuss them separately and try to determine whether or not it is a common issue.

9. The final job of the mediator is to help parties decide what they might concede to each other. The mediator can support each party as it formulates and states what it expects from negotiations and what in turn it might give up. On the basis of his knowledge of issues and facts, the mediator may suggest possible concessions for *all* parties, particularly when the discussion of possible sacrifices is avoided. Pruitt and Johnson (1970), in a fine-grain analysis of conflict, found that concessions were easier to make when combined with ways "to save face."

In their present state these guidelines are more testable hypotheses than firm conclusions. The model of mediation presented here is designed to facilitate rather than substitute for direct negotiation by parties to conflicts. In its present state the model provides one mediator for all parties. It is possible that each party choose its own mediator and that the mediators lead the negotiations. Mediator-led negotiations, whatever their advantages in time-saving, could by-pass or minimize the anger and perceptions of the parties to the conflict and thereby weaken their emotional and intellectual commitment to whatever resolutions are reached.

Summary

This chapter has presented a three-step model for the negotiation of school conflict. First, each party to the conflict should make statements of issues with the direct, verbal expression of anger. Second, each party should agree to common statements of issues and to argue those issues. Third, each party should strike a bargain that involves each making gains and concessions.

The previous chapters are pertinent to some or all of the steps in the negotiation model. Chapters 2, 5, 6 and 7 are pertinent to the first step. Chapter 2, on survival teaching and learning, presented a classification of real conflict issues that resulted from a lack of classroom and curricular choice. Chapter 5, on the direct verbal expression of anger, showed the usefulness of the initial, direct expression of anger structured around specific issues. Chapter 6, on acting angry, showed how the failure to provide verbal expression of anger resulted in violence, intimidation, and coercion. The failure to verbalize the anger or to tie it to the issues that aroused it often results in the displacement of anger on to issues, personal differences, and actions that cannot be negotiated. Chapter 7 also bears on step one in making sure that all parties to the conflict have the chance to make angry statements of issues.

Chapters 3, 4, and 7 pertain to the second step. Chapter 3, on the civic choices of decision-making and dissent, and Chapter 4, on the civic statuses of equality and due process, provide a political context within which common statements of issues can be crystallized and agreed upon. The second step limits the number of issues that can be argued and negotiated at any one time and place. The second step requires agreement by all parties over what they will disagree. Taking this step means that the parties are "agreeing to disagree." Chapter 7 shows how to identify the parties to the conflict. It illustrated how common statements of issues require parties to coordinate and differentiate their points of view. Parties must perceive and describe the common threads of interests.

Several chapters are linked to the third step, striking the bargain. Chapter 2 links bargaining to survival and gourmet learning because it requires each party's clarity about its own priorities. Chapters 3 and 4 link bargaining to democratic rights that are standards for acceptable and unacceptable sacrifices. Chapter 7 links negotiation to decentering which requires the ability of each party to determine what concessions the other parties realistically can make. Bargaining is tied to the temporal perspectives described in Chapter 8 because accurate perspectives clarify current issues and possible concessions by placing events in the proper order and against a background extending from past to future. Bargaining is also linked to the perception of time because each party must see today's concessions against the background of "it's better than I got last time and not as good as I will get the next time."

The negotiation model is not the way to handle all complaints. If the school board in the incident cited agreed with students about starting a black studies program, then there would be no conflict and no need for negotiation. To pursue negotiation as an empty, mechanical exercise probably teaches students little about the resolution of real conflict. Better to start work on the black studies program!

This three-stage model of conflict resolution cuts across the legal model of direct negotiation, mediation, and arbitration. It cuts across the political model of resolution by majority vote. It denies the monarchical model of resolution only by decree from above. It denies the proletarian model of resolution only from below.

It is a working model for democratic participation in school governance. It is pertinent to the high school setting because it provides opportunities for political learning while it resolves genuine conflicts.

The act of negotiation is one of both love and sacrifice. First, it requires school adults to sacrifice the time and trouble to listen to the angry complaints of students. It shows students that adults care enough for them to listen even though they often rebel. Second, it requires adults to share and give up some power. This sacrifice also shows that adults care enough to go through the pain of negotiation.

Even with this care and sacrifice there are no guarantees for success. Sometimes the rage and fear are intense and cannot be constructively channeled into negotiable issues. The need to destroy the opposition becomes more powerful than the need to find a way of living and working together. Sometimes the issues are non-negotiable—when parties feel that they must concede, for example, the equality of their race, sex, or personality or some value or principle. At other times, even after considerable amounts of time and effort by all parties, the negotiation fails. Students are left disillusioned with both the authority figures and the negotiation process. Even with these risks and perils, negotiation still seems to be the most humane alternative we have to dealing with conflict by coercion or to trying to avoid it altogether.

10 Levels of Conflict INTRAPERSONAL, INTERPERSONAL, AND INSTITUTIONAL CONFLICT

THIS BOOK HAS SHOWN HOW school people can look to piecemeal change for solutions of school problems. This final chapter integrates theory, data, and practice in three ways. First, it interrelates the theories of the various chapters: teaching and learning, political socialization, affective expression, and cognitive development. Second, it relates this body of theory to psychoanalytic discussions of adolescent development. Third, it shows how education beyond the formal curriculum uses everyday school conflict for student learning and development.

Piecemeal change is never easy and this may be the reason we resist it for the more beguiling monolithic solutions that promise more change, faster, and with less pain. Piecemeal change requires us to face our daily conflicts, fight openly with the people we are mad at, and negotiate our settlements with them. The practice of honest confrontation, honest anger, and honest negotiation does not come easily to adults who have achieved material and political success as organization men— avoiding fights, suppressing anger, and evading negotiated decisions. It does not come easily to students who have achieved an uneasy truce with authority while retreating behind walls of apathy to waste their lives and talents cutting classes, plugging up toilets, attacking fellow students.

The student who is not allowed to express anger verbally is forced to express it in destructive acts. The relationship between tough school discipline and aggressive athletic teams is a result of this conversion of anger into physical violence (Prescott, 1970). In the extreme case, prevented from physical expression as well, the student will turn away into sullen apathy broken by spurts of rage.

What happens within the individual student over time can happen simultaneously to different members of the group of students. In any conflict, different members of the group are selected to act out the roles of the critic, the ringleader, the scapegoat, the mediator and perhaps others as well. When aggression is repressed in the group, the roles get acted out in violent behavior, walking out of the group, standing apart from the group work and the like. In high schools, violence, vandalism, and drug-taking are expressions of destructive aggression. When expression of each person's point of view is encouraged, including the aggressive components, real negotiation takes place and conflict results in new social roles and new rules of the game (Brown, 1965). In high school the new rules and new roles can make new institutional structures uniquely suited to the needs of each group of students as they pass through the school. There are two kinds of sacrifice required for realistic conflict resolution. One is the sacrifice of the fantasy of the present school equilibrium. The other is the sacrifice of ideal goals for realistic compromise.

Marcuse (1962) described the political forms that arose from a society of scarcity. Concepts of survival teaching and learning extend Marcuse's idea to the schools. They are quantitative and prescriptive ideas of teaching and learning. Quantitative concepts raise questions about how many lessons are taught, chapters read, points scored, and credits accumulated. Prescriptive concepts raise questions about courses and materials, prerequisites, and school schedules. Gourmet teaching and learning are based on theories of choice. Bruner (1966) wrote about the importance of the student's choosing the goal if he engages in learning for the reward of mastery. Piaget's research has shown how learners construct knowledge in the process of assimilating the information the environment makes available. Schools should help students articulate options and become aware of their own choice-making. Gourmet teaching and learning are qualitative and self-determined. They allow students and teachers to add new courses, materials, and activities and to use resources outside the classroom and the school.

Piecemeal change is a way of restoring to the high school the pursuit of its traditional but presently overlooked objective —the political education of young people in democratic society. It is an article of democratic faith that institutions should emerge out of the needs of individuals who comprise them. Citizens are both governors and the governed. Efforts of educational and political leaders to direct and control school reform from their positions of power and responsibility inevitably fail to shore up the tottering school monoliths.

Consider the democratic rights described in Chapters 3 and 4. The right to participate in making decisions that affect one's institutional investments is basic for all individuals— students, teachers, school officials, counselors, office staff, janitors, parents, and so on. For any one high school, this is a large body of decision-makers. Such widespread involvement arouses fears of inefficiency and chaos in many students and adults. The democratic system of checks-and-balances deliberately builds in inefficiency as a way of extending participation in decision-making. It is not the "inefficient" conflicts that immobilize high school but the efforts to avoid and ignore them.

From the point of view of the individual, participation requires time that is an irreplaceable part of life. The time must be used up before one knows what the results will be. In many meetings no decision may be reached. Sometimes unworkable decisions are made. When these results occur the individual feels frustrated and bored. The person may then conclude that time has been wasted. Even when a satisfactory decision is reached the person has used up time. In this way democratic participation is the piecemeal sacrifice of one's life.

The right to participate includes the right not to participate. Not everyone needs or wants to participate in every decision. When one does not participate, however, he is bound by decisions made in his absence by the group. The freedom not to participate, therefore, requires the sacrifice of individual autonomy. The young people who have been educated in the democratic process will be aware that they have to pay for a stake in that process with constant investment of more time and energy.

Dissent also creates tensions. On the one hand it provides the experience necessary for the moral and intellectual independence of young people and adults. To dissent is to make intellectual choices about right and wrong ideas. It requires verbalizing and connecting them to others and the willingness to take the consequences for publicly acting on them. On the other hand it threatens the need for institutional consensus. To put disagreement and criticism always before agreement breeds disunity; to put agreement always before dissent forces conformity. Disunity can be painful, conformity stultifying. Dissent can lead to moral independence; agreement to satisfying joint enterprises. To enjoy a little of each means to sacrifice a little of each.

Equality poses the inescapable tension between separation and integration. All the newly emerging subgroups in the nation and world want integration as the way in which they achieve status, money, and power in the mainstream of society. They also want separation as the way they can celebrate and enjoy their unique heritage. The tension between integration and separation has become so severe that it tears apart individuals, groups, and institutions. The story of the suicide of a black assistant principal of a racially integrated junior high school illustrates this point (*New York Times,* March 19, 1972). The story refers to a three-page suicide letter he left for the school:

Mr. Cabell [the assistant principal] wrote he was weary of fighting "insensitive trainers, also known as teachers." But most of his letter was devoted to his dilemma "Isolated in the middle, never right always wrong. I cannot allow myself to turn against what I know to be right," he said, "on the other hand I cannot be turned against my people." He said that dying was the only way to get the attention of "the vast majority of black students who did not take a stand" and to "impress upon you the need

to stop standing back and force out those 'sick' people who will
never let us black people become equal, because they want
to compete or fight with white folks instead of working [with] and
understanding them."

Clearly the plea in this letter is for more negotiation and for
students to join in dissent.

The equality crisis goes beyond race and sex. Young people
who bid for equality regardless of ethnicity, sex, and age bring
to the high school the same painful tension between separation
and integration.

Due process, the bulwark of democratic society, also creates
institutional tension. There is the tension generated by two
conflicting views of what due process is (Dworkin, 1972).
Judicial activism asserts that men have moral rights against
the government and that the views of these rights change with
fresh moral insight. Judicial deference asserts that decisions
about controversial issues of political morality should not be
made by the courts (using due process) but by other governmental departments. Students and school adults hold both
views. Due process is an elaborate, time-consuming, and expensive process. Outside the school due process works because the
large percentage of the accused plead guilty and thereby spare
the state the time and expense of trials. Inside the school due
process requires serious investment of time and resources (Ladd,
1972). If there must be protection of students' rights, then
school adults and students must sacrifice some of the time and
energy that they would otherwise give to satisfying and valuable
personal pursuits.

Anger can be expressed in words and acts. The expression
of anger in words, in settings provided for this expression, and
in conjunction with the issues that aroused the anger initially,
makes anger permissible. Claude Levi-Strauss (1969) refers
to ritualization of raw emotion as transforming the "raw" into
the "cooked." The "raw" anger is dangerous, the "cooked" anger
acceptable in civilized society. The school can ritualize anger
by providing for counseling, rap groups, grievance procedures,
judicial proceedings, open meetings, and so on. In psycho-

analysis, the individual talks about his feelings and makes them part of the external world so that they can be dealt with (Freud, S. E., Vol. 4). Blos (1962) describes the raw aggression of normal male adolescents. By raw aggression he means aggression not tied to specific issues. With the rapid change in female roles, the adolescent girl also feels free to express such aggression. The developmental section below will explain why there is this sudden unprovoked release of raw aggression in adolescence.

Feshbach's investigations (1970) showed that violence can be an expression of anger through physical acts. He found that verbal expression of anger can be a substitute for physical aggression.

In a discussion of the controlled forms of aggression, Hacker (1972, p. 221) pointed out some of the potentially creative uses of verbal aggression:

Aggression as strategy can be an alerting signal, an alarm sign, a provocation, a cry for help and attention, a frantic communication attempt, a symbol of hope or despair, a cognitive search for novelty, an instrument for group cohesion and identity confirmation as well as defence against anxiety, anonymity, alienation and futility.

Hacker argues for the controlled expression of aggression to reform and repair social institutions. The high school appears to be the social institution with greatest impact on the people who will run all the social institutions of the future. It makes its impact on these people in terms of teaching them to handle their aggressions in the way that will be appropriate for them as adults. The choice is whether to teach students that verbal aggression should be stifled (with the potential increase in violent physical expressions of aggression) or to show them how to use their aggression in verbal forms that serve the varied purposes Hacker suggests.

The theory of anger assumes interpersonal conflict. To understand interpersonal conflict we recast Piaget's theory of cognitive development to analyze how parties to a conflict describe their relationships. Our central concepts were differentiation and coordination. Differentiation is the ability to see how one's own interests differ from those of others. Coordination is the ability to see how one's interests are the same as others. Together the two processes describe the ability to decenter: to see the world as others see it.

Various psychological theories of time can help one to understand conflict and conflict resolution. Piaget (1969) has shown that time can be understood as sequences of events, duration, and a set of measurements. Time also represents varying amounts of delay in gratification (Lewin, 1939). The perception of time is also related to individual states of pleasure and unpleasure (Wiener and Mehrabian, 1968).

Time has its tragic aspects. Teachers harbor ambivalent feelings about the students' inevitable departure. The teachers are in school for an indefinite time while the students are there for a few years. For the students the shortness of their stay in high school is a measure of their success. For teachers the length of their stay is a measure of their success.

The dimensions of interpersonal conflict and time are useful in developing a model of conflict resolution. We also turned to studies of school conflict resolution and mediation of Chesler, BenDor, Guskin, and Pruitt.

Negotiation has three stages: (1) the verbal expression of anger over specific issues directly expressed by all parties to the conflict; (2) the agreement to a common statement of issues; and (3) the bargaining and concessions by both sides.

The model does not guarantee success. It simply shows how to start on a plan of action rather than remain deadlocked in conflict or bogged down in apathy.

There is inherent tragedy in the negotiation of school conflicts, for conflict arouses anger and pain. There is the anger and pain of confrontation for those who speak and listen. Then all parties must endure pain long enough to reach a common statement of issues. Next there is the pain of sacrifice involved in making concessions. Finally, there is the pain of future negotiations involving the new students and school adults who arrive each new school year. No single negotiation will please everybody. Every negotiation, since it involves compromise, will leave each party partly dissatisfied.

Negotiations can be hampered in many ways. Anger can become so intense that the parties never communicate specific grievances—the issues are never clear. Or they cannot agree on a verbal description of the issues—they cannot agree even on what issues they should debate. Finally, they may wait for one side to make all the concessions, hoping that time and events will eventually give them victory without compromise.

There are also intrapsychic obstacles: uncertainty about what the choices are and indecision about which choices to make. The emotional state accompanying uncertainty and indecision is the pain of doubt. The individual may try to avoid decisions and negotiation to avoid this painful emotional state (Rangell, 1971, p. 439).

Doubt can enter the negotiation at different points. Stating the issues arouses intrapsychic uncertainty because it involves scanning the possible issues. Choosing the issue toward which the anger is directed, choosing the common statement of issues, and making concessions arouse intrapsychic indecision.

We have now completed our discussion of the theories used in the analyses of incidents. These theories have dealt with the interpersonal, political, and social conflicts any people engaged in negotiation could have. These theories have been applied to high school.

Negotiation is bargaining. The people at the bargaining table determine the nature of the bargain. In high school conflict the bargainers are adolescents. The next section is about the intrapsychic conflicts of adolescents.

Intrapsychic Conflict: The High School Student as an Adolescent

Not all conflict that students have with the school is the result of institutional inadequacies. Some of the conflict is internal to the students. We can even distinguish between two types of internal conflict. Some internal conflict is characteristic of adolescence. Other conflict is specific to students whose particular life histories make it difficult for them to conform to school.

There are two stages of conflict in adolescence proper (ages 14 to 18) (Blos, 1962). The first is separation and the second individuation. The separation is from perceived parental values. In early adolescence conflict arises between the child's adherence to perceived parental value systems and perceived peer and school adult value systems. In choosing between parent and peer or school values the adolescent divests himself of many parental injunctions.

The second adolescent stage of development is individuation. It involves the consolidation of a unique personal value system. This value system is different than that of teachers and peers as well as parents. The resulting personal system will contain elements derived from parents, peers, and teachers but in a combination unique for each person. Esman (1972) believes that the "reorganization and consolidation of values is as central a task of contemporary adolescence as finding a permanent love object and stabilization of character and defense organization."

The adolescent uses the teacher as a stand-in for the parents. His images of the powerful parent inspired good behavior in childhood just as the voice of conscience punished bad behavior. When adolescence upsets the balance between conscience and powerful parents, on the one hand, and his wishes and impulses, on the other hand, the individual enters a period of turmoil during which he must discard old controls before he can develop new ones. In effect, the adolescent is rebelling against his own infantile conscience. Josselyn (1952, p. 68) describes the struggle:

The infantile conscience was adequate for the adjustment of the small child; its structure as determined by the needs and requirements of childhood. The same standards of adjustment are not satisfactory for adult living, and because the conscience is part of childhood, it becomes a barrier against maturation.

An adolescent feels he must free himself from infantile modes of behavior; he rebels against his own conscience.

The rebellion causes internal conflict. To meet rebellion the conscience becomes more alert and rigid than before. And so high school students swing between an astonishing lack of any inhibitions and severe, self-imposed restrictions:

The adolescent often handles this conflict between the wish to be free of the conscience and slavish devotion to it by verbalization of defiance but with complete compliance with standards in actual behavior. Sometimes, however, the defiance is not only verbal but is acted out, with serious consequences. Usually, then, the acting out that occurs during the phase of defiance results in an overwhelming guilt reaction when the conscience is again in control. The conscience did not succeed in prohibiting the behavior but once the act is committed, it must use all its force to punish.

In this connection Lowenfeld and Lowenfeld (1972, p. 377), using clinical evidence derived from the treatment of adolescents who adopted a hippie life style, have warned against the dangers of unrestricted expression of the drives. They write:

Freud's concepts of the power of the drives led to splits within the analytic movement, the new group more or less denying the dangers of the drives.

In effect, they are arguing for the maintenance of adult standards as a model of reasonable repression of the drives.

Because of their moral conflicts, students have trouble with rules, as shown in the following two incidents reported by students:

In this school there are different problems. The one that I think should be considered is that the students come dressed in every type of clothing. The girls wear slacks and sneakers. Before I went to a school where we wore tie, jackets and I liked it much better. We ate with spoons forks, silver wear. Now we use wooden spoons, forks and the kids throw food around and do not eat as ladies & gentlemen. I think that this should be changed by finding stricter teachers or teachers that care for the kids.

The student in the previous incident asked for stricter rules. He equated enforcing rules with caring for kids. In the following incident the student asks for lenient rules:

All sophmores in Cathedral High School are very dissapointed with the Student Council. Because there has been a lot of arguments about the uniforms we have to wear next year. Nobody like them and everybody is complaining. I don't see why we have to change uniform when nobody likes them. This has created a problem for the school.

When the Student Council met with the principal of the school and discussed the problem nothing changed because the principal said that, that was one rule she could not change. And that we were the first kids to complaint about that. We were very sad when we heard that nothing was going to change. So we protested again and we were decided to win this time. So this time we told the principal that we had our rights to change the uniform because we were the ones who were going to wear it. And she said that it was not a matter of taste and that her decision was still the same. And that was the conclusion. We did not change uniform no matter how hard we tried.

In the second incident the students ask for the right to select their uniforms. Internal adolescent conflict catches the high school in two ways: It is caught (1) between students who want strict rules and students who want no rules and (2) by each student as he alternately responds to the need for rebellion and the need for control. Rules, therefore, must always be renegotiated to meet these swings of conscience and rebellion.

We have viewed the internal conflicts of adolescence in terms of emotional development. The specific conflicts of adolescents have also been studied from the cognitive side.

According to Inhelder and Piaget (1958) adolescent decentering occurs at the same time in thought and emotional processes. Blos (1962, p. 124) integrates cognitive and psychoanalytic views of adolescent thinking and adolescents:

Inhelder and Piaget (1958) studied adolescent thinking in its typical form; their findings bear out this correlative development of "affective life" and "cognitive processes," or drive and ego, to which I am referring. For Inhelder and Piaget it is the "assumption of adult roles" that "involves a total restructuring of the personality in which intellectual transformations are parallel or complementary to the affective transformations." Some of these findings are closely related to my concept of a hierarchical arrangement of ego function in adolescence. The adolescent "begins to consider himself as the equal of adults and to judge them"; he "begins to think of the future—i.e., of his present or future work in society"; he also "has the idea of changing this society." "The adolescent differs from the child above all in that he thinks beyond the present"; he "commits himself to possibilities."

The adolescent, in equating himself to adults, is entering the process of interpersonal decentering—he is coordinating with adults and differentiating from children. In his thoughts about the future he is expanding his sense of time duration.

In essence this is the capacity to think in terms of hypotheses and theories, to see multiple possibilities for solutions to problems, and to examine their world from many points of view. Blos (1962) also agrees with their view that the adolescent constructs theories while the child lacks the capacity for thinking in generalized terms about hypothetical situations. Because of the new cognitive capacity, high school students can grasp the concepts of civic choice and civic status.

This cognitive development enables the adolescent to re-evaluate the world view he obtained from his family (Barnett, 1971, p. 113). Barnett writes:

Prior to adolescence the child is largely a product of his interaction with the family. The cognitive matrix of his interpersonal experience—what he may know and how he may know it—is structured by what I call the implicit family ideology, an implicit system of cognition which determines systems of knowing and of innocence compatible with the specific homeostatic balance maintained in the family. The family ideology is an apprehended system, functionally related to the cultural and characterological values and needs of the parents. By prescription and proscription it defines the limits of knowing, and consequently of the organization of experience and of behavior. It structures implicit assumptions about interpersonal relationships, implicit value systems, preferences and taboos, and thus defines and delineates reality for the child. It is the effective cognitive framework for growth and development during the important years when the child's life is centered around the family, and its restrictions and limitations only become apparent when development leads the child to important and central interpersonal relations outside the family.

Esman (1972, p. 90) describes this adolescent development of values in psychoanalytic terms:

As part of the adaptive functions, the ego (or rather that part of it devoted to self-observation) "screens" the superego-value reservoir as it does external reality, to assess the appropriateness of any thought or impulse and its consistency with the conscious and unconscious value systems.

Much of the adolescent examination and search for values goes on outside of conscious thought and intention. Esman's statement points to the chief value of psychoanalytic theory for understanding adolescent development. The student cannot describe to school adults his intrapsychic conflict because he is unaware of what is happening at that level. On the surface he may appear moody, taciturn, uncooperative, and simply bored. His energies are absorbed inward in these internal conflicts. Teachers sense this withdrawal as personal or professional failure whereas these states are largely beyond their control.

Recognizing the importance and complexity of the emotional development of adolescents, the teacher is not held responsible for fostering their mental health or providing their psychotherapy. The primary function of the school is conceived as helping the students in their cognitive development. Sometimes students, as in the following incident, ask for more:

I once had a teacher who really seemed as if he cared about each of us. He taught me more about life than anything else—things that were worth learning. That's the important thing, knowing that a teacher cares about students as people equal to themselves in every way except, perhaps, experience. You can really tell if a teacher loves you or cares about things like love. Some

people don't get too much at home so its good to find it at the
place where you spend the next most time next to home. I mean
the teacher always made us feel as if we could talk to him
any time about anything. I realize that I didn't take as much
advantage of it as I should have, because of shyness, I guess.
If I were a teacher I would really try to show love to every student.

High school students need educational models. High school is
the time when young people turn away from the family and
satisfy this need outside the home. Peers can also be intellectual
models while the teacher remains the adult model. The student
asks teachers "to show love to every student." He asks them
to be parents to those students who "don't get too much [love]
at home" and to be deities available for anything at any time.
What he does not demand is any help for his cognitive growth.
His demand for love might be more appropriately directed
toward a peer. His demand for time might be appropriately
separated into smaller units of clock and calendar time allotted
to his various needs and requests by different people in different
places. Even the change from survival to gourmet teaching
means that certain choices exclude others and, particularly,
that the choices for learning exclude choices for pure emotional
support.

But love without discipline is not enough (Bettleheim,
1950). The following student demands a disciplinarian:

My problem I think is why do they have behavior officer
because the people who does no how to do the work they say its
bornren. They shouldn't have behavior officer. But they should
have meaner teachers so that pupils would do the lessons and
not mess up the class.

Students in the last two incidents demanded emotional
satisfaction the teachers could not provide. In the former
incident the student asked for unlimited love and in the second
unlimited control. Teachers sometimes supply a little love and
a little control but they cannot give unlimited amounts of either
one, much less of both. Trying to meet these unlimited demands
of students would leave the teacher drained.

Because adolescents make extravagant demands and must shortly leave the school, the school adult must maintain relationships with colleagues as protection against over-involvement with students.

Some school adults respond to student need for nurturance with self-denial. Consider the following incident:

In our school of limited funds, we in the library and with the acquiescence of the staff and principal have formed a paperback club to which all students who wish to read paperbacks contribute 25 cents annually. It is not necessary to belong to the club in order to read, because there is a good selection of hard cover books for those not wishing to pay the 25 cents. However, 95% of the students are reading paperbacks, whether they have paid the 25 cents. They do this by having a club member sign out for them—or by taking advantage of the rush prevailing when signing out books before 9:00 a.m., 1:30, etc. What action should the librarian take? Enforce the policy set down by the staff or accept the idea that the kids are reading and want to read paperbacks they haven't contributed to. I have made an attempt to counsel those students of whom I have knowledge re this situation—inviting them to bring the money at their earliest convenience and trying to make them aware of the honorable things to do in relation to the ones who already paid. But many times I have felt this was defeating the purpose of encouraging kids to read so I have not always carried out my professional duty to staff members (perhaps!!!).

Given the choice between allowing students not to pay the quarter and preserving loyalty to colleagues, the librarian has two reasons for the latter course. First is the unreasonableness of the students who will not make even the smallest payment for what they want. Second is that the students will leave and the librarian and her colleagues will stay. The students' irresponsible demand to read the paperbacks without paying the quarter is evidence of their regression to childish behavior that we now understand to be a necessary part of their adolescent development. Their eventually leaving the school is another essential part of their adolescent development.

In the light of knowledge about adolescent regressions school adults can remain passive or active. When passive they can use this knowledge as a basis for surrendering to adolescent student demands. When active they can maintain adult roles while still listening but not capitulating. The maintenance of adult roles is important because adolescents need school adults as new models of behavior as in this example of adult loyalty to colleagues.

This section on psychoanalytic theory of adolescent development concluded with a description of its relationship to our earlier theories. The earlier theories represent three different levels of analysis: the intrapersonal level for the psychoanalytic theory; the interpersonal level for the cognitive theory; and the social and political level for the political socialization theory. Each theory had two dimensions. For the psychoanalytic theory there is separation and individuation. For the cognitive theory there is differentiation and coordination. For the political socialization theory there is separatism and integration.

Each level of analysis has two dimensions—one of getting things together and the other of sorting things out. Separation is sorting things out at the intrapsychic level. It means discarding family values, separating one's own beliefs from the family ideology, and separating one's image of himself from the family's image. Differentiation is sorting things out at the interpersonal level. It means separating one's goals, values, and interests from those of other individuals. It means separating one's goals, values, and interests from one's group. It also means separating the goals, values, and interests of one's group from other groups. Separatism is sorting things out at the social political level. It is separating the group's ethics and customs from those of the larger society and the group's image of itself from the society's stereotype of it.

Individuation is getting things together at the intrapsychic level. It is consolidating into a system of one's own the values and ideals from various sources. It is restructuring one's image of oneself from materials obtained from various sources. Coordination is getting things together at the interpersonal level.

It is finding the interests and points of view one shares with another individual and with one's group. Integration is getting things together at the social and political level. It is finding the community of interests, ethics, customs and ideals one's group shares with all other social groups. It is finding the community of interests that other groups share with each other —something that requires a high level of coordination.

At each level the processes of sorting out and putting together are occurring at the same time. At any given moment, however, the individual may be concentrating on one dimension to the relative neglect of the other. He may also be concentrating on one level to the relative neglect of the other levels.

At any one historical moment in the school people may appear to be working at cross purposes because they are working at different levels. This difference in concentration may make negotiation difficult because parties to conflict cannot agree on a statement of issues they are working on, issues specific to different levels. Consider the following example. At the social and political level, some students may be interested in forming ethnic studies courses to celebrate their ethnic background (separatism) while other students may be interested in getting fellow students to join a new ecology movement of the Sierra Club (integration). At the interpersonal level, a student may try to organize a chess club so that he can be a president (differentiation) while another student may do the same thing because he wants to find students to share a common interest in chess (coordination). At the intrapersonal level, one student may be refusing to do his English homework because he prefers the image of car mechanic and designer to his parents' image of him as a white collar worker (separation). Another student may study mathematics (a parental value) because it fits his interest in the designing of cars (individuation).

Now turn to considerations of possible relationships of theory to high school practice.

Changing the High School

The model of negotiation is submitted as the basic process of school reform. To see how it differs from other reform models, examine the objectives of a reform program summarized by a follower of John Dewey. In 1938, Everett's *The Community School* provided a summary of objectives and assumptions used by educational programs in the big city ghettos, rural Appalachia, Indian reservations, and prosperous small towns. The objectives and assumptions sound remarkably modern:

1. All life is educative, rather than education takes place only in school.

2. Education requires participation rather than mere passive spectator roles.

3. Adults and children have fundamental common purposes in both work and play rather than limiting adults to work and children to play.

4. Schools should improve the community and social order rather than just pass on the social heritage.

5. The curriculum should consist of community problems rather than traditional subject disciplines.

6. Community change comes through the development of common concerns rather than conflict between subgroups.

7. Public schools should educate adults rather than only children.

8. Teachers should be prepared to carry on this kind of education rather than traditional lecturing in subject areas.

The ideas of the "radical" educators of the seventies, as this list shows, are largely the revival of the ideas of the educational reformers of the twenties and thirties. Since these reforms hardly altered the educational mainstream of American high schools, we can assume that there may be some weaknesses in either the objectives, the ways used to attain them or both.

Consider the statements in that list. We agree, for example, that all life is educative (statement 1) and that participation is vital to education. But exposure to life is no simple guarantee of learning. It is not only the amount of experience but the understanding one brings to and derives from experience. The need for understanding conflict is, therefore, the major emphasis of this book.

The second statement, that education requires participation rather than mere spectator roles, is sound if two qualifications are added. First, participation should be cognitive and emotional as well as behavioral. Students returning to the school from fieldwork should not return to study divorced from their community experiences. They need to analyze their experience through discussion, reading, reporting and so on as well as planning the new activities.

The third statement fails to allow for different interests. Interests can be coordinated at the interpersonal level into group projects involving adults and children and differentiated in projects carried out by one group but not the other.

Not everything can or should be coordinated. To the extent that there is also differentiation and separation there must be conflict as well as cooperation. Kay (1969) points to the importance of interpersonal conflict for the students' moral education:

But on the whole schools do not approve of children whose moral control is personal. These can be awkward and difficult pupils since they tend perpetually to question the established system. They are critical of the quality of life inculcated by the school as an institution and invariably disapprove of the school regulations and general educational practice.

But is participation *required* (statement 2)? If so, required by whom? Statement 3 claims that adults and children have common purposes. But they also have opposed interests. Point 4 is that schools should improve the community and social order. But schools should also learn from and be changed by the community and social order. The curriculum should deal with community problems, as set forth in statement 5, but it should also relate the traditional disciplines to the community problems. We agree with the statement (number 7) that public schools should educate adults as well as children, that teachers should be trained to do more than to lecture.

The fundamental difference between their position and that taken in this book lies in statement 6, which asserts that there can be change and the development of common interests without group conflict. Incidents related in these pages have shown the ubiquity of school conflict. It has been shown how adults and students can use conflict to attain the goals embodied in Everett's list.

The students' anger with high school causes daily conflict. This anger has many sources. Some lie within students because their adolescence subjects them to the pulls and pushes inherent in making the transition from childhood to adulthood. Others lie in their interpersonal and institutional involvements.

Recent proposals for improving the high school have the intent of expanding options for teachers and students. They appear to be some or all of the options that we described as gourmet learning. But new options are not enough for enduring change in the school. The understanding and use of conflict make possible a flow of necessary change.

Conflict is inherent in choice. And choice, as well as conflict, seem to be connecting themes in gourmet learning, political socialization, emotional expression, interpersonal involvement, uses of time, and negotiation.

The multiplication of options leads to the multiplication of conflict if what we seek is individual as well as group commitment to choice and not its mere expansion. To develop one set of options inevitably involves the surrender of another set of choices. And soon the conflicts emerge—within individuals, between individuals and groups, and within the school and school system.

Conflict releases energy that can power renewal of the high school.

APPENDIX A

Paying
Attention CONDUCTING AND
ANALYZING INTERVIEWS ON CONFLICT

THE MODEL OF CONFLICT resolution described in Chapter 9 requires that each party to the conflict state the issues as seen from that party's own side. Statements of the issues are then compared in order to find out where they agree, where they disagree and where an issue addressed by one side is not even seen as an issue by another. The partisan statements are then transformed into a mutually acceptable statement of issues to be negotiated. The checklist below is intended to be used in transforming partisan statements into forms more suitable to the production of a mutually acceptable statement.

Paying attention to both student and adult views of school conflict is a two-step process. First, the conflict must be described (see Conflict Interview Form, Figure 1). Then the checklist can be used to summarize each written statement. If one party to the conflict cannot or will not write his statement in his own words, then the mediator can write it from that party's dictation. The statement should be read back in order to make sure that it represents the point of view of the party to the conflict rather than that of the mediator who wrote it out.

Using the checklist as a substitute for the conflict description could abort negotiation. Students and teachers could be repelled by the mechanical nature of the list format. They would certainly be denied the experience of expressing their views in all the living color of their feelings about the conflict. And without that expression of feelings, the statements become mere formal exercises, incapable of converting the anger aroused by conflict into energy for the creative resolution of that conflict. Figure 2 reproduces the checklist.

FIGURE 1:   CONFLICT INTERVIEW FORM*

Sometimes a group has trouble being as democratic as its members would like it to be. Sometimes a person is not sure what is the democratic thing to do. Other times it seems as if no one can change the way things are enough to make a democracy work in a place like a school or a town. When someone wants to do new things or do things in a new way, it can start a fuss. Please write about one time when something like this happened to you or you saw something like this happen in your group or your school.

C. Please reread what you wrote now and check to see that you have put in something about each topic below. As you find each item, check it off in the space below. Please add to your story any items you do not already have in it.

Where it happened	( )
Who started it	( )
Who else was there	( )
What problems came up	( )
How were the problems handled	( )
How else could the problems have been handled	( )

Now: we would like to know which of our names for problems in democratic behavior fits your story best. Please put number one (1) next to the name that fits best, number two (2) next to the name that fits second best, and so on.

Your story raised problem of:

Dissent	Criticizing, protesting, or refusing to take part in a group.	( )
Equality	Getting the same chances in life no matter what your race, religion, sex, or how well off your parents are.	( )
Decision-making	Having a voice in what rules should be made and how they should be enforced.	( )

* This is a shortened version of the form actually used. The first page consisted of the opening paragraphs ("Sometimes . . .") and lined space for the writer to describe the conflict. The second page consisted of entirely lined space. The third page consisted of everything below the first paragraph shown in the above form.

Due process	Giving a person who has been accused of something a fair chance to defend himself.	( )

FIGURE 2: SCHOOL CONFLICT CHECKLIST

	YES	NO
1. Does authoritarian decision-making extend survival teaching into the classroom by specifying:		
A. Amount of work to be done?	—	—
B. Selection of courses, materials, activities?	—	—
C. Order of courses or activities?	—	—
D. Evaluation and goal selection?	—	—
2. Is gourmet innovation encouraged in:		
A. New materials, activities and courses?	—	—
B. Learning outside the classroom?	—	—
C. Student prepared materials?	—	—
D. Creative solutions to conflicts?	—	—
3. Does the conflict involve the school as a democratic institution by raising issues of:		
A. Participation in decision-making?	—	—
B. Dissent, objecting, refusing to take part?	—	—
C. Equality of race, religion, sex, income?	—	—
D. Due process in charges stated, open hearing, advice of counsel and separation of judge from enforcer?	—	—
4. Is the anger of students expressed by:		
A. Talking?	—	—
B. Action? (Or refusal to listen?)	—	—
5. Is the anger of school adults expressed by:		
A. Talking?	—	—
B. Action? (Or refusal to listen?)	—	—
6. Does the action feature, as the first party (the "good guy"):		
A. "I": the writer himself or herself?	—	—
B. "We": the writer and his group?	—	—
C. "He" or "She": another individual?	—	—
D. "They": a group not including the writer?	—	—

	YES	NO
7. Does the action depict as the second party (the opposition):		
A. An individual student?	—	—
B. An individual school adult?	—	—
C. A student group?	—	—
D. An adult group?	—	—
8. Is the conflict described as:		
A. A series of separate events?	—	—
B. Ordered or numbered in time?	—	—
C. Ongoing with future consequences?	—	—
D. Related to clock and calendar time?	—	—
9. Does the writer state explicit alternatives for resolving the current situation?	—	—
10. Has negotiation proceeded as far as:		
A. All sides stating their positions?	—	—
B. All sides expressing their feelings?	—	—
C. Agreement on which issues to discuss?	—	—
D. Bargaining with each side giving something and getting something?	—	—

An example of the use of the checklist follows. The written statement is quite long and gives a full description of the writer's point of view. This is followed by a filled-out version of the checklist. Finally, a rationale for the way the checklist was filled out is given. Several shorter statements and the checklist analysis follow the long example.

One day a certain student was late for homeroom period at 3 o'clock because she had stayed after at the period before, which was Math, so the teacher could explain a certain problem which she had not understood. Now, upon arriving at the homeroom, the teacher was calling the role, but this student's name had been passed. There were other students whose names had been called before they got there. When finishing the role the teacher said "All those who got here after their name was called will stay after for one extra hour." The student who was late because she had to talk to the math teacher went up and told the teacher this. The teacher just replied by telling the student to sit down. The student had to stay after school for one hour extra until four o'clock.

Now as a result of this many of the students who had to stay
after such a petty thing were mad, but especially the student
who had a perfectly legitimate reason for being late. The students
had appointments to make and some had to get home right after
school to go home, etc. When the other students heard of this
incident they protested to the president of the student council.
(Now the problem comes. Can a student even though president
of the student council, go and question a teacher in authority?)
How was this solved? Well it wasn't for soon the incident
blew over and everything was back to normal. It could have been
solved by talking to the teacher or else talking to the principal,
who in turn could talk to the teacher. If I had been the teacher
I would have handled the situation in a completely different way.
First, I would have listened to all those who had excuses
for being late. Then decide if the reason was good enough.
Then dismiss the students who had perfectly legitimate reasons,
and then warn those who were late and didn't have an excuse
not to let it happen again. If the incident was then repeated,
I would find it necessary to punish the student who had no excuse
for being late a second time. However, I find very irresponsible
of the teacher. She wouldn't accept an excuse, and would not
excuse those who had things to do on that day, even if she required
them to stay after on another day. The teacher also harmed
herself by those actions. For example, the teacher now is generally
disliked throughout the school because now the students consider
her unfair. Her reputation is being ruined. I am sure that
the teacher has many good qualities in her that could make her
a well-liked figure about the school.

FIGURE 3: SCHOOL CONFLICT CHECKLIST

		YES	NO
1.	Does authoritarian decision-making extend survival teaching into the classroom by specifying:		
	A. Amount of work to be done?	—	—
	B. Selection of courses, materials, activities?	✓	—
	C. Order of courses or activities?	✓	—
	D. Evaluation and goal selection?	✓	—
2.	Is gourmet innovation encouraged in:		
	A. New materials, activities and courses?	—	✓
	B. Learning outside the classroom?	—	✓

	YES	NO
C. Student prepared materials?	—	—
D. Creative solutions to conflicts?	—	✓

3. Does the conflict involve the school as a democratic institution by raising issues of:

	YES	NO
A. Participation in decision-making?	✓	—
B. Dissent, objecting, refusing to take part?	—	—
C. Equality of race, religion, sex, income?	—	—
D. Due process in charges stated, open hearing, advice of counsel and separation of judge from enforcer?	✓	—

4. Is the anger of students expressed by:

	YES	NO
A. Talking?	✓	—
B. Action? (Or refusal to listen?)	—	—

5. Is the anger of school adults expressed by:

	YES	NO
A. Talking?		
B. Action? (Or refusal to listen?)	✓	—

6. Does the action feature, as the first party (the "good guy"):

	YES	NO
A. "I": the writer himself or herself?	—	—
B. "We": the writer and his group?	—	—
C. "He" or "She": another individual?	✓	—
D. "They": a group not including the writer?	—	—

7. Does the action depict as the second party (the opposition):

	YES	NO
A. An individual student?	—	—
B. An individual school adult?	✓	—
C. A student group?	—	—
D. An adult group?	—	—

8. Is the conflict described as:

	YES	NO
A. A series of separate events?	✓	—
B. Ordered or numbered in time?	✓	—
C. Ongoing with future consequences?	✓	—
D. Related to clock and calendar time?	✓	—

9. Does the writer state explicit alternatives for resolving the current situation?

	YES	NO
	✓	—

	YES	NO
10. Has negotiation proceeded as far as:		
A. All sides expressing their positions?	—	✓
B. All sides expressing their feelings?	—	✓
C. Agreement on which issues to discuss?	—	✓
D. Bargaining with each side giving something and getting something?	—	✓

The checklist is only a tool to use in the first stage of conflict resolution. When all parties to the conflict have expressed their views, the checklist is applied to each of their statements. The discrepancies between statements revealed by the checklists can become the starting points for negotiation between the parties.

The general pattern is to (1) include those items in the agenda to be negotiated which both parties agree are sources of conflict, (2) discuss placing on the agenda of negotiable issues those which at least one party checks as a source of conflict, and (3) eliminate all other items. This procedure simplifies the negotiations, mostly by excluding irrelevant issues. For example, if both sides agreed that item 1C about order of courses or activities represented an area of conflict, both would check "No" for 1C. Then the item would go on the bargaining agenda. If only one of the parties checked "No" for item 1C, it would be put on the list of items to discuss prior to bargaining in order to agree about whether it should be on the agenda for bargaining at all. If none of the parties checked "No" on this item, it would not enter into the negotiation.

The issues involving the school as a democratic institution can similarly be used in deciding the bargaining agenda. The items on expression of anger reflect the method to be used in negotiation more than substantive issues. By checking these items, the parties become aware of their feelings about what they have done and are doing by putting them into words. Only when they put the anger into words is it available for conflict resolution. As long as they are putting it into actions, they are avoiding negotiation. Each party may be able to become aware of their actions when they are confronted with the information on what the other party thinks they are doing.

The statement of the first party or "good guy" may match up for all parties, but it is more likely to be different for each of the parties to the conflict since they are each likely to see themselves as right and the other parties as wrong. Negotiations can often benefit from widening the scope of the parties to the conflict so that an individual teacher is not held responsible for the interests of all teachers or a specific student is not made into a scapegoat for all students.

The statement of time over which the conflict has been taking place allows the parties to the conflict to see whether they are actually dealing with the same issues. When it forces the party to specify his complaint, it helps reduce conflict to concrete, manageable proportions. It is obviously easier to solve a problem when one conceives of it in terms of, for example, yesterday's late slips rather than "what that teacher always does to me!"

As soon as the parties to a conflict are able to see all the alternative resolutions to that conflict, the preferred one can be selected. The statement of alternatives gives the parties a chance to bargain in a creative way. They may think up alternatives that everyone would prefer to the conflict situation. One party may find an alternative proposed by the other party is even better than its own original proposal. In other conflicts, the need to state alternatives may demonstrate to one or more parties that they do not prefer any alternatives to that provided in the status quo. In such conflicts, the mere lack of alternatives may avert further conflict by both parties realizing that they have nothing to gain by prolonging it.

The question on the stage of negotiation currently reached may enable the realistic setting of an agenda to take place. If the parties disagree on what stage the negotiation has reached, they can begin the negotiation by discussing which stage they are in and taking up the negotiation at the earliest stage any of the parties sees as unfinished.

APPENDIX B

Research
Summary

THE PURPOSE OF THIS appendix is to present a summary of the research upon which the book is based for those readers interested in its details. The appendix describes how the investigation was tied to the development of objectives for civic education for the seventies. It describes the research methodology (group interview), the overall findings, and the conclusions drawn from the findings. Finally it lists the goals and guidelines for civic education in American high schools.

This appendix is a summary of *Civic Education for the Seventies: An Alternative to Repression and Revolution* by De Cecco, Richards, *et al.*, and of subsequent research (1970-1973) in schools in the San Francisco Bay Area. The original research was supported by a $500,000 grant from the Bureau of Comprehensive and Vocational Education, United States Office of Education. The research in the metropolitan areas of New York, Philadelphia, and San Francisco constitutes the basis for the book.

The original research and development goal was to specify citizenship objectives in behavioral terms. These behavioral objectives were to be used in the development of civic educational materials for high school teachers and students. The first project document was *Civic Participation and Education in a Crisis Age.* The document summarized a large body of literature on contemporary American political institutions. A shorter version of that document appears in *Civic Education for the Seventies* (Chapter 1). Its major conclusion was:

[C]ivic education is the student's participation in the governance of the school and community. We believe that the new civic education will occur as we (adults) help young people transform vertical governance of the school and community into horizontal governance that shares decision-making with students, parents and teachers. . . . The civic education of high school students in the seventies should largely consist of their learning how to form partnerships with principals, teachers, and parents and taking more and more responsibility for their self-governance.

Methodology

The purpose of the original research was to discover how junior and senior high school students perceived the need to participate in school governance. To obtain these data we developed the interview form described in Appendix A. The form is a modification of the critical incident technique developed by Flanagan (Flanagan and Schmid, 1959). The students were asked to describe "dilemma incidents" they have experienced or observed which left them with two or more alternative ways of acting and in which the "democratic thing to do" was not immediately clear. Many preliminary versions of the form were tried out before we settled on this one.

The original data were collected from March 1 to May 15 in 1969. We collected 6,783 written interviews. The sample included urban and suburban elementary, junior high, and senior high school students, comprising an extensive mix of socioeconomic status, race, nationality, religion, and school entrance requirements. In the high schools, a whole class would be interviewed at one time, each member writing his own responses. In the elementary schools we used individual interviews. To insure student privacy no identifying data were collected. The data analysis is by schools only. The interviewers were college and first-year graduate students. They visited more than thirty suburban and urban schools. The protocols were coded by trained graduate students.

Of the total number of students interviewed, 317 (4.7%) refused to answer or returned blank interview forms. Students were urged but not required to participate. There were 953 students (14.05%) who wrote complaints, tirades, and so on. These were classified as non-incidents and were coded as far as possible. The total number of cases, therefore, varied from item to item as well as from code to code. The original codes and their relationship to later codes used for this book will now be described.

Political socialization codes

As explained in Chapter 1, students were asked to rank from 1 to 4 the four categories of political socialization, assigning a rank of 1 to the category that best applied. The adult coders independently assigned ranks to the same incidents. These codes were the civic choices of participation in decision-making and dissent and the civic statuses of equality and due process. The political socialization codes were derived from Alan Westin's theory of civic participation (De Cecco, 1969). The definitions for these codes as they appear on the Conflict Interview Form (Appendix A), were developed with the help of a panel of high school students, teachers, and administrators, who coded taped incidents. By adding these codes to the interview form the students could code their own incidents and use the interview as a learning situation. It also showed how closely the students' understanding of the political socialization codes approximated those of professional political scientists.

Content codes

The content codes, unlike the political socialization codes, were derived empirically from the data. Staff members read incident descriptions until there were no new categories derived from reading another hundred incidents. At that point about 2,000 incidents had been read. Forty-one categories were originally derived. For greater reliability in coding they were grouped into the following six categories: (1) issues relating to courses and curriculum; (2) political issues pertaining to political units larger than the school; (3) issues involving infractions of legal codes of units larger than the school; (4) issues involving aspects of school organization other than academic issues; (5) out-of-school social issues involving peers and adult society, but not in legal or political contexts; and (6) issues of individual rights involving authorities, mainly in school, or involving others outside of school but which became problems because they involved the school (e.g., parents' objecting to student's long hair because the school objected). Categories 4 and 6 were grouped together in the data analysis since those issues could be dealt with through school governance. These two content categories parallel the decision-making code in the political socialization codes. Categories 1 (courses and curriculum), 4 (school organization), and 6 (individual rights) are largely the basis for the chapter on survival teaching and learning.

Affect codes

The affect codes proved to be the most difficult to develop. For the original data analysis these codes were limited to two categories —tension level and satisfaction with outcome. The tension level was coded as raised or lowered by the way in which the conflict was handled. The outcome (the final termination or resolution of the conflict) was coded as satisfactory (good) or unsatisfactory (bad).

In subsequent data analyses (1970-1971) we used categories derived from Davitz (1969) and Wiener and Mehrabian (1968). We developed six affect categories: (1) global satisfaction—a Nirvana state; (2) specific satisfaction—an active involvement with specific achievement; (3) global anger and rage; (4) specific anger—an active involvement in specific issues; (5) global apathy—an avoidance of all conflict; and (6) specific apathy—the avoidance of specific conflicts. Although these codes proved to be useful and reliable, we had only intuitive notions of how they interrelated and how they explained specific failures and successes in negotiations.

With the application of these six affect codes it became clear that the central emotional issue of conflicts is how the parties handled their anger. We then turned to psychoanalytic theory which distinguished the effects on behavior of anger that is directly and verbally expressed and anger that is left unverbalized. In the latter case the unverbalized anger is displaced on to issues and parties not central to the conflict. Such displacements of anger made negotiation difficult or impossible because parties engaged in acts of violence, coercion, and avoidance that greatly impeded the joining of issues by all parties. Since psychoanalytic theory tied emotional states to negotiating and non-negotiating behavior, we found it the most useful affective analysis.

Decentering codes

These codes were derived from theories of child and adolescent development, particularly those of Piaget and Inhelder. There were two sets of decentering codes: (1) those dealing with how the writer of the incident viewed his relationship with the parties to conflict, and (2) those dealing with perceived alternatives to handling the conflict. The decentering codes were based on the writer's choice of pronouns in describing the conflict. Also the writer could choose different pronouns to describe the two parties to the conflict.

We distinguished various dimensions of decentering: coordination and distance. The operational definition of coordination was group size. As for group size, the writer could describe either party as an individual or a group. If the writer used "I," "she," "it," or "he," we said he was describing an individual. If he used "we" or "they," we said he was describing a group. For distance, the writer's use of "I" or "we" was less distant than his use of "she," "he," or "it." Finally, for relative status, the writer could depict his conflict as occurring between parties of equal or peer status or unequal or adult status.

The operational definitions of distance for the first party were as follows: (1) if the writer used "I" or "we" to describe the first party, this indicated less distance than if the writer used "she," "he," "it," or "they," and (2) if the writer described the second party to be of equal or similar status, then we said that there was less distance. We used "near" to describe conflicts between peers (e.g., two teachers, two subjects, two groups of subjects, and so on). We used the word "far" to describe parties on different status levels. Distance was equated with relative status for the second party while it was equated with the writer's own participation for the first party. In this book we have emphasized the process of differentiation that results in distance.

The second set of decentering codes dealt with alternative conflict resolutions. The codes distinguished between conflict descriptions that provided *no* alternatives and those that provided *one or more* alternatives. The codes also distinguished between alternatives that were based on expediency, conviction, or competing convictions. Cases in which there was a choice between a conviction and expedient act were combined with cases in which the choice was between competing convictions. The alternative resolution codes were based on psychological theory and moral philosophy. To make choices one must perceive alternatives. According to Piagetian theory of moral development, convictions or ideals become more influential in shaping choices as people mature.

Conflict resolution codes

The original codes distinguished between coercive and non-coercive methods for terminating or resolving conflict. The coercive methods included decision by authority and the use of physical assault or physical restraint. The non-coercive methods involved negotiation: direct negotiation, mediation, and arbitration. The original resolution codes were not mutually exclusive. The same incident could be coded as many times as necessary to determine all methods attempted. Voting, petition, and verbal threats were considered non-coercive methods.

Few methods of conflict resolution occurred often enough to warrant detailed analysis. Decision by authority was the method used most often to terminate conflict. Negotiation was used to describe any attempt at resolution by talking with the other parties involved in the conflict. This definition of negotiation was less precise than the later one. Decision by authority, however, was strictly defined to refer only to those cases in which the conflict was terminated by official decision.

In the present book, coercive methods for dealing with conflict are dealt with in Chapter 6. That chapter now includes physical assault, physical restraint, verbal threat, and institutional force (as in the use of suspension and expulsion). This new classification enabled us to distinguish between essentially verbal and non-verbal expressions of anger.

Data analysis

For determining reliability, 193 interviews were randomly selected. They were coded by a different coder and the codings were compared. Inter-rater reliabilities are shown in Table 1. All the categories shown were judged to be reliable enough to warrant further data interpretation. The data are shown as frequencies and percentages. The Chi-square statistic was used to determine significance levels. A summary of findings now follows.

TABLE 1: INTER-RATER RELIABILITY

VARIABLE	AGREE	PERCENT	R	TOTAL
Incident—Non-incident	156	80.82	.656	193
Content I[1]	149	77.20	.593	193
Content I[2]	168	87.04	.757	193
Content I[3]	176	91.19	.828	193
Interpersonal Involvement[4]	141	73.05	.533	193
Interpersonal Involvement[5]	146	75.65	.578	193
Person vs. Institution[6]	141	73.05	.533	193
Person vs. Institution[7]	146	75.65	.578	193
Peer vs. Authority	148	76.68	.593	193
Alternatives	148	76.68	.593	193
Conviction vs. Expediency	140	72.53	.533	193
Resolution Process I[8]	140	72.53	.533	193
Negotiation	145	75.12	.562	193
Violence from Peers	176	91.19	.828	193
Violence from Subordinates	181	93.78	.884	193
Violence from Authorities	167	86.52	.757	193
Decision by Authority	136	70.46	.490	193
Formal Vote—Elections	187	96.89	.941	193
Mediation	189	97.92	.960	193
Arbitration	178	92.22	.846	193
Verbal Threats	165	85.49	.722	193
Petitions	170	88.08	.774	193
Affect Outcome[9]	136	70.46	.490	193
Affect Outcome[10]	153	79.27	.624	193
Tension Level[11]	147	76.16	.578	193

Except as noted below, reliability was figured on a one-to-one basis.

[1] Content I: 1-2-3-5 vs. 4-4.
[2] Content I: 2 vs. all (political issues vs. other).
[3] Content I: 5 vs. all (out-of-school social issues vs. other).
[4] Interpersonal Involvement: 1-2 vs. 3-4 (I-We vs. He-They).
[5] Interpersonal Involvement: 1-3 vs. 2-4 (I-He vs. We-They).
[6] Person vs. Institution: 1 vs. all (individual adversary vs. plural adversary).
[7] Person vs. Institution: 4 vs. all (institutional adversary vs. non-institutional).
[8] Resolution Process I: 1 vs. all (complete participation vs. partial or none).
[9] Affect Outcome: 1 vs. all (bad vs. good, mixed, and unclear).
[10] Affect Outcome: 2 vs. all (good vs. bad, mixed, and unclear).
[11] Tension Level: 2 vs. all (lowered vs. raised, unchanged, unclear).

Results

Political socialization categories

Tables 2 and 3 show how the theoretical categories of political socialization fit the experience of high school students. The tables constitute a macroscopic overall view and a microscopic school by school view of the same four political socialization categories for a few representative schools. Tables 2 and 3 contain percentages inflated by students who ranked more than one category as the best title for their incident. In Table 2, the number of incidents ranked is given next to each percentage rather than frequency within ranking. The reader can compute frequencies if desired from the numbers and percentages displayed here. In addition, Tables 2 and 3 both require careful reading because the percentages add up to 200% rather than 100%. This is due to our having combined categories ranked *either* first or second.

The outstanding finding is that participation in decision-making is the category most frequently ranked first as the title for the conflict. This is true in the overall totals, for every level of school, for both urban and suburban schools and for both graduate student coders and the high school students ranking the titles for their own incidents. The lack of systematic difference between students' own ranking of titles for their incidents and coders' ranking for the same incidents is notable.

TABLE 2: POLITICAL SOCIALIZATION CATEGORIES OF IN-
         CIDENTS AS RANKED 1 OR 2 BY STUDENTS AND
         CODERS

	GRADUATE STUDENT CODERS		HIGH SCHOOL STUDENTS	
	PERCENT	NUMBER RANKED	PERCENT	NUMBER RANKED
Dissent	49.29	6,463	48.91	5,278
Equality	43.10	6,459	45.37	5,216
Decision-making	68.47	6,460	69.55	5,417
Due Process	39.33	6,454	47.09	5,251

TABLE 3:   CROSS SECTIONAL COMPARISON OF POLITICAL
SOCIALIZATION CATEGORIES RANKED 1 OR 2 BY
STUDENTS AND CODERS

SCHOOLS	TOTAL INTER-VIEWED		DISSENT %	EQUALITY %	DECISION-MAKING %	DUE PROCESS %	CHI-SQUARE (BETWEEN STUDENT & CODER RANKINGS)
City H.S.	353	S	57.76	53.77	65.57	39.33	
I		C	62.34	44.62	65.29	28.16	
							43.87
City J.H.S.	454	S	46.34	48.73	61.76	53.04	
I		C	43.99	51.40	63.36	39.91	
							6.67
City Grade	105	S	49.47	43.62	54.74	54.26	
School		C	30.39	49.51	80.58	49.59	
							12.03
Suburb H.S.	1,311	S	56.43	31.56	83.09	47.51	
I		C	59.33	31.05	72.89	36.98	
							18.75
Suburb J.H.S.	616	S	41.63	43.56	61.52	62.06	
I		C	37.21	45.18	58.04	59.63	
							1.32
Suburb H.S.	333	S	46.80	44.10	81.40	33.80	
II		C	56.00	34.15	76.10	32.61	
							6.92
Suburb J.H.S.	471	S	52.50	38.80	67.90	40.30	
II		C	47.80	37.40	75.20	38.90	
							3.27
City H.S.	166	S	54.61	55.79	76.87	29.01	
II		C	60.87	49.04	60.81	25.32	
							5.174
City J.H.S.	95	S	63.41	51.85	74.75	22.00	
II		C	70.00	44.44	66.67	25.00	
							1.810

S = Student ranking   C = Coder ranking
Chi-square of 7.815 required for significance at $p = .05$ level.

Content codes

Taken together, non-academic school issues and individual rights accounted for over half the problems in democracy reported by students. As can be seen in Table 4, non-academic school issues alone were 26.97% of the overall sample; individual rights issues were 24.88% More than half (51.85%) of all the issues raised by the students were issues of school governance.

TABLE 4:   CONTENT CODES: CONTENT OF INCIDENTS
DESCRIBED BY STUDENTS

CONTENT CATEGORY	PERCENT STUDENTS	NUMBER OF STUDENTS
Courses and Curriculum	12.79	843
Political Issues	6.47	440
Illegal Acts	10.23	696
Non-Academic School Issues	26.97	1,831
Out-of-School Social Issues	10.24	697
Individual Rights	24.88	1,690
Total*	91.58	6,197

* Total possible 100%. Non-incidents and unclassified incidents plus refusals account for remaining 8.42%.

Decentering codes

SELF, OTHER: As can be seen in Table 5, most students (61.32%) were concerned with their own, rather than other's problems. Only 30.98% of the incidents were described as having "other" second parties, "he" or "they."

TABLE 5:   DECENTERING CODES: FIRST PARTY TO
THE CONFLICT (THE GOOD GUYS)

			PERCENT	NUMBER
(Undifferentiated)	Self:	I and We	61.32	4,160
(Differentiated)	Other:	He and They	30.98	2,102
			92.30	6,262
(Uncoordinated)	Individual:	I and He	45.68	3,099
(Coordinated)	Group:	We and They	46.62	3,163
			92.30	6,262

GROUP SIZE: In the overall sample (Table 5), about the same percentage of students wrote incidents in terms of "I" or "he" as in terms of "we" or "they." Students described issues as involving individual protagonists equally as often as group protagonists and, clearly, political issues were still seen as personal and individual by high school students.

RELATIVE STATUS: As seen in Table 6, in the overall sample most incidents described conflict with authority (67.65%) rather than peers (19.47%). Thus, students' concept of the democratic process involves inequities in status.

PERSONIFICATION: In the overall sample (Table 6), more incidents were reported as conflict with persons (45.65%) than as conflict with institutions (23.45%). Thus, adolescents may be moving toward an impersonal, abstract view of social conflict, but they do not see all their conflicts *sub specie aeternis* by the high school years.

TABLE 6:   DECENTERING CODES: SECOND PARTY TO THE CONFLICT (THE BAD GUYS)

		PERCENT	NUMBER
Distance:	Peer (Undifferentiated)	19.47	1,319
	Authority (Differentiated)	67.65	4,589
		87.12	5,908
Group Size:	Person (Uncoordinated)	45.65	3,097
	Institution (Coordinated)	23.45	1,591
		69.10	4,688

Alternatives and convictions

ALTERNATIVES: In the overall sample (Table 7) only 18.22% of the incidents included descriptions of alternatives to the protagonist's actions in events as they actually occurred. Most students felt, or at least wrote as if they felt, relatively powerless, constrained and limited by the events they experienced. More than four-fifths of the students were either unable or unwilling to articulate their choices.

Table 7: ALTERNATIVES, CONVICTIONS AND EXPEDIENCY

		PERCENT	NUMBER
Original Sample:			
One or more alternatives*		18.22	1,236
No alternative		81.77	5,547
	Total	99.99	6,783
Convictions		79.87	1,024
Expediency only		20.12	258
	Total	99.99	1,282
Suburban High School:			
One or more alternatives		2.77	2
No alternatives		97.22	70
	Total	99.99	72

* A suggestion made by Professor Mark Chesler that the paucity of alternatives in our data may have been due to inadequate probing was tested by giving 72 students at a suburban high school a version of the questionnaire with a separate page on which to write an alternative and clear instructions to do that. The results are displayed above. They clearly show that the students were not misunderstanding the intent of the question, but were *unable* to describe an alternative either because there were none or the students could not articulate them.

CONVICTIONS: Since convictions (Table 7) could only be mentioned as affecting choices in those incidents in which a choice was articulated, few (1,024) incidents were analyzed for the presence or absence of conviction in the alternatives considered. Still, almost four-fifths (79.87%) of those incidents in which a choice was discussed *did* mention convictions as a factor in that choice. This finding indicates that awareness of alternatives goes along with a relatively high level of moral development.

Conflict resolution

NEGOTIATION: As a means of conflict resolution, negotiation (Table 8) was mentioned in only 16.60% of the incidents in the overall sample. By contrast, resolution by authority decision was mentioned in 55.32% of the incidents. Most of the students in our sample defined "problem in democracy" in terms of conflicts decided by unilateral decisions of authorities.

TABLE 8:   CONFLICT RESOLUTION: NEGOTIATION vs. DECISION BY AUTHORITY

	PERCENT	NUMBER
Negotiation	16.60	1,126
Decision by Authority	55.32	3,753
Total	71.92	4,879

DECISION-MAKING: As can be seen in the overall results in Table 8, few modes of conflict resolution by negotiation occurred often enough in the incidents described to warrant detailed analysis.

USE OF FORCE: In the overall sample (Table 9), 18.92% of the incidents involved use of force. This may be seen as a small percentage since less than one-fifth of the incidents led to use of force. On the other hand, one may not wish to condone use of force in the resolution of almost one-fifth of the conflicts experienced by high school students. One may contrast use of force among peers (5.54%) with use by authorities (10.55%). Use of force from subordinates against authorities was mentioned in 2.83% of the incidents in the overall sample. Evidently, students either refrained from use of force against authorities more often than they refrained from use of force against their peers *or* avoided mentioning or even being aware of such actions. In either case, students seemed to have been aware that use of force against authorities was inappropriate. By contrast, use of force by authorities was mentioned in 10.55% of the incidents. Students perceived (whether or not it actually was so, or would be so reported by authorities) that authorities used force almost five times as often against them as they used it against authorities. Students reported adults using relatively more force and less negotiation than they themselves used.

TABLE 9: CONFLICT RESOLUTION: USE OF FORCE

	PERCENT	NUMBER
By Peers	5.54	376
By Subordinates°	2.83	192
By Authorities	10.55	716
Total Violence	18.92	1,284

° Includes any use of force by students against teachers, principals, etc.

Affect categories

OUTCOME: As shown in Table 10, the outcome of 61.46% of the incidents in the overall sample was evaluated as bad; of a mere 9.25% as good. Overwhelmingly, problems in democracy are seen as having outcomes that are unsatisfying. If people tend to avoid situations found unpleasant in the past, it might be expected that they would be "turned off" by their political experiences in the schools more than educators would want them to be.

TABLE 10: OUTCOME AND TENSION LEVEL

		PERCENT	NUMBER
Outcome:	Bad	61.46	4,169
	Good	9.25	628
Tension Level:	Lowered	9.14	620
	Not lowered	90.86	6,163

TENSION LEVEL: The tension level (Table 10) was reported as lowered in so small a percentage of incidents (9.14%) that few conflicts reported can be presumed to have decreased the potential for violence in future conflicts. Indeed, the outlook for de-escalation of affect and the use of reason in future conflicts is bleak. Modes of conflict resolution used in these schools in 1969 were not conducive to learning how to resolve conflicts in a way that would be satisfying to the participants.

Conclusions

In evaluating our results, it must be kept in mind that the schools do *not* constitute a random sample of all schools in the country.

Data from individual schools have been analyzed separately for those schools selected as representative of particular types. For example, evidence from the tables in the urban-suburban comparison suggests that a particular junior high school may be representative of suburban junior high schools in communities with mixed socioeconomic status. Therefore, a junior high school in a similar community may be especially interested in the data from this school and may find it far more useful to look at this in detail than to use the general sample to try to draw conclusions about its own situation.

Our data suggest the following:

1. The majority of high school students see "dilemma in democracy" as referring to a situation in which they cannot cope with an experience of injustice. In other words, they see themselves as relatively powerless.

2. More incidents described by students as dilemmas in democracy involved decision-making than due process, equality or dissent. The latter three categories were used to label approximately equal percentages of incidents, while decision-making was the label chosen for many more incidents than any of the other three alternatives.

3. Many incidents involved allegations of arbitrary behavior on the part of teachers. Relatively few incidents reflected concerns with political units larger than the school. Since few conflicts involved questions of professional expertise, the content codes suggest that many school conflicts *are* negotiable.

4. Many incidents were reported in personal terms, fewer in terms of other persons. Many involved interpersonal conflict between individuals, many more between an individual and the school as an institution.

5. The vast majority of incidents described no alternative courses of action for the writer or second party. There was a great sense of helplessness, of having been forced into actions rather than having chosen to act. Insofar as this reflects a real lack of choice, it indicates that choices must be made available if students are to have experience in making social and political decisions. Where alternatives are available but the students are either unable to perceive or unable to articulate them, this may indicate a need for getting students to articulate their alternatives so that their decisions are both rational and communicable. Since many convictions were mentioned as

factors in making choices, moral-value-governed behavior may be fostered by encouraging students to articulate choices.

6. Those incidents described as resolved were most often described as resolved by unilateral decision—rarely was a situation described in which there was a resolution achieved with the participation of more than one person. Schools are seen as a model of force and violence. This must change so that students become aware that negotiation and not violence is the democratic means of resolving conflicts approved by the adults in our society.

7. Dissatisfaction and raised tension levels resulting from incidents were almost universal.

Objectives

The objectives of the 1970 study were presented as a manual of objectives and guidelines for high school civic education. These objectives and guidelines are listed below:

1. The democratic citizen participates in the decision-making processes of his society.

2. The citizen makes use of alternative courses of action. If he finds no viable options open, he creates new alternatives for democratic action.

3. The citizen analyzes courses of action for their democratic bases, feasibility, and anticipated and actual consequences.

4. The citizen employs negotiation, mediation, and arbitration in resolving conflicts.

5. The citizen understands and analyzes issues from more viewpoints than his own.

6. The citizen sees democratic issues in the problems of others as well as in his own problems.

7. The citizen recognizes the value and utilizes the power of group action.

8. The citizen distinguishes personal issues and conflicts from institutional issues and conflicts, and handles them accordingly.

9. The citizen grasps and acts on the democratic principles involved in particular conflicts.

10. The citizen can exemplify democratic principles by relating relevant conflicts.

Guidelines (Based on Comparisons of Junior and Senior High School Students)

1. Junior high school students' problems are focused more on the students themselves than are those of senior high school students.

2. Senior high school students are more concerned with group problems than junior high students, and the latter are more involved with the conflicts of individuals.

3. Junior high students have more conflicts with their peers than do high school students, while the latter report more conflicts with authority figures than do the former.

4. Problems with institutions occur much more frequently in the senior than in the junior high school, while problems with persons are more common in the latter than the former.

5. High school students have a more highly developed abstractive capacity than do junior high students.

A Guide to the Content of Civic Education

The study pointed up some of the more pressing areas of student interest. It is true, of course, that the interests of students are not the same in all schools and are continually changing within a school, and for this reason no fixed course content can ever be devised for a civic curriculum. The interview and analysis procedures described in Appendix A can be used on a regular basis in schools to determine changes that can be made in the content of the civic education curriculum. The issues presented here are those students wrote about in 1969. This part of Appendix B, therefore, is intended to provide clues to the type of student interests the teacher can expect to encounter, rather than a prescription of what to teach.

The content issues were divided into six categories: courses and curriculum, political issues, illegal acts, non-academic school issues, out-of-school social issues, and individual rights. Of these groupings, two accounted for the majority of the incidents reported: non-academic school issues and individual rights. All other incidents were divided about evenly among the other categories, except that "political issues" contained significantly fewer incidents than the other groups.

Predominant non-academic school issues are: the school calendar, attendance regulations, both non-verbal and verbal misbehavior, school government, and racial and ethnic conflict in school. The most significant "individual rights" issues are: teacher favoritism, dress and appearance, the expression of opinions, and parental freedom. All of these issues are concrete and immediate; they directly affect the students' lives.

This is true of all categories except "political issues." "Courses and curriculum" includes incidents dealing with choice of courses, grades, exams, admission requirements, and teaching methods. The category of "illegal acts" embraces incidents involving loitering, smoking, thievery and drugs. "Out of school social issues" involve peer quarrels, social clubs, and racial and ethnic conflict. All these types of incidents are to be found in the daily lives of the students. Only concern with "political issues" requires abstracting to a wider field of interest.

The results of the content analysis, therefore, mesh with the approach of the objectives themselves. If the goal of civic education is to develop civic participants, the content of the curriculum must consist of the issues in which citizens wish to participate. These issues are predominantly the concrete problems students face in their daily lives.

Table 11 includes all the issues used in the coding and the percentages of each.

TABLE 11:   CONTENT ANALYSIS

I. Courses and Curriculum....12.79%
    Black studies
    Courses
    Grades
    Exams
    Teaching methods
    Admission requirements

II. Political Issues.....................6.47%
     Pledge
     War and political issues
     Political speakers
     In-school demonstrations
     Out-of-school demonstra-
       tions

III. Illegal Acts..........................10.23%
      Drinking
      Thievery
      Loitering
      Disruptions
      Drugs
      Smoking
      Harassment

IV. Non-Academic School
     Issues 26.97%
     Racial, ethnic conflict
       in school

School calendar
Attendance
Extra-curricular school
  events
Verbal misbehavior
Non-verbal misbehavior
Food
School government
Police

V. Out-of-School Social
    Issues 10.24%
    Social clubs
    Community projects
    Jobs
    Racial or ethnic conflicts
    Peer quarrels

VI. Individual Rights...............24.88%
     Privacy
     Teacher favoritism
     Right to leave class
     Freedom of movement
     Appearance
     Parental freedom
     Expression of opinions
     Use of school facilities

Not-Classifiable 8.42%

References

Adler, N. and C. H. Harrington, *The Learning of Political Behavior*. Glenview, Ill.: Scott, Foresman, 1970.

Aries, P., *Centuries of Childhood: A Social History of Family Life*. New York: Vintage Books, 1965.

Arlow, J. A. and C. Brenner, *Psychoanalytic Concepts and the Structural Theory*. Journal of the American Psychoanalytic Association Monograph Series Number Three. New York: International Universities Press, 1964.

Barnett, J., "Dependency Conflicts in Young Adults," *Psychoanalytic Review*, 1971, 58, 111-125.

Bellack, A., "What Shall the High School Teach?" *1956 Yearbook*, Association for Curriculum Development. Washington, D.C.: National Education Association, 1956, p. 103.

Berlyne, D. E., *Conflict, Arousal, and Curiosity*. New York, McGraw-Hill, 1960.

Bettleheim, B., *Love Is Not Enough*. Chicago: The Free Press, 1950.

Blake, R. R. and J. S. Mouton, "The Fifth Amendment," *Journal of Applied Behavioral Science*, 1970, 6, 413-426.

Blos, P., *On Adolescence: A Psychoanalytic Interpretation*. New York: The Free Press, 1962.

Brown, R., *Social Psychology*. New York: The Free Press, 1965.

Bruner, J. S., *Toward a Theory of Instruction*. Cambridge, Mass.: Harvard University Press, 1966.

Bruner, J. S., J. J. Goodnow and G. A. Austin, *A Study of Thinking*. New York: John Wiley & Sons, 1956.

Chesler, M. and J. F. BenDor, "Crisis Intervention in School Conflict," in *Regeneration of the School*, ed. J. De Cecco. New York: Holt, Rinehart & Winston, 1972, pp. 490-500.

Coleman, J. B., "Education in the Age of Computers and Mass Communication," in *Computers, Communication and the Public Interest,* ed. M. Greenberger. Baltimore: The Johns Hopkins University Press, 1971.

Coser, L., *The Functions of Social Conflict.* Chicago: The Free Press, 1956.

Davitz, J. R., *The Language of Emotions.* New York: Academic Press, 1969.

De Cecco, J. P., *Civic Participation and Education in a Crisis Age.* New York: Teachers College, Columbia University, 1969. ERIC No. ED-043-554.

De Cecco, J. P., "Attitude Change in the Classroom," *Encyclopedia of Education.* New York: Macmillan, 1971, 1, 396-402.

De Cecco, J. P., A. K. Richards, *et al., Civic Education for the Seventies: An Alternative to Repression and Revolution.* New York: Teachers College, Columbia University, 1970. ERIC No. ED-041-810.

De Rivera, A., "On Desegregating Stuyvesant High," in *Sisterhood Is Powerful,* ed. R. Morgan. New York: Vintage Books, 1970, p. 370.

Deutsch, M., "Conflicts: Productive and Destructive," *The Journal of Social Issues,* 1969, 25, 7-41.

Dewey, J., Democracy and Education. New York: Macmillan, 1916.

Dworkin, R., "The Jurisprudence of Richard Nixon," *The New York Review,* May 4, 1972, pp. 27-35.

Erikson, E. H., *Identity, Youth and Crisis.* New York: W. W. Norton, 1968.

Esman, A. H., "Adolescence and the Consolidation of Values," in *Moral Values and the Superego Concept in Psychoanalysis.* New York: International Universities Press, 1972, pp. 87-100.

Everett, S., *et al., The Community School.* New York: D. Appleton-Century Company, 1938.

Fantini, M. and G. Weinstein, *The Disadvantaged.* New York: Harper & Row, 1968.

Feshbach, S., "Aggression," in *Carmichael's Manual of Child Psychology,* ed. P. H. Mussen. New York: John Wiley & Sons, 1970 (3rd edition), 2, 261-360.

Flanagan, J. and F. W. Schmid, "The Critical Incident Technique in Psychopathology," *Journal of Clinical Psychology,* 1959, 15, 136-139.

Frank, A. D., "Conflict in the Classroom," in *Conflict Resolution Through Communication,* ed. F. E. Jandt. New York: Harper & Row, 1973, pp. 240-309.

Freud, S., "The Interpretation of Dreams" (1900), *Standard Edition of the Complete Psychological Works of Sigmund Freud.* London: Hogarth Press, 4.

Freud, S, "A Case of Hysteria, Three Essays on Sexuality and Other Works" (1901-1905), *Standard Edition of the Complete Psychological Works of Sigmund Freud*. London: Hogarth Press, 7, 119.

Friedenberg, E. Z., *Coming of Age in America*. New York: Random House, 1963.

Getzels, J. W. and P. W. Jackson, *Creativity and Intelligence*. New York: John Wiley & Sons, 1962.

Glasser, G., *Schools Without Failure*. New York: Harper & Row, 1969.

Goodman, P., *Growing Up Absurd*. New York: Random House, 1960.

Guskin, A., *High Schools in Crisis*. Ann Arbor: Community Resources Limited, 1971.

Hacker, F. J., "Sublimation Revisited," *International Journal of Psychoanalysis*, 1972, 53, 221-219.

Havighurst, R. J., "An Educator Looks at Education and Responsible Behavior," in *Approaches to Education for Character*, eds. C. H. Faust and J. Geingold. New York: Columbia University Press, 1969, p. 103.

Herndon, J., *The Way It Spozed To Be*. New York: Simon & Schuster, 1968.

Herndon, J., *How to Survive in Your Native Land*. New York: Simon & Schuster, 1971.

Hess, R. D. and J. V. Torney, *The Development of Political Attitudes in Children*. Chicago: Aldine, 1967.

Hudson, L., *Contrary Imagination*. Middlesex, England: Penguin Books, 1966.

Illich, I., *Deschooling Society*. New York: Harper & Row, 1971.

Inhelder, B. and J. Piaget, *The Growth of Logical Thinking From Childhood to Adolescence: An Essay on the Construction of Formal Operational Structures*. New York: Basic Books, 1958.

Jacobson, E., "Adolescent Minds and the Remodeling of the Psychic Structures in Adolescence," *The Psychoanalytic Study of the Child*. New York: International Universities Press, 1961, pp. 164-186.

Jones, H. E., *Development in Adolescence*. New York: Appleton-Century, 1943.

Josselyn, I. M., *The Adolescent and His World*. New York: Family Service Association of America, 1952.

Kagan, J. and N. Kogan, "Individual Variation in Cognitive Processes," in *Carmichael's Manual of Child Psychology*, ed. P. Mussen. New York: John Wiley & Sons, 1970.

Kane, M. B., *Minorities in Education*, Chicago: Quadrangle Books, 1970.

Katz, M. L., "Attitudinal Modernity, Classroom Power, and Status Characteristics An Investigation." Paper read at American Educational Research Association annual meeting, Chicago, April 5, 1972.

Kay, A. W., *Moral Development: A Psychological Study of Moral Growth from Childhood to Adolescence.* New York: Schocken Books, 1969.

Keniston, K., *Young Radicals.* New York: Harcourt, Brace & World, 1968.

Kohlberg, L., "Moral Education in the Schools: A Developmental View," *The School Review,* 1966, 74, 1-30.

Ladd, E., "Civil Liberties for Students—At What Age?" Paper delivered at First Annual Study Conference in School Psychology, Philadelphia, Temple University, June 22, 1972.

Lelyveld, J., "Where 78% of the People are 'Others'," in *Prejudice and Race Relations,* ed. R. W. Mack. Chicago: Quadrangle Books, 1970, p. 85.

Levi-Strauss, C., *Raw and the Cooked: Introduction to a Science of Mythology.* New York: Harper & Row, 1969, Vol. 1.

Lewin, K., "The Field Theory Approach to Adolescence," *American Journal of Sociology,* 1939, 44, 868-897.

Lowenfeld, H. and Y. Lowenfeld, "Our Permissive Society and the Superego: Some Current Thoughts about Freud's Cultural Concepts," in *Moral Values and the Superego Concept in Psychoanalysis.* New York: International Universities Press, Inc., 1972, pp. 375-397.

Mack, R. W. and R. C. Snyder, "The Analysis of Social Conflict: Toward an Overview and Synthesis," *Journal of Conflict Resolution,* 1957, 1, 212-248.

Marcuse, H., *Eros and Civilization: A Philosophical Inquiry into Freud.* New York: Vintage Books, 1962.

Meerloo, J. A. M., "The Time Sense in Psychiatry," in *The Voices of Time,* ed. J. T. Fraser. New York: George Braziller, 1966, pp. 235-252.

Meltzer, H., *Children's Social Concepts: A Study of Their Nature and Development.* New York: Teachers College, Columbia University, 1925.

Mill, J. S., *On Liberty.* In E. A. Burtt, ed., *The English Philosophers from Bacon to Mill.* New York: Modern Library, 1939, p. 998.

New York Times, March 19, 1972, p. 58.

Oliver, D. W. and J. P. Shaver, *Teaching Public Issues in the High School.* Boston: Houghton Mifflin, 1966.

Piaget, J., *Science of Education and the Psychology of the Child.* New York: Viking Press, 1969.

Piaget, J. and B. Inhelder, *The Psychology of the Child.* New York: Basic Books, 1969.

Prescott, P. S., *A World of Our Own: Notes on Life and Learning in a Boys' Preparatory School.* New York: Coward, McCann & Geoghegan, 1970, p. 103.

Pruitt, D. G. and D. F. Johnson, "Mediation as an Aid to Face-Saving in Negotiation," *Journal of Personality and Social Psychology,* 1970, 14, 239-246.

Rangell, L., "The Decision-Making Process: A Contribution from Psychoanalysis," in *The Psychoanalytic Study of the Child.* New York: Quadrangle Books, 1971, 26, 425-452.

"Redstockings Manifesto," in *Sisterhood Is Powerful,* ed. R. Morgan. New York: Vintage Books, 1970, pp. 533-535.

Reitman, A., J. Follman and E. Ladd, *Corporal Punishment in the Public Schools: The Use of Force in Controlling Student Behavior.* New York: A.C.L.U., 1972.

Rice, A. K., "Individual, Group, and Intergroup Process," *Human Relations,* 1969, 22, 565-584.

Rustin, B., "A Way Out of the Exploding Ghetto," in *Prejudice and Race Relations,* ed. R. W. Mack. Chicago: Quadrangle Books, 1970, p. 261.

Sebald, H., *Adolescence: A Sociological Analysis.* New York: Appleton-Century-Crofts, 1968.

Silberman, C. E., *Crisis in the Classroom: The Remaking of American Education.* New York: Random House, 1970.

Skinner, B. F., *Beyond Freedom and Dignity.* New York: Knopf, 1971.

Soreno, K. K. and C. D. Mortenson, "The Effects of Ego-Involved Attitudes on Conflict Negotiation Dyada," *Speech Monographs,* 1969, 36, 8-12.

Underwood, B., "Verbal Learning and the Educative Process," *Harvard Educational Review,* 1959, 29, 107-117.

Westin, A., Civic Participation in Current Dilemmas of American Society: A Background for Considering Possible Reforms in the Civic Education Process for the 1970's. Columbia University, Center for Research and Education in American Liberties, 1968, *in mimeo.* Summarized in J. P. De Cecco, *Civic Participation and Education in a Crisis Age,* pp. 62-69 (listed above).

Wiener, M. and A. Mehrabian, *Language Within Language: Immediacy, a Channel in Verbal Communication.* New York: Appleton-Century-Crofts, 1968.

Wolfson, B. J. and S. Nash, "Perceptions of Decision-Making in Elementary-School Classrooms," *The Elementary School Journal,* 1968, 69, 89-93.

Zigler, H., *The Political World of the High School Teacher.* Eugene, Oregon: The Center for the Advanced Study of Educational Administration, University of Oregon, 1966.